FRANCE–GERMANY, 1983–1993

FRANCE–GERMANY, 1983–1993

The Struggle to Cooperate

Edited by
Patrick McCarthy

St. Martin's Press
New York

First published in the United States of America 1993

Printed in the United States of America

ISBN 0-312-08524-9

Library of Congress Cataloging-in-Publication Data

France–Germany, 1983-1993 : the struggle to cooperate / edited by
    Patrick McCarthy.
        p. cm.
    Includes bibliographical references and index.
    ISBN 0-312-08524-9
    1. France—Foreign relations—Germany. 2. Germany—Foreign
relations—France. 3. France—Politics and government—1981-
4. Germany—Politics and government—1945- 5. International
cooperation. I. McCarthy, Patrick, 1941- .
DC423.F725 1993
327.44043—dc20   93-12551
                                                               CIP

For Kate, Noah, Alexander and Sebastian,
all of whom arrived after Mitterrand's speech to the Bundestag

TABLE OF CONTENTS

ABBREVIATIONS

CAP	Common Agricultural Policy
CDU	Christian Democratic Union
EBRD	European Bank for Reconstruction and Development
EC	European Community
ECSC	European Coal and Steel Community
EDC	European Defense Community
EMS	European Monetary System
EMU	Economic and Monetary Union
FDP	German Liberal Party
FRG	Federal Republic of Germany
GATT	General Agreement on Tariffs and Trade
IGC	Intergovernmental Conference
IGC–EMU	Conference on Economic and Monetary Union
IGC–POL	Conference on Political Union
IMF	International Monetary Fund
NATO	North Atlantic Treaty Organization
OEEC	Organization for European Economic Cooperation
PCI	Italian Communist Party
PS	Parti socialiste
SDI	Strategic Defense Initiative
SPD	Socialist Party of Germany
WEU	Western European Union

INTRODUCTION

Patrick McCarthy

This book began life as a series of discussions in the European Studies department of the Paul H. Nitze School of Advanced International Studies. A group of us at the Washington and Bologna campuses decided to concentrate our research on what we considered the most significant Western European development of the 1980s and early 1990s, namely, the revived, constantly imperiled but curiously necessary Franco–German relationship. We were inspired in part by two excellent Ph.D. theses, written by Philip Gordon and Jörg Boche, on French security policy and on the economic aspects of the Franco–German relationship. If these analyzed important themes of the dialogue between the two countries, then the place that their cooperation might assume in the post–Cold War world was in part suggested to us by David Calleo's work on the end of American hegemony.

The decision to begin in 1983 was simple enough: this was the year of the French switch to rigor and of Mitterrand's speech to the Bundestag. There was also the practical consideration that the earlier period of Franco–German cooperation has been well covered, notably by F. R. Willis and H. Simonian. Not, however, that post–war history may be taken for granted. The late 1970s, when the European Monetary System was set up, look quite different from the perspective of the late 1980s when the EMS was working better than many had foreseen. In September 1992 they looked different again! So chapter 1 retraces the Franco–German dialogue from 1944 to 1983 partly to provide an introduction for the general reader and partly to introduce themes that recur later.

Perhaps the most important of these is that Franco–German cooperation is the product of two national strategies which overlapped and conflicted.

Put crudely, France wished to embrace–enmesh Germany, which was eager to be so embraced–enmeshed. Germany used France first to recover a measure of autonomy and then to expand her influence in Europe without reawakening historic fears. France sought to calm her own fears by exercising some control over Germany, which in turn increased her power in Europe and in the world. Often these operations could be reconciled—examples would be the Coal and Steel Pool and the joint defense ventures of the 1980s—and sometimes they could not—the Elysée Treaty and the early phase of German reunification.

These strategies were played out in a series of circles. Within the Franco–German circle lay the two domestic spheres: before the EMS could be successful the Bundesbank had to win the struggle for control of German macroeconomic policy in the aftermath of the 1973 oil crisis; conversely, the French Socialists could only become suitable partners for Germany by changing many of their policies in 1983. Beyond the two countries lay "Europe," where they competed for the support of other countries even as they exercised joint leadership. Outside Europe lay the circle of the superpowers and, although each country pursued its own relations with each of them, Franco–German cooperation was also a means to gain freedom from them and move towards a multipolar world. That this was—and is—more a French than a German goal is just another tension in the struggle to cooperate.

To emphasize the Western European state's determination to survive by entwining itself with other nation–states is, in the aftermath of Maastricht, less of a novelty than ever. More important for the structure of this book is the theme that the gamble of interdependence–autonomy invaded all areas of political and economic life. In the 1960s the German Christian Democrats split between "Gaullists" and "Atlanticists," while at present defenders and critics of the close tie with Germany vie for leadership of the French Gaullists. So the method we have chosen is to approach the last decade from many different angles.

Thus chapters 2 and 3 are complementary, each depicting how the political elites of one country viewed, used, and were used by those of the other. These accounts raise economic issues which are discussed more fully in chapter 4. Then Roger Morgan shows how France and Germany are inventing a more united Europe, while Erik Jones describes how the small countries, especially the Benelux, have invented for themselves special national roles within the framework of their neighbors' cooperation. Philip Gordon deals with the vital issue of security, which leads naturally into Julius Friend's chapter on the U.S. view of the Franco–German entity. Finally,

David Calleo examines the future prospects of cooperation. Important issues like reunification are thus discussed in several chapters from various and overlapping viewpoints.

The authors are familiar with one another's work, and most of them have read most of the chapters. If this enables us to "tell a story" rather than offering a series of fragments, it does not mean that there is unanimous agreement on what the story means. To mention only one example, Roger Morgan provides a useful antidote against excessive reliance on the national strategy approach.

More importantly, several judgements go against prevailing wisdom. Present opinions of post–Maastricht Europe are negative—inspired by a fresh bout of europessimism and a surge of faith in the new Clinton administration—but Calleo warns against such simplicities. Conversely, if judgements on the Franco–German bond are generally positive, Gordon stresses the difficulties that lie in the path of security cooperation. Similarly, my own chapter 3 takes issue with the view, dear to many—especially French—observers, that France is too weak not to be stifled by the German embrace.

The essays were written in the autumn of 1992, and authors were asked to take account, where relevant, of the French referendum on Maastricht and the September monetary crisis. They were free to speculate on the future of cooperation, as Dana Allin does in his interesting comments on the next generation of German leaders. However, no attempt has been made to update the volume in order to treat very recent developments. The pace of events in Europe renders such efforts futile, and it is worth reiterating that academic publications cannot and should not compete with good journalism. If our story is at all convincing, the reader will be able to add extra chapters on her own. One of our themes is that no conclusion is in sight.

I wish to thank all the people who have helped with this project, especially two Bologna Center directors, Stephen Low and Robert Evans, the Center's library and secretarial staff, and my research assistant, Christine Knudsen, without whose calm efficiency this book would probably have ended its life as a jumble of manuscripts on my desk.

Bologna, Italy
January 1993

Chapter 1

Condemned to Partnership: The Franco–German Relationship, 1944–1983

Patrick McCarthy

INTRODUCTION

Franco–German cooperation in the postwar period has been a matter of hard–headed realism. Initially, it had to be promoted by elites against public opinion. When Hubert Beuve–Méry told a group of Resistance fighters in 1944 that in the future French and German army officers should be trained in the same academies, he was almost lynched for his pains.[1] Inevitably, painful French memories of the Nazi occupation persisted, and the Oradour trial of 1953 played a part in blocking the European Defense Community. On the German side there was suspicion of French designs on the Saar and the Ruhr, and this feeling may have resurfaced recently in the shape of worry about French designs on the mark. Certainly French fears of German militarism reemerged in the 1970s, transformed into a concern about German economic might.

Political leaders have had to engage in pedagogy, but they have not received much help from culture. At the turn of the century, when relations with Germany were bad, Frenchmen admired German thought: Kant, Schopenhauer and Nietzsche were all much read, albeit in different circles; French businessmen praised the Bismarckian partnership between state and industry, while the French Socialists accepted the hegemony of the SPD. During the postwar period there has been no such fascination, if one excepts the lasting presence in France of Martin Heidegger. A writer like Michel Tournier who proclaims his love of German culture is an oddity indeed. In the postwar years the American novel and cinema exerted greater influence than any German works, and English is overwhelmingly the first foreign language. Nor has postwar Germany produced a figure like Ernst Robert Curtius, whose interventions in the 1920s' Pontigny *décades* were memorable.[2]

Political memories of the interwar years have of course been vital. Even today, when the "postwar" is supposedly over, German policy is guided in part by Adenauer's belief that a German state can only exist if it is intertwined with the French state. On the French side, the Liberation saw a debate begin between those who wished to punish Germany and those who wished to embrace her, the second group believing that "we had to take care not to repeat the error we had committed between the wars when we conceded nothing to democratic Germany and refused nothing to the Nazis."[3] Certain wartime experiences led certain Frenchmen to become pro–German: the role of ex–prisoners' associations in seeking reconciliation was important, while the Vichy technocrats, like Jean Bichelonne, had offered an example of economic cooperation.

However, the embrace was a means to enmesh. The special trait of the Franco–German relationship is that it has been riddled with conflict because it is not primarily an alliance of two friendly powers against outside forces, but rather a way for one power to control the other and for the other to control itself, as it had not done in the first half of the century. This is one reason why the two are condemned to partnership, and it explains the tension that exploded in the 1940s, in 1963, in the early 1970s, and in 1989. Each country seeks in its different way to expand, and not to relinquish sovereignty.

Outside forces are also important. The alliance has been a way to improve security against the Soviet Union and to increase autonomy from the U.S. This goal has been generally more important for France than for Germany, but the German attitude towards America's world role has been changing in the last two decades. The struggle to gain leverage against the outside world constitutes the second reason why the two nations are condemned to partnership, but it does not mean that they can or wish to establish a self-sufficient bloc. On the contrary, they have often invoked other powers to regulate their differences—as with the EDC—and their cooperation has grown inside broader groupings like the Atlantic Alliance and the EC. Their partnership has allowed France and Germany to influence these organizations at the price of allowing themselves to be influenced by Britain or the Netherlands. Conflict and cooperation exist without as well as within the partnership.

1944-1958

From the vantage point of the end of the Cold War and a reunited Germany it is interesting to glance back at the mid-1940s when East–West relations were still cordial and Germany was divided into zones rather than into states. Or at least it is interesting to consider France. Germany was silent until the Cold War allowed her to speak: the Federal Republic was born in the same year as the Atlantic Alliance. But France talked much of Germany in the period 1944–47, and the question is whether any part of what she said remained important.

At first sight it appears not. De Gaulle and Bidault followed what may, imprecisely, be called the "Poincaré" line in seeking to prevent the reemergence of a threat by dismembering Germany. They wished to annex the Saar, detach the left bank of the Rhine, and establish a separate authority in the Ruhr. Economic and security goals went together. Coal from the Saar and Ruhr would drive the French steel industry, which would become the largest in continental Europe, while the French troops stationed on the Rhine guarded against the formation of a centralized, much less rearmed, German state.

This plan was slowed by Anglo–American opposition, and was wrecked by the breakdown of East–West relations, but it would not have worked anyway. Its economic weakness was inherited from the 1920s: the French steel industry could not flourish without a healthy West European economy, which in turn was not possible if Germany were not allowed to revive her industries. More important in 1944 was de Gaulle's failure to enlist Soviet support for his views. The Russians wanted to keep Germany united in order to obtain reparations and had a shrewd suspicion that they would have little control over a separate Ruhr authority.

More generally, they accorded a low priority to France as a partner, and while the collapse of 1940 seems the obvious explanation for their misgivings, it does not constitute the whole story. Earlier memories played a part, and the unfulfilled promises of the Laval Pact partially eclipsed the successful collaboration in the First World War. The outlines of a Franco–Soviet deal were present in de Gaulle's visit to Moscow in December 1944: in return for Soviet support on the Rhine, the Ruhr, and the Saar, France would recognize the Oder–Neisse frontier, and the two countries would present their plan to the British and the Americans.[4] But Stalin was not interested.

One might argue that throughout the post–1944 period France has never succeeded in conducting a fruitful dialogue with the USSR over Germany. De Gaulle had limited success when he turned east after the Bundestag ruined his 1963 treaty with Adenauer. While relations between France and such East bloc countries as Poland were improved, as were relations between France and a USSR that was pleased at de Gaulle's decision to leave the NATO military structure, no progress was made on the German issue, and the French *Ostpolitik* collapsed with the Prague invasion.

If this failure could be explained away by the corroding influence of the Cold War, the same is not true of the attempt by Mitterrand to win Gorbachev's support during the crisis of German reunification. Yet the Kiev meeting of December 1989 produced no joint plan for France and the USSR to "guarantee" the process of bringing together what they had helped to divide, although Mitterrand was eager to demonstrate that France could play such a role. Instead, Gorbachev preferred to trade his consent directly to the Kohl government. One can only conclude that the USSR, which in 1944 looked to the Anglo–Saxons as bargaining partners, had now opted for Germany as well, but was still neglecting France. Nor is there much evidence that France is able to compete commercially with Germany in the ex-Communist countries: Czechoslovakia's decision to opt for Volkswagen rather than Renault as a partner for Skoda is revealing.[5]

The other strand in French policy at the Liberation was the construction of "Europe." The concept of a united, federal Europe was present in the Resistance movements like *Combat,* but de Gaulle's vision was different, and in 1945 he foresaw a Europe of states. It would be made up of the countries "that border the Rhine, the Alps and the Pyrenees," and it would become "the arbiter between the Soviet and Anglo–Saxon camps."[6] Other French leaders were less ready to assign Britain to a non–European, Anglo–Saxon camp. In March 1947 Britain and France signed the Dunkirk Treaty and the French politicians who supported the EDC hoped that Britain would join.

However, on this one point de Gaulle was proven right. The Dunkirk Treaty was only a part of Britain's attempt to help strengthen France. She had fought for France to have an occupation zone and a permanent seat on the UN Security Council. But Britain's aim was to help rebuild France in order to fill a dangerous vacuum on the continent rather than to engage with her in constructing any kind of "Europe." This policy would continue via Britain's refusal to join the ECSC and the EDC, to her half–hearted first attempt to join the EC, and beyond.

De Gaulle's two vetoes of 1963 and 1967 were the logical conclusions of this noncooperation, which survived the Pompidou–Heath alliance of 1970–1974. Although a member of the EC, Britain adopted a minimalist stance, departing from it in the mid–1980s to press for the Internal Market, reverting to it with Thatcher's 1988 Bruges speech, and sticking to it at Maastricht. Britain simply did not share France's goal of creating a "Europe" that would control Germany and offer a measure of freedom from the U.S. The first of these tasks was, in British eyes, to be accomplished by NATO, and the second was best achieved through the special relationship. Britain thus cooperated with Germany in NATO and provided a focus for the elements in German politics—Ludwig Erhard or the SPD—that were less enthusiastic about France.[7]

For the rest, de Gaulle's 1945 view of Europe was unrealizable, and not merely because the Cold War left no space for arbiters. Without Germany such a Europe was too weak, and if Germany were to be included as de Gaulle implied, then she could hardly be dismembered.

But the period 1944–47 leaves traces that are not obliterated by the impact of the Cold War. The economic goal of building up France as a modern industrial power precedes the Marshall Plan and determines the way that France sought to use U.S. aid. The "Poincaré" approach to Germany was given up in favor of what might, with equal imprecision, be called the "Briand" approach of reaching agreements with Germany in order to bind her to France. A policy of hostility gave way to a policy of friendship that deployed different methods to attain the same end.

The concept of "Europe" was changed but it was not abandoned. Since Europe could not be constructed with Moscow or London, then it would be constructed with Bonn. This made it all the more difficult to maintain the second goal of "Europe," namely, an edge of independence from the U.S., because Bonn was dependent on, and indeed created by, the U.S.[8] But France did not quite give up that goal, which may be seen as a milder version of arbitrating between East and West.[9]

It remains true that the breakdown of East–West relations had a dramatic effect on French policy towards Germany. It drove the U.S. to seek first the creation of a West German state with a central, though federal, government and a strong economy, and then the rearmament of that state: precisely the French nightmare. French attempts to keep Germany out of the Organization for European Economic Cooperation and the European Payments Union, which were created to administer Marshall Aid, were unsuccessful, and Germany achieved qualified membership in both. At the same time, the Soviet threat increased French dependence on the U.S. Finally, it gave power to West Germany, as Adenauer was quick to realize.

"I believed that the conflict between the Soviet Union and the Free World grew steadily. America needed the development of a strong Western Europe. For this Germany was essential. A nation in chains cannot be a worthwhile partner. In my opinion our chains would gradually fall away."[10] Adenauer was lucky that the Soviet threat, which he exaggerated, created his opportunity, and he was clever enough—which the SPD leader, Kurt Schumacher, was not—to see that the recovery of German sovereignty and the integration of Germany into the West went together. Adenauer simply ceded to the ECSC or to NATO pieces of power that were held by the Occupation authorities; other pieces of power were acquired by the Federal Republic.

Adenauer shaped West German public opinion, which, while suspicious of France, was generically pro–Europe. He knew that France could not be ignored and that she was, along with the U.S., Germany's principal partner. His dealings were easier with the U.S., which wanted West Germany to be self–supporting, knew that the Marshall Plan could not work without Germany, and sought German rearmament. Only the last of these was unpopular in Germany, and even here Adenauer could use such unpopularity to wring concessions from the Allies. The Bonn Convention, which ended the occupation status, was signed the day before the EDC pact in May 1952.

France was almost as necessary a partner, for the new German state had to be rooted in "Europe." She was also more difficult, even if the fortunate arrival of the Cold War helped rid Adenauer of the Poincaré approach. However, after France agreed to the creation of the Federal Republic, there remained the questions of the Saar, which France wished to annex, and the Ruhr, where she wanted to keep a watchful eye on German heavy industry. In general, Adenauer tried to conciliate France by offering economic concessions. In 1949 he worked to separate the issues of Saar coal and Saar annexation by offering France control over the mines but not the territory. Meanwhile he flaunted his willingness to engage in political reconciliation by proposing in 1950 that France and West Germany should merge. He showed a benign tolerance for French weaknesses—a strong communist party and a penchant for costly strikes. He thus helped France to make the leap from dismembering Germany to smothering her with affection.

It has been argued that the Cold War robbed France of her freedom of maneuver: "internationally her role had become almost entirely passive."[11] But this judgement has been revised, for France in fact reacted to both the great U.S. projects, the Marshall Plan and the Atlantic Alliance, with initiatives of her own.

In the former case she was successful. France used the European Reconstruction Programme to meet the targets of her Monnet Plan and ignored American pressure to set up a unified European market. She joined with Britain in obstructing the American attempt to use the OEEC as an instrument of economic union. Having resisted the U.S. version of European unity, in 1950 she offered her own version in the shape of the Schuman Plan.

Economically, the plan was consistent with the postwar French goal of obtaining access to German coal, because Ruhr coal would be allotted by a

High Authority on which France would be represented, while French domination of the Saar would be cloaked in Europeanism. This was a gamble since Adenauer welcomed moves to Europeanize the Saar in order to block annexation by France.

Politically, the Schuman Plan gave France a measure of control over Germany's war–making capacity. Moreover, it established a close Franco–German relationship which became the focus of a broader European group. This in turn brought about the exclusion of Britain, which did not wish to join the ECSC but was irritated that it had been formed without her. Although the U.S. supported the Coal and Steel Pool, it was not the kind of economic union American officials had hoped for. Rather than a free market in steel and coal, it represented a patchwork of intergovernment deals where Italy retained tariffs, the price of coal was fixed, and harmonized freight charges were not realized. In short, France had imposed elements of her *dirigisme* on Europe.[12]

How had she achieved this? In part because Italy and other members of the ECSC were following the same path of rebuilding their economies in a national context before moving outward towards Europe. But the Schuman Plan also reveals that France was not as weak as she seemed in 1950. The U.S. could not realize its goal of a strong, united Western Europe without her, especially since Britain had opted out. One might suggest that throughout the postwar period France has been neither as weak as she seemed under the Fourth Republic nor as strong as she has sometimes appeared under the Fifth Republic. The successive waves of lament and self–congratulation are to be explained as aspects of French political culture. They are perception rather than reality.

Another reason for French success was Konrad Adenauer. His economics minister, Ludwig Erhard, resisted the ECSC in the name of free markets, but Adenauer could see that the powerful German economy needed above all a solid national and international political framework. Integration of the Federal Republic into a stable Europe would more than compensate for supplying France with German coal. To Adenauer, the ECSC was "a lasting foundation for a European Federation," and even the embryo of a "third force in a united Europe."[13] That the ECSC was also a means of extending the sovereignty of the Federal Republic did not seem contradictory to him. West Germany gained a share of control over her steel industry by dividing that share with France.

Overlapping with the Schuman Plan was the proposal for a European Defense Community, but here France's task was more difficult. Her aims were once again to smother Germany by setting up joint armed forces under French leadership, and to create within the Atlantic Alliance an enclave where Europe, once more led by France, would enjoy some autonomy. West Germany would be rearmed and rewarded with greater sovereignty through the ending of the Occupation status, but she would be enveloped in a network of military and political organizations dominated by France and—until she announced she would not participate—Britain. Germany would not be a member of NATO, except indirectly via her membership in the EDC. There would be a European Minister of Defense to run the enclave.

From the start, however, the Pleven Plan seemed a desperate expedient to minimize German rearmament. Adenauer saw in rearmament the chance to obtain *Gleichberechtigung*: "Germany must be treated in exactly the same way as the other European peoples. If we were to have the same duties we should enjoy the same rights."[14] Repeated French attempts to limit the size of German units, to leave the Germans as the only troops not commanded by their officers, and not to allow them on French soil went against *Gleichberechtigung*. Adenauer wanted a commitment that Germany, on joining the EDC, would also be allowed at some future time to join NATO.

This time the two countries could not extend their sovereignty by merging it. On the French side there were two special obstacles to the watered down version of the Pleven Plan which the National Assembly debated in 1954. The first was that, whereas coke and pig iron were of interest only to elites, soldiers and flags attracted mass attention. The second reason was the opposition of the Gaullists, who were determined to maintain the link between the nation and its army. To de Gaulle there were different kinds of sovereignty, and the power to defend oneself was the last to be shared. The EDC was qualitatively different from the ECSC.

Pressure from the U.S. had strengthened Germany's case. The U.S. wanted large German divisions for reasons of military efficacy. Disputes about the number of soldiers in a unit were a distraction to an administration that had originally sought German entry into NATO and saw in the EDC primarily a way to achieve this.

Moreover, the autonomy of the European enclave did not amount to much even in the original Pleven Plan because of the overwhelming French need for American protection. By 1952 it had been further whittled down, and the European Minister of Defense, who would most probably have been French, had become a Board of Commissioners. It is unlikely that this displeased the U.S., which had from the outset insisted that the EDC should be an integral part of the NATO structure.[15] It has been argued that Marshall Aid and the Atlantic Alliance represented different ways of dealing with Europe and that the former left the Europeans greater freedom.[16] The U.S. has been jealous of its authority in NATO and is reluctant to share it even today. After the

EDC was defeated in the French parliament, the Anglo–Saxons were able to impose their own solution, which appeased both Germany and France even as it left them dissatisfied with each other. Germany entered NATO and France retained control over her own forces. Britain acted as broker by dreaming up the Western European Union and by offering to maintain troops in Germany. This provides an example of how France and Germany have had to call in outside powers to regulate their relationship.

Meanwhile, France continued to seek a measure of autonomy within NATO, and found it in the development of her nuclear force, which also offered her a means of control over a Germany rearmed and endowed with the legitimacy that came from membership in NATO.[17] She saw no contradiction between economic cooperation and a national *force de frappe*. The Franco–German partnership does not develop at an equal pace in all areas.

Indeed, economic integration once more became the motor of friendship, which in turn spurred movement towards the Rome treaty. Other countries, like the Benelux group, were significant as catalysts, and in general the EC prevented Franco–German cooperation from appearing menacing and divisive. However, the Rome Treaty was essentially a compromise between the now rebuilt French and German economies. By the mid–1950s France was Germany's largest customer and second largest supplier, while Germany was France's second largest customer and supplier.

French industry was to be exposed to international competition despite the doubts of some industrialists like the mechanical engineering employers. German industry was offered assured markets, although here again Ludwig Erhard, who distrusted French mercantilism and would have preferred a broader free trade area, had to be overruled by Adenauer. The domestic debate in Germany about the value of letting oneself be embraced–enmeshed by France would not explode until 1963. For the moment, it found expression only in West German pressure for low external tariffs.

To compensate France for her expected industrial difficulties, the Common Agricultural Policy (CAP) was set up to provide markets for her growing agricultural surplus and to transfer the subsidizing of her agriculture onto Europe. Germany, where food represented 35 percent of total imports, was to constitute the main market. Although it took another decade to sort out how the mechanism of the CAP was to work, the integration of French and German trade was irreversible. The questions of macroeconomic harmonization and monetary coordination were left for the future, but the detaching of the left bank of the Rhine lay light years in the past. On the agenda was political cooperation, and in September 1958 President de Gaulle and Adenauer held their first meeting.

1958–1969

Just as we considered how Adenauer perceived France, so the first question in this period is what de Gaulle asked of and offered to Germany. In 1945 his concern was to ensure that there could be no revival of German militarism, but now he sought above all to enlist Germany in France's struggle for greater independence. From enemy Germany was to come an ally in the battle against superpower domination of Europe, particularly American hegemony. As the ECSC had demonstrated, this view was not altogether new, but de Gaulle placed such emphasis on it that the Franco–German relationship was qualitatively changed. Although de Gaulle took care to maintain power over Germany, he did not fear her, and indeed his years may be seen as an interlude between the postwar French fear of German military strength and the worry about German economic supremacy which would grow in the 1970s.

Despite or because of this, de Gaulle had no intention of accepting West Germany as an equal. When Kissinger asked him how he intended to keep Germany in line, he reportedly replied "by war,"[18] and certainly the *force de frappe* was designed in part to ensure French military domination. Other advantages held by France were the way the Nazi past delegitimized the West German government, and France's residual control over Germany as a victor in the Second World War.[19] De Gaulle, who believed—all too much—in the autonomy of politics, felt that the division of Germany and the Fifth Republic's strong state more than compensated for West Germany's reviving economic strength.

The assumption of superiority became one source of conflict with Germany, while the goal of independence constituted another. De Gaulle felt that he needed to restore French self–confidence after the crushing defeat of 1940 and the dubious victory of 1944, and that his position vis–à–vis the U.S. remained too weak to allow him to make concessions. The apparent strength of the Fifth Republic did not deceive de Gaulle, who compared his own action with that of the comic strip character Tintin.[20] Nor did de Gaulle ever hold the naive belief that a sovereign state could act without restraints; he merely tried to increase France's power to make her own decisions in a world where all too many constraints had been placed on her. France might not be strong, but she should not be afraid; self–assertion would make her stronger. Yet de Gaulle's perception of himself as a rebel did not prevent the Germans from frequently seeing him as an oppressor who made decisions that involved them—like the refusal to admit Britain to the EC—without consulting them.

Although a heretic, de Gaulle was the man who imposed on France a new orthodoxy: independence, the ability to defend herself, the creation of a national ambition. In the case of Germany, orthodoxy was the Franco–German relationship as the cornerstone of a more autonomous Europe. The 1963 treaty, with its clauses on intergovernmental consultation in such areas as economics and defense, was the model to which Mitterrand and Kohl could return when they relaunched the alliance in 1983. Yet de Gaulle's heresy was that he made more demands on the French and the Germans alike than any of his successors would dare to do.

Of the Germans, he demanded that they choose between France and the U.S., while of the French he asked that they treat the franc as a weapon in the struggle against American hegemony. When the Germans said no in 1963, de Gaulle turned away from them and neglected the treaty. When the French eventually rebelled, de Gaulle declared that "they would do nothing for France," and resigned.[21] So it is wrong to overemphasize the continuity between de Gaulle and his successors and to see in their foreign policy nothing more than Gaullism by any other name. Pompidou gave priority to domestic economic policy, which meant that his foreign policy was more modest. Yet in turn this was possible only because de Gaulle had been intransigent: Pompidou's concessions were made from a position of strength.

If de Gaulle's historical achievement is to have ushered France from a position of weakness to a necessary self–assertion as U.S. power weakened, his actions had, paradoxically, the same effect on Germany. By offering her the alliance, he assisted her in the task of rehabilitation; by making excessive demands, he provoked her towards her own brand of independence. Brandt's *Ostpolitik* would barely have been possible without de Gaulle's. It is not a wild exaggeration to state that de Gaulle brought about the downfall of Adenauer, the most pro–French of German leaders, by embracing him, and of Erhard, the most anti–French of German leaders, by neglecting him. The long–term effect was to bring Brandt, who had other foreign policy priorities, to power. Yet this effort of German self–assertion was as necessary as the French cultivation of modesty for the revival of Franco–German cooperation.

De Gaulle's goal of independence was immutable, but the strategies and tactics he used to pursue it were diverse. Skeptical of humans, ideas, and ideologies, he maneuvered his policies as he had maneuvered his tanks. His years in power may for our purposes be divided into two periods, each with its German strategy; and the first strategy, that of 1958 to 1963, may be subdivided into three tactics.

During these years, de Gaulle sought to harness German support for France's policy of independence. He offered Germany the full trappings of an alliance, complete with regular meetings between heads of government, and capped his campaign with the pomp of his state visit in September 1962. No Fourth Republic leader had been so explicit. For a West German government still pursuing rehabilitation, this was a triumph in itself.

De Gaulle also offered Germany support on Berlin, where the Anglo–Saxons appeared to Adenauer to be willing to compromise with Soviet demands. It is, however, too simple to state that France was supporting German policies in the East in return for German support in the West, because at their first meeting de Gaulle told Adenauer he intended to recognize the Oder–Neisse line, which foreshadowed his aim of improving relations with the Soviet bloc.

That he was offering West Germany legitimacy but not equality was demonstrated by the memorandum tactic: his proposal of a triumvirate composed of the U.S., Britain, and France to run NATO. Germany, like the other continental European countries, was excluded; this was made all the more pointed by two features of the memorandum. The first was that de Gaulle proposed extending NATO's responsibilities worldwide, so that a distinction was established between France, a power with a world role, and Germany, with no such role. The second was that, in demanding a certain degree of control over America's use of her nuclear weapons, de Gaulle was meeting the fear that the improvement in Soviet nuclear weapons made the American guarantee to Western Europe less reliable, because U.S. weapons could no longer be deployed without inviting the risk of Soviet retaliation against the U.S. This view was shared by Germany, whose dependence on American protection was greater than France's. Yet de Gaulle did not consider formulating a common approach to the U.S.[22]

When, predictably, the memorandum tactic failed, de Gaulle did seek to organize continental Europe through the Fouchet Plan. His argument was that only an EC that was a political confederation, rather than either a free–trade area or a federal entity, would be strong enough to negotiate with the U.S. Although Germany supported a federal Europe, this form of European unity was sufficiently tempting for her to support it initially. The plan, which allowed for regular meetings of national governments to hammer out political agreements, expressed the French vision of Europe's structure and would presumably have produced policies pleasing to France. For that very reason it was rejected by such countries as the Netherlands.

This prompted de Gaulle to invent a bilateral version of it in the form of the Franco–German Treaty, which was for Adenauer both triumph and embarrassment. Such a formal arrangement represented the culmination of his attempt to intertwine the French and West German states, but it came immediately after de Gaulle's veto of British entry. Moreover, the cooperation clauses were designed to produce Franco–German agreements which would then be carried into such international fora as NATO. Both this form and the policies it seemed likely to produce would make Germany chose between France and the U.S.

Thus the Bundestag's preamble, which subordinated Germany's participation in the treaty to her membership of organizations like NATO and GATT, was pure Atlanticism. It marked the end of the Adenauer policy of courting France, and the emergence of an alliance, however fragile, between the SPD and the Erhard wing of the CDU. As Chancellor, Erhard sought compromises with France over the CAP but gave priority to a successful completion of the Kennedy Round, where de Gaulle was willing to compromise. Meanwhile, Erhard sought a different solution to the problem of the increasing unreliability of U.S. nuclear protection via the Multinational Nuclear Force. This irritated France without producing results, since Lyndon Johnson shelved the MLF in December 1964.

If Johnson was demonstrating the perils of Atlanticism, then the Bundestag's preamble made the treaty useless to de Gaulle. Hidden away in the complex series of events was the issue of whether the treaty might have offered a better solution to Germany's security demands; in short, whether defense cooperation might have meant a French nuclear guarantee to Germany. In the short term the answer was clearly no, if only because the *force de frappe* was then militarily insignificant and probably seemed to the Soviets nothing more than "a pleasant new source of trouble for the Atlantic Alliance."[23] In the long run this would, however, change, leaving open the political issue.

It has recently been emphasized that there was a Europeanist strand to de Gaulle's thinking. As early as 1963 Pierre Messmer stated that the *force de frappe* would become a "cornerstone" in the construction of Europe,[24] and yet de Gaulle also believed that the nation–state derived its legitimacy from its ability to defend its citizens. This contradiction has plagued his successors. In 1963, however, de Gaulle could not in any case offer the *force de frappe* as the deterrent of an independent Europe because the notion of such a Europe was so fragile. To survive at all, independence must remain a national policy. Dilution would mean destruction.

For this reason de Gaulle was unable to form with Germany the alliance that he needed, and that would later come about in part—albeit only in part—because of him. The same was true of monetary issues. While de Gaulle converted dollars into gold in order to demonstrate the privileged role of the dollar in the world economy, the German government agreed not to turn into gold the dollars spent in Germany by the U.S. armed forces, and also to buy U.S. medium–term government bonds.[25] The problem was the same: the overextension of the U.S., the vulnerability/abuse of the dollar, and the American government's understandable belief that the Europeans were getting security on the cheap. However, the attempted solutions were different and it would not be until the Giscard–Schmidt years that a common approach would be found in the form of the European Monetary System.

From 1963 to 1968, de Gaulle deployed a new strategy where West Germany was a pawn rather than an ally. In his battle against superpower condominium, his privileged interlocutor was the Soviet Union, for if he could remove the Soviet threat, he would eliminate Western Europe's dependence on the U.S. So he sought to reassure the Soviets against the fear of a Western attack, and at the same time to remove the special fear of a new German onslaught which, arguably, compelled them to impose their rule on Eastern Europe. His 1966 decision to leave the military wing of the NATO alliance and his visits to Moscow and to other Eastern Europe capitals were designed as harbingers of what Europe would be once bipolarity was left behind.

This vision has a perhaps spurious modernity about it. It looks forward to the post–1989 era but it implies a Soviet willingness to change. In fact, change had to be forced on the Soviets by economic necessity, and in the 1960s they were unwilling to allow their satellites any freedom. The invasion of Czechoslovakia put an end to de Gaulle's policy. Even had the Soviet leaders been tempted by the vision of a Europe with a reduced U.S. presence (but on this account more unruly), they would have had to have faith in France to keep such unruliness under control. As of 1945 they did not.

For Germany, de Gaulle envisaged some sort of resolution of the postwar division—source of superpower rivalry and hence condominium—but in a way that did not leave the USSR (and France) facing an independent and potentially hostile Germany. The solution was an international agreement where France would act as the guarantor of German behavior, but here again this did not convince the Soviets. It was also different from the way German reunification came about in 1990, which perturbed Mitterrand, who was thinking in precisely these Gaullist terms.

In short, de Gaulle perhaps deliberately overestimated French might and isolated himself. His crusade against the Vietnam War was certainly correct, and his vision of an America that was overextended and hence weak behind a façade of strength was prophetic; but if, when that became apparent in the early 1970s, there was no united European response to it, it was in part de Gaulle's responsibility.

In part, but not entirely. It has been said that de Gaulle's neglect of the EC after 1963 left European leadership to West Germany,[26] but in fact the stagnation of the EC in the mid–sixties demonstrates that without and against France little could be done. Monnet's adage that "only France could create Europe" was still valid.[27] Not until ten years later could Helmut Schmidt's Germany take a lead, and even then only in partnership with Giscard's France.

In the meantime, however, the illusion of the Fifth Republic's grandeur and the reality of West Germany's economic, if not yet political, might became apparent in 1968. The deflationary policies designed to create a strong franc for the battle against the dollar, and the hypercentralized government that was so effective in the foreign policy arena, produced their backlash in the wave of strikes and student protests which undermined that foreign policy. Then in November 1968, West Germany refused to revalue the mark in order to spare France the humiliation of a sharp devaluation of the franc.

De Gaulle reacted with a doomed attempt to save the franc, but in other areas he demonstrated how mobile and realistic he could be. At home he set about reforming the education system and decentralizing the state, while abroad he drew closer to the U.S., which had been helpful with the franc. This is another example of how outside powers are left to resolve Franco–German differences which the partners cannot resolve.

1969–1983

These were years when, despite a difficult beginning, the Franco–German relationship grew stronger, and one might argue that after the 1973 oil crisis the partners attempted to offer a leadership that the U.S. was no longer able to provide. Reluctant to engage in energy conservation, the Ford and Carter administrations chose the easy economic solution of letting the dollar go down. The only serious attempt to reestablish monetary stability was the European Monetary System. However, the EMS was no more than a first step which protected intra–European trade while leaving untouched the broader issue of the dollar's increasing inability to serve as the main currency of the world economy. Moreover, it took the French and Germans the entire decade to achieve what they did.

The construction of a more united and more independent European bloc was going to be slow, and it was held back by a power struggle between the two partners. This took place on several fronts, but on the most important issue of macroeconomics it ended in a victory for Germany. Here again, however, the result was not clear-cut since Giscard d'Estaing used Germany to impose on France his policy of austerity. *Modell Deutschland* could work only if it suited the other countries.

Although it troubled France, the new German self–assertion was necessary if the Franco–German relationship were to work as France had hoped. In the late 1970s Schmidt showed greater independence of the U.S. than Erhard had done in the mid–1960s. Similarly, France was gradually, albeit sporadically, able to confront this new Germany. Pompidou was more distrustful, Giscard d'Estaing more realistic.

From the EC's Hague summit of 1969 onward, Pompidou and Brandt tried to strengthen ties that had been weak since 1963, but the memory of November 1968 haunted France. In particular it fed the distrust which Pompidou felt for the *Ostpolitik*. Although Brandt's turn eastward presupposed that West Germany was firmly rooted in the EC as well as in NATO, the switch of emphasis was clear and it provoked in the French government three separate but overlapping fears. The first and most justified was that Germany was replacing France as the privileged interlocutor of the Soviet Union. Brandt had taken over de Gaulle's policy and had changed it. He made fewer demands on the Soviets to change the way they ruled Eastern Europe—indeed, the novelty of his policy was that he accepted the existing situation—and he had more economic help to offer.[28]

This in turn revived the postwar French fear of a second Rapallo revamped as a concern that Germany would drift into neutralism along some new *Sonderweg*. In the 1980s this theme would reach crescendo, but from 1970 on it served to mask the third and least avowable fear—that West Germany was growing less easy to control. In particular, Brandt was freeing West Germany from its Nazi past by facing it more openly than Adenauer had done, thereby removing a source of French influence. This is surely the real reason why Pompidou disliked Brandt's genuflections. Since this could not be stated openly, Pompidou and Jobert were left declaring that "Germany is edging away from Europe," and that she must choose between East and West.[29]

When Brandt looked west he was well–meaning but vague. Some of his plans for relaunching the EC, such as initiating a real social policy and instituting direct elections to the European parliament, made no appeal to Pompidou. When the West Germans pressed for British entry, Pompidou successfully outflanked them by establishing a working relationship with Heath. But Heath lost the 1974 elections and once more the French and the Germans were left alone with each other. Outside forces could not replace the partnership.

The real issue now was monetary stability. France wanted some sort of monetary union because without it the recently completed CAP would be unworkable. Meanwhile, the U.S. was pressing for the revaluation of the

European currencies to help U.S. exports, and Nixon forced the issue by uncoupling the dollar from gold in August 1971.

Although it is impossible here to do justice to the complex debate that took place over the following years, one point may be stressed: the need for and difficulty of harmonizing French and German macroeconomic policy.[30] Thus France wanted fixed rates of European currencies, both one against the others and all against the dollar, enforced by currency controls. West Germany, however, opted after much internal debate for a float against the dollar, which sent the mark up and, while damaging German competitiveness, gave the Bundesbank more control over inflation by ending the need to exchange marks for an overvalued dollar. West Germany would have liked a joint float in order to avoid loss of competitiveness in Europe, but France resisted this, fearing that either the franc would go up or that it would have to be supported by high interest rates. In either case French growth would be damaged. When France did enter a joint float—the snake—it left it in January 1974, despite the risks to the CAP and the blow struck at European unity vis-à-vis the U.S., rather than deflate.

Pompidou's motives were largely domestic, dictated by the switch of priorities away from foreign policy. The key to his presidency is the quest for growth which he perceived as a solution to the social tensions that had exploded in 1968. In 1973 he accepted an inflation rate of 7.3 percent in return for a growth rate of 5.4 percent. But the foreign policy aspect of this choice was the need to overtake West Germany; in 1971 he declared that France must double her industrial capacity over the next ten years in order to equal Germany's. The drawback that the race for growth unleashed a vicious circle of inflation and a weak franc which then undermined growth, would not become apparent until the late 1970s.

In the meantime there could be no monetary union between France and Germany, much less in the broader EC. The clash between the "economist" approach of the Germans and the "monetarist" approach of the French was illusory because only the economist approach could work. Both countries had a vested interest in some form of monetary system that could protect Europe against the imperial vagaries of the dollar, but they could not achieve it without harmonizing their macroeconomic policies, unless West Germany were willing to subsidize France massively—which she was not.

Moreover, although the revaluation of the mark was undertaken in Germany as a gesture of conciliation to the U.S., whose support was needed for the *Ostpolitik* and who was a more significant trading partner for Bonn than for Paris, it was the German emphasis on deflation and a strong currency which offered the real defense against the U.S. Jobert's criticism of the way that the

American government ignored the European interests during the 1973 Arab–Israeli war was well founded, but would have remained mere rhetoric without the rigor of the Bundesbank. France and Germany were changing roles.

This was not, however, apparent when Pompidou died and Brandt left office in 1974. Franco–German cooperation did not appear to be flourishing, as the continued squabble over the CAP demonstrated. However, the limits of the *Ostpolitik* and the need to correct the shortcomings of Pompidou's economic policy—as well as the invasive presence of the U.S. and the persistent absence of Britain and Italy—brought into being the most promising phase of the relationship.

By the mid–1970s the *Ostpolitik* could go no further. The Soviets had gained from it the recognition of their power in Eastern Europe and had no interest in allowing West Germany more influence; West Germany had to gamble that in the long run the influence she had gained would corrode Soviet and East German rule. The U.S.–Soviet detente, which had made the *Ostpolitik* possible, was fading as American critics of SALT II confronted a Brezhnev who was engaging in military adventures in Africa and deploying the SS20s in Europe. The German government's task, which caused less friction with France, was to ensure that the U.S. would continue as protector but prevent Germany from being caught up in a new cold war. The methods it would employ were to press, not without misgivings, for the NATO decision to install the Pershing and cruise missiles and to attempt bilateral negotiations with the U.S. and the USSR.[31]

But his dealings with the new Carter administration convinced Schmidt that the U.S. was no longer capable of providing leadership for the West. Carter's human rights policies, his confusion over arms control, and above all his refusal to draw up an economic policy to deal with the effects of the oil crisis infuriated Schmidt. Since there was little to be gained in the East or across the Atlantic, Schmidt turned to Western Europe. For him this was not new; he had enjoyed good relations with Giscard d'Estaing when they were the finance ministers of their respective countries. He would have liked closer ties with the Labor government in Britain, but its obdurate Atlanticism and minimalist attitude towards the EC made that impossible. Similarly Italy, plagued by inflation and the—to Schmidt—incomprehensible historic compromise, could not be a partner.

Not that Schmidt was a francophile, as Adenauer had been, or that he had a plan for Western Europe, however vague it might be, as Brandt had. Schmidt was primarily concerned with the well–being of the German economy, but this led him to take measures that changed the EC. He was able to do so because the oil crisis and the ways the various countries responded to it left West Germany in a position of leadership. It has been argued that the real task facing the European states was not merely to execute a deflation that would compensate for the slice of revenue that was transferred to the OPEC countries, but to undertake a more fundamental redistribution within their societies which would transfer wealth from labor and from the share of government spending that went to welfare towards business. Wages and health care must be adjusted to permit increased profit margins.[32]

For well-known cultural reasons such as a skepticism about Keynesianism and an obsession with inflation, West Germany was able to undertake this plan and had started even before the oil price increase. Whereas in 1972 real domestic demand rose by 4 percent in Germany and by 4.8 percent in France, in 1973 the figures were 3.3 percent and 6.3 percent. Although in 1974 fiscal policy was used in the counter–cyclical manner to maintain flagging demand, and trade unions obtained high increases in the wage round, the Bundesbank imposed a tight monetary policy which brought about a recession and pushed unemployment above one million. This reduced wage demands in 1975 and led to generally good years from 1976 to 1979.

The political result was that while Britain had to call in the IMF, and Italy the PCI, West Germany had got its recession out of the way. Unemployment was lower in 1978 than in 1975; 3.5 percent compared with 3.6 percent. *Modell Deutschland* was launched. There was a shift of power within Germany where the Bundesbank, which could control speculation better because of the floating mark, gained influence. But internationally the prestige accrued to Helmut Schmidt, who used it to find a partial and European solution to the problem of the dollar, which fell sharply in the winter of 1977–78.

The EMS was designed to limit the damage that a high mark created for West Germany. First, by reestablishing nearly fixed parities, it protected German competitiveness within the EC, and second, by creating monetary stability among Germany's major trading partners, it benefitted German exports. Although it was hoped that the EMS would also shelter the mark against the plunges of the dollar by making other European currencies like the franc equally desirable, this did not take place. Indeed, there was a contradiction between this aim and the previous one, which implied extend-ing German monetary stability to other European countries: the exposed mark was the unwelcome price of leadership.

The Bundesbank opposed the EMS, fearing that the weaker EC countries would succeed in exporting their inflation to West Germany and dragging down the mark, but the government circumvented this obstacle by insisting on the grid formula rather than the basket which was favored by Italy. In the argument with the bank Schmidt was inspired not by any kind of "Euro-idealism" but by a broader sense of the national interest. However, this led him to consider political as well as economic issues and to adopt a European rather than a merely German perspective.[33]

His gamble was that the risk of having to bail out France or Italy was smaller than the risk of being caught up in the whirlpool of the dollar. The debates about the EMS coincided with the pressure from the U.S. to act as the locomotive of world economic revival. Schmidt bowed to this pressure, and while the precise effects of the 1978 expansion are unclear, it ushered in a more troubled period where initial high growth—4 percent in 1979—gave way to recession, confused government policies, and clashes with the Bundesbank. It is likely that the EMS was designed to protect West Germany against the consequences of the locomotive role, but it could not do this, constituting further proof that a Franco–German (or, indeed, EC) agreement cannot really work without U.S. cooperation. Yet the intent indicates that the bid for a measure of autonomy from the U.S. inspired West Germany's first attempt at leadership in Western Europe.

The EMS could not have been instituted without French cooperation, which was accorded for a different set of reasons. In 1974 Giscard d'Estaing was elected president by a narrow margin over Mitterrand. This made him reluctant to undertake a sustained policy of deflation, which would have jeopardized his project of a reformist center able to win support both from the left and the Gaullist right. After running a 13.7 percent inflation rate in 1974, he had to cut back, but when in 1975 GDP dropped by 0.3 percent, his prime minister Jacques Chirac once more expanded. Since government spending and real wages were rising, the oil crisis was essentially paid for by industry. Moreover, the state, which had helped create the "thirty glorious" years of prosperity by its *dirigisme,* was looking weak.

In 1976 Giscard changed prime ministers, and Raymond Barre gave priority to the battle against inflation. Judgements on Barre's success vary, and a contemporary observer distinguished hard and soft elements in his policy.[34] While he stabilized the franc, ended the current account deficit, and brought domestic demand below the G7 average from 1977 to 1979, he could not contract the money supply sufficiently to hold down inflation and could not restore the level of business profits. This is the context in which to set Giscard's role in setting up the EMS—he wished, unlike Pompidou, to have a macroeconomic policy like West Germany's, but for political reasons he could not. The solution was to call in the Bundesbank to help him. In 1975 the franc had gone back into the snake, but it had departed again in March 1976. Two years of austerity later the franc was ready to enter the EMS, a move which was both the reward of virtue and the promise—which was not kept—that there would be no backsliding.

The close tie with West Germany was an essential feature of Giscard's redefined project. In *Démocratie française* he offered Germany as a model; a country with few ideologies and much social cohesion where alternation of parties in power could take place and inflation could be combatted. *Modell Deutschland* was proposed, and in a way created, by France. From this time on there is, unlike during the postwar period, a cultural admiration for Germany. It was not universal, for Sartre and Genet were fulminating against the authoritarian methods the SPD was using to combat the Rote Armee Fraktion terrorists, but from the late 1970s there has been a current of interest in such German institutions as the apprenticeship program.[35]

Here the difference between de Gaulle and his successor is clear: Giscard was more realistic in his view of France's strength. However, it is too simple to speak of French acceptance of German supremacy in Europe when France was in fact using the Bundesbank to increase her own strength. The French state had lost control over the distribution of value added between capital and labor and needed German help to regain it. Giscard was trading in one kind of power for another.

He was also successfully pursuing the by now traditional goals of tying West Germany to France after the troubling years of the *Ostpolitik,* and increasing French participation and hence power in Europe after the erratic period of the later de Gaulle. If his acceptance of direct elections to the European Parliament may be seen as a concession to the German vision of Europe, then the formalization of the Council of Ministers meetings was a victory for the French vision. Moreover, Giscard tried to increase French influence over Germany by offering her military protection.

At least arguably, Giscard was following up the neglected European strand in de Gaulle's security thinking. Giscard admitted that France could not define sanctuary simply in terms of territory and could not stand aside from an eventual battle of Germany. The solution was the concept of "enlarged sanctuary," which would mark a stronger commitment to defend Germany.[36] There were two features of this new approach which might be expected to appeal to the West German government. The first was that France was offering to participate more fully with conventional weapons and Theater Nuclear Weapons in the battle of Germany rather than using such weapons as warnings before the *force de frappe* was unleashed. The second was that France would be cooperating more with NATO forces, on which West Germany relied.

Giscard was once more being modest. The purely national option was not credible for France, and the conception of a European defense could become credible only when Europe was politically more united. In the meantime it must be blended with Atlanticism. Under Giscard's presidency French relations with the U.S. had improved after the theatrics of Kissinger and Jobert, and the U.S. supported the French intervention in Katanga. Moreover, Giscard was not repeating the 1963 mistake of forcing West Germany to chose between France and the U.S. In the long run the combination of greater West German independence, American overextension, and Franco–German military cooperation might lead to a European security system. The immediate benefit was that France's superiority in defense could counterbalance German economic power.

Yet Giscard did not follow through on his innovations and after 1977 he spoke less of enlargened sanctuary. The most probable reason is the opposition from the orthodox Gaullists who feared that his policy would lead to military integration into NATO. Having many battles to fight and being unable to create a strong center, Giscard chose to concentrate on the Barre Plan and the EMS. This was the third time that Franco–German military cooperation had failed, and it would be left to Mitterrand and Kohl to try again.

In the early 1980s Franco–German cooperation went through another of its periodic lapses, but both the decline and the recovery indicated the logic of the alliance. Economic difficulties in both countries had to be confronted nationally before the solutions could be reinforced by international agreements. In Germany the *Wende* was necessary before cuts in government spending and investment grants for industry could reverse the downward trend that started in 1979. In France the Keynesian expansion of 1981–83 demonstrated the old truth that the EMS could not work without harmony of macroeconomic policy. Conversely, the adoption of *rigueur* permitted the relaunching of cooperation with West Germany.

Political developments indicated that France and Germany were condemned to be partners. Mitterrand came to power in 1981 as the critic of a relationship that he considered too close and too exclusive. The French Socialists and the SPD had disagreements such as their reactions to the imposition of military rule in Poland, where Mitterrand was more critical of Jaruzelski than Schmidt was. But hard facts drew the two countries back together. The very size of the German trade surplus with France in 1982 made it impossible for Kohl not to help Mitterrand stabilize the franc. The threat that the Soviet military build–up posed to French security drove Mitterrand to support Kohl over the installation of the cruise missiles. The vicissitudes of the dollar and the anti–European tirades of Thatcher excluded other options, and in 1983 Franco–German cooperation was relaunched.

CONCLUSION

The dominant theme of the partnership has been the pursuit of national interest by France and Germany, but this consistency has left space for variables. There has been a discrepancy between the rapid pace of economic integration and the slower pace of political accord, between the spurts of cooperation and the ebbs that follow them. Such movements spring from the structure of the ballet, a *pas de deux* where the dancers embrace while remaining apart and seeking other partners. Over our period there were two changes in the choreography. West Germany grew stronger even if France proved able to adapt, and the collective strength of the partners grew as well. For the decade after World War II they scraped for "increased leverage" within the U.S.'s domain, while in the 1960s de Gaulle undertook his great rebellion. By 1980 there were signs that the French and Germans were getting ready to bargain with the U.S. about the creation of a multipolar world.[37]

NOTES

1. Laurent Greilsamer, *Hubert Beuve-Méry* (Paris: Fayard, 1990), p. 199.
2. For the French turn-of-the-century interest in Germany, see Theodore Zeldin, *France 1848–1945* vol. 2 (Oxford: Clarendon, 1977), p. 113. For Michel Tournier, see his autobiography *Le Vent Paraclet* (Paris: Gallimard, 1977). For an overview of Franco–German cultural relations, see Robert Picht, "Kulturelle Beziehungen als Voraussetzungen deutsch–franzoesischer Kommunikation," in Robert Picht (ed.), *Deutschland, Frankreich, Europa* (Munich: Piper, 1978), pp. 243–267.
3. Edgar Faure, *Mémoires* vol. 2 (Paris: Pion, 1984), p. 147.
4. Charles de Gaulle, *Mémoires de guerre—Le Salut* (Paris: Plon, 1959), p. 62.
5. This was already one of Pompidou's fears. See Georges Pompidou, *Entretiens et discours 1968–1974* vol. 2 (Paris: Plon, 1975), p. 163.
6. De Gaulle, *Mémoires de guerre*, p. 179.
7. Roger Morgan argues that Britain and Germany cooperated in NATO, while France and Germany moved towards economic interdependence. See Roger Morgan and Caroline Bray (eds.), *Partners and Rivals in Western Europe: Britain, France and Germany* (London: Gower, 1986), Preface, p. xi.
8. Alfred Grosser, "Vorwort," in Picht, *Deutschland,* p. 7.
9. David Calleo has argued that there is a fundamental difference between seeking "a substitution for American hegemony" and "increasing European leverage

within it." See *Beyond American Hegemony* (New York: Basic Books, 1987), p. 36. My thesis is that France and Germany have accepted U.S. hegemony where it suited them or where they had no choice, but they have sought to transform it into something like the balance of power which Calleo recommends; see the conclusion to this chapter.

10. Konrad Adenauer, *Erinnerungen 1945–1953* (Stuttgart: Deutsche Verlags–Anstalt, 1963), p. 245.

11. Alexander Werth, *France 1940–1955* (Boston: Beacon Press, 1966), p. 389. For the way France and other countries seek to expand sovereignty by engaging in the construction of Europe, see my "France and the EC: Can a Gaullist World Power Find Happiness in a Regional Bloc?" *Johns Hopkins University Bologna Center Occasional Papers,* 1992.

12. For this account of the French role in the ECSC I have drawn heavily on Alan Milward, *The Reconstruction of Western Europe 1945–1951* (London: Methuen, 1984), pp. 362–420.

13. Adenauer, *Erinnerungen,* pp. 335, 330.

14. Ibid., p. 345. Wolfram Hanrieder has argued that for Adenauer "the primary pay–off came in equality rather than independence." This is true but equal treatment increased independence. See W. Hanrieder and G. Anton, *The Foreign Policies of West Germany, France and Britain* (Englewood Cliffs: Prentice Hall, 1980), p. 29.

15. Irvin M. Wall, *The U.S. and the Making of Post–War France* (Cambridge: Cambridge University Press, 1991), p. 203.

16. Calleo, *American Hegemony,* p. 32.

17. Hanrieder, *Foreign Policies,* p. 103. See also Michael M. Harrison, *The Reluctant Ally: France and Atlantic Security* (Baltimore: Johns Hopkins University Press, 1981), chapter I.

18. Henry A. Kissinger, "De Gaulle: What Would He Do Now?" *International Herald Tribune,* 7 May 1990.

19. Alfred Grosser, "France–Allemagne 1936–1986," *Politique étrangère* 1 (1986), pp. 247–255.

20. André Malraux, *Les chênes qu'on abat* (Paris: Gallimard, 1971), p. 176.

21. Ibid., p. 23.

22. For this section I have drawn on Edward Kolodziej, *French International Policy Under de Gaulle and Pompidou* (Ithaca: Cornell University Press, 1974), p. 74 and following. For a good account of de Gaulle's dealings with Adenauer, see Julius W. Friend, *The Linchpin: French–German Relations 1950–1990* (New York: Praeger, 1991), chapter 2.

23. Philip H. Gordon, *A Certain Idea of France: French Security Policy and the Gaullist Legacy* (Princeton: Princeton University Press, 1993), p. 41.

24. Pierre Messmer, "Notre politique militaire," *Revue de défence nationale,* May 1963, p. 761.

25. For Germany see Hanrieder, *Foreign Policies,* p. 16. For France see Kolodziej, *French International Policy,* p. 185.

26. Kolodziej, *French International Policy,* p. 256.

27. Jean Monnet, quoted in *Le Monde,* 9 May 1970.

28. Hanrieder, *Foreign Policies,* p. 129.

29. Georges Pompidou, quoted in Daniel Calard, "Convergences et divergences politiques," *Documents* 2/1974, p. 95. For Jobert, see "Michel Jobert au Spiegel," *Documents* 4/1973, p. 11.

30. For the economics of the 1970s I have drawn much on Jörg Boche, "Franco–German Economic Relations: National Strategies and Cooperation in the European Community," Ph.D. diss., Johns Hopkins University Paul H. Nitze School of Advanced International Studies, 1992, chapters 3, 4, 7, and 8.

31. For information on Helmut Schmidt I have drawn on Klaus Wiegrefe, "Die Sowjetunionpolitik H. Schmidt 1977–1982," M.A. thesis, Universität Hamburg, 1989.

32. Boche, *Economic Relations,* p. 40–53.

33. My interpretation leaves Schmidt as the key figure in the creation of the EMS. Haig Simonian inclines to the view that Schmidt was deferring to Giscard d'Estaing, in *The Privileged Partnership: Franco–German Relations in the EC 1969–1984* (Oxford: Clarendon Press, 1985), p. 279. For my view of Giscard's role, see below. The most complete account of the decision–making process remains Peter Ludlow, *The Making of the EMS: A Case Study in the Politics of the EC* (London: Butterworth, 1982).

34. Yann de l'Ecotais, "Le bilan économique du septennat," *Express,* 28 March 1981, p. 45.

35. Valéry Giscard D'Estaing, *Démocratie française* (Paris: Fayard, 1976), p. 127. For an overview of Franco–German cultural exchange at this period, see Henri Ménudier, "Die Rolle der Information in den deutsch–franzoesischen Beziehungen," in Robert Picht (ed.), *Deutschland,* pp. 307–349. French interest in the German cinema has increased now, but of course directors like Rainer Werner Fassbinder paint an unfavorable picture of West Germany.

36. Gordon, *A Certain Idea of France,* pp. 85–88.

37. I wish to thank Randy Arndt, who worked as my research assistant for this chapter and for chapter 3.

Chapter 2

Germany Looks at France

Dana H. Allin

Three weeks after the first German multitudes poured west through the Berlin Wall, Chancellor Kohl's foreign policy adviser found himself in a tense interview with the Bonn correspondent of *Le Monde*. Why, the French journalist demanded, had Kohl failed to consult French President François Mitterrand before unveiling, on 28 November 1989, a ten–point plan for German reunification? Because, answered Horst Teltschik, the German and French leaders had already exhaustively discussed the "German question"— and besides, would Mitterrand ask German permission before speaking out on a matter of basic national interest? The Frenchman was far from satisfied. He feared dire consequences from the whole turn of events. Mikhail Gorbachev's reform efforts were endangered. European integration could be derailed. The Franco–German partnership, carefully nurtured over four decades, would end. France would have to fall back on old alliances. (Teltschik took this last dark hint to mean a Franco–Soviet combination against Germany.)[1]

The year of German reunification, starting in November 1989, did indeed prove a troubled one for Franco–German relations. Since then, things have improved. In part, the improvement is the natural consequence of prosaic realities supplanting lurid nightmares. Gorbachev did fall, the Soviet Union itself collapsed, but despite the heartwrenching travails of the former Soviet peoples and renewed savagery in the Balkans, there has been no return to the suicidal diplomatic gyrations of 1914. In part, the improvement comes from a realization that the specter of a domineering Germany will be at least delayed by the difficulties of integrating a poor and embittered eastern population. And in large part, the improvement resulted from the fulfillment of a German promise. Throughout the year of unification, countless German officials repeatedly offered some variation of this promise: German unity would be an accelerator rather than a brake on European integration. A unified Europe was to be the gilded cage that would restrain German power and reassure Germany's neighbors—France in particular.

To the extent they were able, and in the face of considerable skepticism, the Germans have proven true to their word. Yet the reunification remains unsettling to Franco–German relations for at least two reasons. First, despite its current difficulties, the bigger Germany does seem likely to wield power that, by a number of (primarily economic) measures, will be disproportionate to France's. Second, the blank check that German officials wrote for European unity seems, paradoxically, to have cast uncertainty over the entire project. In the autumn of 1992, on the heels of a European currency crisis, one could detect a pervasive sense of unease, an anxiety that the rush to European unity was taking place without any clear agreement on the meaning of the final goal.

German reunification is the obvious pivotal event of this essay. The chapter's plan is to trace, from a German perspective, the postwar partnership with France and its somewhat surprising strengthening by Kohl and Mitterrand between 1983 and 1989. It will then consider in greater detail the disturbances to that cooperation introduced by the collapse of the Berlin Wall. Finally, it will explore how German elites rate the likelihood and necessity of recovering and expanding their French connection.

BEFORE 1983

The modern antagonism between Germany and France produced three wars, starting in 1870 and ratcheting steadily upward in savagery and fury until the *Götterdämmerung* of 1945. The Franco–German enmity, in other words, spanned no more than a single lifetime, and it was congruent with the rise and spectacular fall of Bismarck's unified German state.[2] After the fall, in the western zones of occupied Germany, two men who had lived through most of this drama led a debate over how to avoid such disasters in the future. The socialist Kurt Schumacher blamed the Nazi misadventure on a mixture of militarism and monopoly capitalism. His solution was to be a humane German socialism, distinct from both Stalinist communism and American capitalism. The German state would be unarmed and neutral in the emerging

East–West conflict. In Schumacher's very plausible view, such neutrality offered the only short–term hope of reuniting his country and coaxing foreign forces out.[3]

However, it was Schumacher's conservative rival, Konrad Adenauer, who had the opportunity to chart western Germany's actual postwar course. In his analysis of recent disasters, the Federal Republic's first Chancellor seemed inclined to fault the Prussian character of Bismarck's creation. For Adenauer, the dark spirits of German history all came from the East. Although denying the charge that he was a Rhineland separatist, Adenauer was determined to create a Federal Republic of Germany that was anchored—politically, militarily, economically, and culturally—to the West. In large part "the West" meant, specifically, France. The spiritual bridging of the Rhine would begin in earnest after 1958, when the Algerian crisis brought General Charles de Gaulle back to power. The two old men discovered some surprising affinities—they had much in common that their nations' recent baleful histories could not erase. Both men combined a Catholic conservatism, a geographic sense of history, and an antipathy toward the British. Even de Gaulle's eternal battle against American hegemony found a certain sympathy in Adenauer, who, while dependent upon and certainly grateful to the Americans, was shrewd enough to recognize the opportunity that a Franco–American balancing act offered in terms of increased German autonomy. Above all, the Gaullist plan for building the European Economic Community upon a Franco–German deal—French agriculture for German manufactures—fit nicely with Adenauer's vision of a Rhine–centered Europe.[4]

It might well be objected that this vision had more to do with simple prejudice than with historical analysis. Adenauer's unconcealed distaste for eastern Germany left him vulnerable to the charge that he was in no great hurry to see his country reunited. "Once the night train from Cologne to Berlin crossed the Elbe," he once famously remarked, "I got no more sleep."[5]

And yet, traumatic as the experience was for the hapless East Germans, Germany's postwar division arguably served European stability, for reasons of geopolitical balance rather than geographical culture. The Federal Republic was roughly equal in population to and considerably smaller in area than France. The French, and other West Europeans, could be more comfortable getting into bed with a German state that had been, literally, cut down to size.[6]

Thus could Adenauer, in league with de Gaulle and cruel circumstance, establish a remarkable alliance of former foes. Adenauer's successors maintained this alliance. As Patrick McCarthy details in chapter 1, however, their attention to rival demands—from across the Atlantic and across the Elbe—led to periodic bouts of bad feeling between Bonn and Paris. In the first decade after Adenauer's 1963 retirement, Bonn was stubborn in refusing to subordinate these rival demands to the Franco–German partnership. Ludwig Erhard's Atlanticism and Willy Brandt's *Ostpolitik* irritated and alarmed the French mightily.

But this Franco–German chill was short–lived. After a spy scandal rocked the chancellery, Brandt was replaced by fellow Socialist Helmut Schmidt. Schmidt hardly abandoned the Brandt *Ostpolitik* (which had become very popular among West Germans) but his general *Weltanschauung* was evidently more westward–oriented. Paris was once again a principal lodestar for this orientation, due in part to a paradox of personality: Schmidt was a lifelong Atlanticist who had by far the worst personal relations of any German chancellor with an American president (Jimmy Carter). For this mutual incomprehension between Washington and Bonn, Schmidt compensated by reviving a warm understanding with France, in the person of French President Valéry Giscard d'Estaing.[7] The most significant product of their collaboration was the European Monetary System (EMS) of semi–fixed currency rates.

Soon after raising this institutional monument, both creators fell victim to political change. Mitterrand's Parti socialiste replaced the center–right in 1981, while a 1982 coalition switch by the small German Liberal Party (FDP) brought Christian Democrat Union (CDU) leader Helmut Kohl into the chancellery.

MITTERRAND AND KOHL, 1983–1989

For the Bonn government, François Mitterrand turned out to be a pleasant surprise. The change of governments that swept the amicable Schmidt–Giscard team from their respective offices represented a turn to the right for Germany and a sharper turn to the left for France. The divergence immediately had a damaging effect on economic ties. In general one might reasonably have expected more prickly relations.

In fact, however, the period from 1983 to 1989 proved to be among the most fruitful seven years in the entire history of Franco–German collaboration. Kohl and Mitterrand rivalled Adenauer and de Gaulle in their ability to harmonize their respective national interests. To understand why, we should look in detail at their principal arenas of cooperation: economic policy, the closely related area of European policy, and cold war/military policy.

Economic Policy

The French left's electoral triumph in 1981 led directly to a crisis in the European Monetary System. To maintain parity between currencies required convincing financial markets that inflation rates in member countries would be roughly equivalent, or that interest rate differentials would compensate. This meant, in general, that inflation–prone countries had to maintain relatively higher interest rates and in other ways dampen the pace of economic activity. In his first two years of office, however, François Mitterrand and his government did the opposite. They implemented a leftist program of nationalizations and Keynesian demand expansion that spurred capital flight, high inflation, and a deteriorating trade balance. Neither three consecutive franc devaluations nor capital controls could sufficiently relieve the pressure. France had to either jettison the Socialists' economic program or leave the EMS.[8] Such was the grim choice faced by Mitterrand, but the situation for Germany was hardly more palatable. Had France withdrawn from the EMS, the effort to create a stable currency zone would have failed, and along with it, the hope for stability and predictability in traded–goods prices so valued by German exporters. As it happened, however, the French government decided to accept the constraints imposed by integration with the German economy. Mitterrand instituted a deflationary package that was "alleged to be the largest single dose of deflation in Western Europe" since 1966.[9]

The major burden of this adjustment fell, of course, on the French. The Bundesbank did try, however, to give at least the appearance of a shared adjustment: along with the franc's third devaluation of 2.5 percent, the mark was revalued by 5.5 percent (revaluations of the mark had also accompanied the franc's two previous devaluations).[10] The Germans were bound to feel ambivalent about such revaluations since allowing the mark to appreciate hurts export competitiveness. On the other hand, maintaining it against upward pressure would have required the Bundesbank to intervene by selling marks, thus increasing the money supply and threatening its anti–inflation strategy.

The entire crisis has rightly been interpreted as a watershed in Germany's economic relations with France. A singular defeat for autarkic neo–Keynesianism, it likewise represented a triumph for the German model of monetary conservatism. Despite an unemployment rate that hovered above 10 percent throughout the rest of the decade, the French government remained zealous in its newfound crusade against inflation, which fell to 2.9 percent by early 1986.[11] Indeed, for months after Germany's reunification, France's inflation rate was consistently lower than the German rate.[12]

For Germany, the benefit of this success went far beyond the added prestige accruing to the *Modell Deutschland*. As Schmidt had originally hoped, EMS stability helped shelter the mark from the gyrations of the dollar—which soared on the back of high U.S. interest rates to DM 2.85 in 1985, then plummeted to DM 1.59 in 1987 (a record low at the time), as financial markets began to take panicky note of America's budget deficit and general indebtedness.[13] Despite such turbulent external conditions, Franco–German and, more generally, inter–European trade boomed. Pessimistic diagnoses of a degenerative "Eurosclerosis" were quickly forgotten. The German export machine produced regular surpluses, yet financial markets were so mesmerized by French price stability that they didn't seem to notice the corresponding French trade deficits. By the second half of the decade, then, the EMS had established the institutional framework for a powerful and solidly anchored mark zone. The Bundesbank operated in virtual independence, according to the dictates of German philosophy and interests, while Germany's most important trading partner (along with much of the rest of Europe) followed its lead with few complaints.

Given the virtues of this status quo for Germany, it is difficult to explain the favorable German response to the idea of a common European currency and central bank. In early 1988, French officials proposed such a monetary union. Many commentators dismissed the proposal as a manifestation of the traditional French fixation on the dangers of floating exchange rates, and a backhanded attempt to dilute the power of the Bundesbank.

But despite marked skepticism from the Bundesbank, German politicians did not join this negative chorus. By midyear, they had reached agreement on a series of conferences to study the issue and make specific proposals. More surprising yet, Bonn reacted with remarkable equanimity when, the following year, the so–called "Delors Commission" put forth a three–step plan for a common currency.[14]

German elites were seriously entertaining the prospect of putting German monetary policy in the hands of a central bank run by only a minority of Germans. Despite disclaimers about safeguarding this Eurobank's independence after the Bundesbank model, such a scheme had to represent a dilution of German monetary sovereignty and, by fair implication, a relaxation of the German inflation–phobia.

There were, to be sure, a couple of strictly economic explanations for this German position. For one, French success in the fight against inflation had astounded many of West Germany's economic policymakers, allowing them to take the prospect of a monetary convergence more seriously.[15] At the same time, German exporters worried about continued French trade deficits;

however sanguine financial markets might be for the moment, those structural deficits always posed the risk of a currency realignment. A common currency would end that risk.[16] Yet these economic arguments were not really strong enough for the leap in the dark that a common currency implied. What this idea's stealthily gathering momentum really represented was a triumph of ideology over economic interest. The idea of a united Europe seemed (for a time) to be more powerful than the German determination to defend the power of the Bundesbank.

European Policy

To discuss enthusiasm for European integration under the rubric of "ideology" may seem overblown, especially insofar as the rhetoric and stated aims of European integrationists so often take on a vague, something–for–everyone aspect. But the concept of a united Europe had always been an ideological battleground. The original European Coal and Steel Community stemmed from a consensus of border–region Christian Democrats—the French Schuman, Italian de Gasperi, and German Adenauer. In Germany the idea quickly came under attack from socialists, who saw an attempt to create a market space large enough for the nefarious workings of monopoly capitalism. But the subsequent SPD reform process and abandonment of "class struggle" included a marked warming to Europe until, as we have already seen, the socialist Chancellor Schmidt made himself prime architect of what is perhaps the single most important EC institution.

In France the socialist conversion occurred more recently. The disparate factions that Mitterrand reconstituted as the *Parti socialiste* had included, to be sure, traditional pro–Europeans. But Mitterrand's "Alliance of the Left" with the French Communists had featured a hostility to the EC that was distinctly reminiscent of the SPD in the 1950s. Yet after the 1983 turnaround, as Patrick McCarthy observes in chapter 3, Mitterrand's party needed a new centerpiece for "socialist" politics. They found it, somewhat ironically, in "Europe."[17]

Of course, for a united Europe to be even vaguely "socialist," it had to be constructed around some basic social–democratic principles. And in practical terms, it had to be constructed in continued partnership with Germany. To understand the success of the Mitterrand–Kohl collaboration in this matter, we must understand how French socialist and German center–right governments could agree on a European program that envisioned combining virtually borderless trade with a commonly regulated "social space." To many critics on the left, the answer will be obvious: the PS had abandoned socialism; the social space was a fig leaf to cover naked capitalism. But the other answer is that the center–right government of Chancellor Helmut Kohl was a fairly faithful representative of German social democracy. Christian Democracy stems from a Catholic tradition that stresses social solidarity as much as, or more than, free markets. Moreover, by the early 1980s, most social achievements of the SPD's thirteen years in power were recognized as politically unchallengeable. There was a wide consensus among Germany's mainstream parties about preserving the advanced German welfare state. There was a similar consensus in favor of progress on European unity.[18]

Franco–German unity was dramatized by the antagonism that opened up between Kohl and Mitterrand on one hand, and British Prime Minister Margaret Thatcher on the other. Within EC councils, Thatcher conducted a campaign of sustained diplomatic skirmishes against the allegedly "statist," *dirigiste* proclivities of the continental Europeans.

Cold War Issues

The breakdown of East–West detente in the late 1970s had a polarizing effect on domestic politics in most member nations of the Atlantic Alliance. In West Germany this polarization helped, in a peculiar way, solidify the Kohl–Mitterrand partnership.

For the first three decades after World War II, German social democrats had been among the most zealous of cold warriors. It is true that Schumacher had hoped to escape the clutches of an American–led anti-Soviet alliance. But the socialists had a bitter quarrel with Stalinist communism that was, in its own way, more ideologically intense than most other varieties of anti-communism—born, as it were, of the 1917 schism of German Social Democracy.[19] Schumacher himself had fought communists in the streets, and once memorably remarked, "a communist is a Nazi varnished red." In the Berlin "spy war" of the 1950s, Social Democrats were enthusiastic partners of the CIA. Willy Brandt, Berlin mayor when the Wall went up, became an international symbol of European resistance to Soviet tyranny. Throughout the 1960s, the SPD was strongly Atlanticist; susceptibility to Gaullist blandishments more often occurred on the German right.

Yet the *Ostpolitik* that Brandt charted, although it presupposed a continued harboring within NATO, probably helped guide the SPD into ideological straits. German socialists took justified pride in a diplomatic achievement that eased the pains of a divided Germany and very possibly hastened the end of the Cold War. They had a political stake in detente, however, that made them politically vulnerable as Soviet foreign policy veered into geriatric bellicosity. Moreover, a new generation of leftist Germans, veterans of the 1968 student movement, was outraged by the American war in Vietnam (and untouched by the inhibitions of such socialists as Brandt, who felt that he owed and needed the Americans too much to voice his own deep misgivings about the war).[20] Those new–leftists who were not permanently alienated from mainstream politics naturally gravitated to the SPD, creating there a strong current of skepticism about American leadership.

Such was the situation in 1977 as Chancellor Helmut Schmidt became alarmed by the buildup of Soviet intermediate–range missiles aimed at Western Europe. Schmidt gave a speech that year in which he warned that U.S.–Soviet efforts to negotiate a balance in intercontinental nuclear weapons might perversely magnify the significance of Soviet nuclear superiority in the European theater.[21] After consultations within NATO, the Carter administration responded with the offer of a new generation of ballistic and cruise missiles that could strike Soviet territory from bases in Britain, Italy, the Netherlands, and West Germany.

But when it came time to implement the program, Schmidt faced emotional opposition throughout Germany and open revolt within his own party. Whether in political panic or out of genuine conviction, he proposed a moratorium on deployments to give negotiations a better chance. Carter administration officials concluded bitterly that he was trying to waffle out of a weapons program that he himself had instigated.[22]

In reality, there was a considerable element of exaggeration in the alarms about Moscow's potential to exert nuclear blackmail over Western Europe. The NATO "Euromissile" deployments were, at any rate, a rather incoherent strategic response to the problem.[23] However, the opposition of a large part of the SPD, along with Greens, church groups, and a broad swath of German civil society was at least equally faulty in its logic. The West German peace movement seemed hysterically anti-nuclear, loaded down with pacifist clichés, and, as Henry Kissinger complained, "in most respects addressed to the wrong governments."[24] The movement lent partial credence to the fears of many pessimists, that Germans were already so cowed by Soviet military intimidation that the FRG had opted, spiritually if not formally, out of NATO.[25]

No one was more alarmed at this prospect than the French. As Philip Gordon describes in chapter 7, the *Parti socialiste,* by the time of its triumph in France's 1981 election, had embraced neo–conservative views of a resurging Soviet threat. Mitterrand gave dramatic testimony to these views when he stood before the Bundestag in 1983 and implored the Germans to accept deployment of the American Euromissiles. German socialists were bitter at this intervention from an ostensible ideological ally.[26] Kohl's Christian Democrats, who had assumed the chancellery but still had to face the electorate on a prodeployment platform, were correspondingly grateful. East–West strategic policy could be added to the areas of a remarkable Kohl–Mitterrand consensus—and this despite the "very different [French and German] perspectives on international security." Military provisions of the Franco–German treaty were reactivated, including creation of a (largely symbolic) Franco–German brigade.[27]

It must be emphasized that the Kohl–Mitterrand strategic partnership went well beyond simple anti–Soviet ideology, or support for America's nuclear umbrella. Kohl needed a somewhat more flexible support than he received from the U.S. Reagan administration, which pushed Bonn to be vigilant about the Soviet threat and tended to hector when this vigilance was (in American eyes) insufficient. Paris was far more willing to follow the tactical shifts that Kohl—in alliance with the popular Liberal Foreign Minister Hans Dietrich Genscher—deemed necessary. Kohl and Genscher made clear that, however committed they were to a strengthened U.S. nuclear deterrent, they had no intention of joining the Americans in repudiating detente. They refused, for example, to cancel the massive project for a modern pipeline linking Western Europe with natural–gas fields in Siberia. In this refusal they enjoyed strong support from France, which had its own heavy financial involvement in the project.[28] Likewise, the Germans and French were united in opposition to President Reagan's Strategic Defense Initiative (SDI) because it violated their notion of a "pure" nuclear deterrence based on mutual vulnerability.

In 1985 Mikhail Gorbachev was named Soviet Communist Party General Secretary and began, tentatively at first, the reform process that would lead in a few short years to revolution throughout Eastern and Central Europe. The West Germans were at once enthusiastic: Genscher in particular saw a potential vindication of the *Ostpolitik* he had conducted under both SPD– and CDU–led governments. Paris retained much of its neo–conservative skepticism for a while longer. Even so, the FRG could continue to count on French support for both its *Ost–* and *Westpolitik.*

Again, this French support seemed steady even when the valence of Bonn's policy switched. Thus, Paris and Bonn together registered strong opposition to the utopian plans for complete abolition of nuclear weapons that Reagan and Gorbachev entertained at their 1986 summit meeting in

Iceland. Then, after George Bush replaced Reagan as president, the Americans tried to push one weapons program too many. Many members of the Bush administration were determined to reverse what they saw as the sentimental trust in Gorbachev that had characterized Reagan's last two years. So despite the Reagan–Gorbachev treaty to dismantle all intermediate–range Euromissiles, U.S. officials decided that early 1989 was the time to reaffirm the centrality of nuclear deterrence for NATO strategy. The vehicle of this reaffirmation was to be a new generation of short–range nuclear weapons in Western Europe (mainly West Germany). The American army would replace its two–decade–old Lance missile with a new model of four–times–greater range (450 km, just under the 500 km limit set by the INF treaty). It would also get new nuclear artillery shells. The air force would deploy a new air–launched missile with a range also just under the 500–km limit.[29]

The program ran into heavy German resistance. The CDU leadership had no heart for a replay of the Euromissile trauma. The government's prospects in the 1990 elections were looking increasingly grim anyway. The SPD, correspondingly confident, was sure to make the government pay politically if it accepted the deployments. Moreover, Kohl was also under pressure from his coalition partners: Genscher was strongly opposed to the "modernization." The ground–launched Lance missiles were particularly offensive to German sensibilities since they could only reach as far as western Poland or, more probably, East Germany (hence the grim slogan, "the shorter the range, the deader the German").

In April 1989 Kohl sent Genscher and Defense Minister Gerhard Stoltenberg to Washington to plead for U.S.–Soviet negotiations that might forestall the deployments. The Bush administration rejected the appeal and muttered darkly, both in public and private, about German loss of nerve, denuclearization, and "Genscherism."

Paris, notwithstanding its own strong allergy to German nuclear pacifism, once more decisively backed the Bonn government. Mitterrand could see that Washington's efforts to force the modernization were, given German realities, politically senseless (it was also not very sensible militarily— rationales for the program were quite fuzzy). In the end, the Americans (and British) backed down; the Franco–German position prevailed.

These repeated manifestations of Paris–Bonn unity were starting to look impressive. Despite very divergent strategic cultures in Germany and France, close observers were starting to count on a "continental" (as opposed to "Anglo–Saxon") position on military matters, along with stable collaboration in economics and diplomacy.[30]

THE YEAR THAT HISTORY TURNED

But this comfortable alliance was shaken in late summer 1989 by the decision of the Hungarian government to let vacationing East Germans cross into Austria. With that decision it became clear: the pressures on the East German government that had started with Gorbachev's reform process, intensified with a wave of asylum seekers in Western embassies, and given rise to emotional demonstrations throughout the GDR, could not now be turned off. Barring a bloody repression, the Berlin Wall was effectively nullified. In November the collapsing regime accepted this reality and opened it up. The only remaining question was whether any East German state would survive.

In chapter 3, Patrick McCarthy discusses Mitterrand's reaction to what he apparently considered a reckless campaign by Bonn to encourage the GDR's disintegration. German officials protested, on the other hand, that they were only trying to catch up with events, the pace of which was being set by the thousands of East Germans crossing daily to the West.[31]

Two weeks after the Wall was opened, the Elysée announced that Mitterrand would meet GDR chief Egon Krenz in late December, in Berlin. Kohl and his aides were infuriated, insofar as they had decided to put off Kohl's own official visit until the East German regime's legitimacy (under daily challenge from mass demonstrations) was better clarified. They did not, in fact, expect Krenz to last.[32]

In early December, Mitterrand met Gorbachev in Kiev. The two leaders issued separate communiqués with vaguely worded warnings to the Germans: Mitterrand's text cautioned that "no country" could ignore "the situation deriving from the war."[33] In Germany there circled an explosive rumor that Mitterrand had asked Gorbachev to block unification.[34]

From a German perspective, however, the Soviet leadership was considerably more friendly than the French. A few days after the inner–German border was opened, Gorbachev "electrified" chancellery officials by hinting at eventual support for reunification.[35] The following summer (1990) he astonished the world by agreeing that a unified Germany could be a member of NATO. German officials were likewise pleased by the support they enjoyed from Washington.[36] Vernon Walters, the U.S. ambassador to Bonn, was probably the first Allied official to explicitly welcome the prospect of German unity. The Bush administration swiftly backed Walters's statement.

Bonn officials were full of resentment when they compared the superpowers' relative warmth with the chill from Paris (and London). In the run–up to official reunification in October 1990, German elites continued to interpret various Mitterrand acts as hostile signals. For example, Mitterrand announced the withdrawal of French troops in Germany despite German pleas that they stay.[37] He also reaffirmed his determination to proceed with production of the Hades short–range missiles, which under any plausible scenario could only strike German territory.[38]

Unification had thrown a philosophical divergence into sharp relief. As one close German observer of Franco–German relations noted, the French tended to interpret events in political terms, while Germans interpreted them economically.[39] A German foreign ministry official extended this analysis: throughout 1990, he said, the French problem consisted of interpreting events with a nineteenth–century Great Power vocabulary.[40] (A Gaullist–trained Frenchman would have a ready answer: you Germans are powerful enough and deluded enough to pretend that those concepts no longer matter.)

Unification had also suggested a new imbalance in potential power. It is important to stress the word "potential." In the first year of the new Germany's existence, most criticism concerned the appearance of weakness in Germany's response to the Persian Gulf war. In fact, hardly anyone expected a German military contribution to the war, and the financial contribution turned out to be considerable. But too soon for comfort, the war revealed a paralyzing lack of consensus within German society about the just use of military force. The world witnessed an embarrassing debate about sending aircraft to NATO ally Turkey, and the beginnings of a desultory, although in many ways more serious, discussion of whether Germany would ever send troops abroad.[41]

The French did not generally join in these attacks: as Alfred Grosser observed, they were likely pleased with the demonstration that France was a global military power and Germany was not.[42] The more immediate shadow over Franco–German relations was cast by economic power. Yet here again the immediate product of unification was hardly a spurt of dynamism. Eastern Germany turned out to be a deeper economic quagmire than most experts had predicted. The task of absorbing and rebuilding this productive wasteland was clearly going to absorb the lion's share of German capital and energies for years. In 1991, the German Federal Government's net transfers to eastern Germany were DM 140 billion. The budget deficit grew to DM 180 billion, and German price inflation, at 4.2 percent, surpassed the French rate.[43]

German long–term interest rates remained low, however, reflecting a financial–market confidence that had two likely sources. First, and most vaguely, there was ample reason to assume that after a painful period of reconstruction and rationalization, the former GDR would become part of a revived German powerhouse. Second, and more tangibly, the Bundesbank was doing its utmost to maintain the credibility of its anti–inflation drive. In response to the mounting federal spending for the East, the Bank pushed real short–term interest rates sharply higher, causing dismay among its European partners (and, in late 1992, a full–blown crisis in the EMS). Effective monetary hegemony was, then, the most salient form of real German power in the early 1990s.[44]

A third specter haunting the French involved German influence in Eastern Europe. French elites have often seemed preoccupied with the historical theme of Rapallo—the interwar German–Soviet rapprochement. Like most historical analogies, this one has glaring weaknesses. Weimar Germany and Bolshevik Russia were both desperately isolated from the international community, hardly today's situation. But is Germany, nonetheless, assuming a commanding position in Eastern Europe that might increase its power and set off a destabilizing competition with France and other European nations?

The evidence as of this writing is mixed. Certainly Germany has delivered the greatest share of direct aid to the Soviet Union and its successor states. This factor might very well have influenced Gorbachev in 1989 as he pondered Mitterrand's request to slow the drive to unity; it certainly affected his 1990 acceptance of German NATO membership. But profit–seeking German investment in Russia and the rest of Eastern Europe has fallen short of expectations, due perhaps to the heavy demand for capital in eastern Germany. German firms are indeed quite active in Hungary, Czechoslovakia, and Poland, but in terms of direct–investment share they are rivalled by Americans and Italians.[45]

By far the most contentious element of the new Germany's *Ostpolitik* has been its emotional involvement in Yugoslavia's civil war. Again, it is difficult to make any definitive judgment about that involvement. On the one hand, an observer of contemporary German politics is struck by one point of absolute unanimity: if there is ever to be a major international military intervention, German troops cannot participate. World War II memories are too fresh. On the other hand, the Balkan war is the area of recent controversy in which the Germans have 'most unceremoniously forced their position upon the French. As the war broke out in the summer of 1991, German and Austrian public and official opinion quickly fell in with the Slovenians and Croatians. The French, British and American governments were initially more sympathetic to Serbia. There were unsinister explanations for this alignment: Germany has a large Croatian community within its borders, and the French, British, and Americans were reluctant to sanction the breakup of any European nation. But nervous historians and Serbian propagandists could not help noticing that this line–up was the same as in World War II.

As the fighting grew in ferocity, the German leadership felt increasing pressure to grant the moral support of official recognition to the two break-away republics. Bonn held back, hoping for a common EC position. But in December Kohl delivered an ultimatum to Mitterrand: either join Germany in an official act of recognition or face the ignominy of an open split in EC ranks.[46] In January 1992, on the basis of a complicated face–saving compromise, France went along. The effect is hard to gauge: some observers argue that this German policy helped establish the cease–fire in Croatia; others, that it precipitated the Bosnian declaration of independence and the ensuing slaughter there.

REPAIRING THE DAMAGE

Conor Cruise O'Brien has written eloquently about the continuously rolling film reel that projects a nation's historical consciousness. For Israelis and other Jews it is a film of the Holocaust. For Palestinians, the Irgun massacre at Deir Yassein. For the Northern–Irish Catholics, the Blacks and Tans.[47]

Modern Germans are, in this as in many other respects, unique: they too have an historical film playing in the back of their heads, but it is very often someone else's movie. It is hard to imagine another nation in which political elites are so preoccupied with their country's image abroad. In the 1990 national election campaign, the SPD's candidate for chancellor, Oscar Lafontaine, tried to make an issue of the government squandering its friendship with France. It was part of his general argument that the government was rushing intemperately into reunification.[48] The argument did not help his campaign very much, but it certainly suggested a historical irony: Lafontaine, the socialist candidate, was posing as champion of Adenauer's Germany. Kohl (to push the analogy perhaps past the breaking point) was the new Schumacher. More decisive than political alignments was the generational difference. A younger generation of elites knew, but did not really take seriously, the 40–year promise that Germany would one day reunite. Their Europe was the Europe of Brussels, Bonn, and Paris. They were, regardless of political affiliation, very much Adenauer's children. Yet, by a quirk of history, the Soviet empire unravelled just a few years before this generation was to take power. The generation still in power—that of Kohl, Genscher, Brandt and Bahr—was emotionally committed to an event that few believed would ever happen. But after it did happen, both genera-tions revealed themselves as eager to repair the damage to French relations. In Germany, as opposed to Britain for example, there is nearly unanimous support for European unity and its Franco–German core among the major political parties. Kohl could not long play Schumacher, whom a French Fourth Republic president once compared, absurdly but vividly, to Hitler.[49] From almost the moment that the Berlin Wall was breached, German officials from Kohl down were repeatedly showing, in words if not always in deeds, that they understood French fears and were determined to ease them. The only way to do so was by agreeing to an accelerated schedule for European unity. The German government, according to Kohl's adviser Horst Teltschik, "found itself in the situation of having to approve practically every French initiative for Europe."[50]

In an April 1990 meeting in Paris, Kohl and Mitterrand vowed that "German and European unity would be two sides of the same coin."[51] The following year, in one of the more dramatic examples of Bonn's urgent desire to please Paris, the Germans agreed to turn the largely symbolic Franco-German brigade into a 35,000–strong joint corps. The United States, seeing competition for NATO, registered strong unhappiness with the plan, and although leading German figures insisted they wanted to avoid the old Gaullist choice of France or America, it is significant that they seemed more concerned with keeping Paris happy.[52]

The two–year burst of Euro–enthusiasm appeared to reach a climax with the December 1991 Maastricht Treaty on European economic and political union. But after Maastricht many Europeans started to wonder if the German mantra of reassurance was leading everyone too far too fast. The Danes, most dramatically, rejected the treaty in a referendum. France missed doing the same by only a narrow margin of votes. Britain's Conservative Party found itself bitterly divided over this issue.

Although the Bundestag ratified the treaty by an overwhelming majority, Germans in general were not immune to these misgivings. Their deepest disquiet came in the area of greatest German strength. The Maastricht Treaty anticipated a European central bank and a common currency as early as 1999. Was it really a good idea, many Germans asked, to sacrifice the mark, that overriding symbol of Germany's postwar success and stability?[53]

In retrospect, what seems surprising is not this later disquiet but the earlier lack of any serious German resistance to the idea. The "D–Mark society"—an almost emotional identification of many Germans with their money—is easily parodied. But its effects seem benign, even beneficial, when compared to some of the more romantic German impulses of this century. After Maastricht, Germans seemed to wake up en masse to the implications of abolishing the mark. Polls showed a clear majority against the move.[54] A group of leading German economists issued a manifesto challenging the wisdom of the plan. Somewhat surprisingly, a consortium of leading banks joined together in a counter–statement to support the union.[55] The Bundesbank maintained a position of malign neutrality. It was generally assumed that German central bank officials did not like the idea, but recognized its political imperative.[56]

The choice of integration is often described as a willful surrender of sovereignty. But it is also argued that in economic matters national sovereignty is generally illusory. National economies have grown too interdependent. Moreover, economic policymakers have learned that economic growth cannot be purchased forever with Keynesian expansion: there is no long–term trade–off between unemployment and inflation. If this is true, the French government did not surrender real sovereignty in 1983. The choice of *austérité* was the only rational one, even if France had not belonged to an EMS.

Arguably, however, it is the Germans—and only the Germans— who are now being asked to give up real sovereignty. The argument is a simple one. Whereas the French cannot long afford a loose money policy and its attendant outflow of capital, the Bundesbank can always tighten interest rates and force Paris, Rome or London to follow suit. To dismantle the Bundesbank in deference to a European central bank (even one based in Frankfurt and committed to Germanic monetary conservatism) is to give up tangible power. Small wonder that German economists are nervous.

There is, however, the possibility of a sophisticated rejoinder from Eurocurrency defenders. The dilution of German monetary power, in a new monetary regime with certain guarantees of stability, might seem preferable to the breakup of the EMS. And the survival of an amicable semi–fixed currency system based on effective German hegemony in monetary affairs— a fair description of the EMS system up to 1992—assumes continued good relations between Germany and its EMS partners. When relations sour, those partners do have the option of breaking free from the system, even if the decision seems irrational in its inflationary consequences. There is presumably some limit beyond which the French or British will no longer accept Bundesbank dictates.

In September 1992, an EMS crisis suggested that the Bundesbank had found the British limit. Proximate cause of the market turmoil was the upcoming French referendum on Maastricht. A deeper cause was the high interest rates that the Bundesbank insisted upon to counteract Bonn's deficit spending for Eastern reconstruction. Unable to hold the value of the pound against these high German interest rates and market speculation, the U.K. and Italy withdrew from the EMS exchange rate mechanism. The franc also came under pressure, but joint Franco–German central bank interventions held it within its designated band.

On the surface this crisis bolstered rather than weakened Franco–German ties. An extraordinary, bitter shouting match between London and Bonn (joined by Frankfurt) once more underscored the gap between "Anglo–Saxon" and "continental" visions for Europe's future.[57] The Bundesbank's success in keeping the franc afloat, in marked contrast to the plunging pound, was noted with irritation in Whitehall and satisfaction in Paris.[58]

And the fact that two of Western Europe's four largest economies no longer belonged to the EMS exchange–rate mechanism encouraged those Germans who argued that a much smaller monetary union—essentially between Germany, France, and the Benelux countries—was the only rational plan.[59] Such suggestions of an immediate Franco–German monetary union might be seen as a German attempt to call the French bluff: we are ready for union now, but with you alone. Under such circumstances, France would face German power on its own, without allies in a Eurobank council to face down Frankfurt rigor.

Officially, however, Bonn was not raising this prospect.[60] A "two–speed" Europe has always been something of a taboo in European councils, raising the specter of marginalizing the slower members. But many German elites nonetheless argued that a Franco–German monetary union could take place almost immediately, whereas a wider union would court disaster.

Foremost proponent of this view was Karl Otto Pöhl, the recently retired Bundesbank chief.[61] Pöhl rooted his argument in Germany's recent experience with its own monetary union, between East and West. The theory of that union had been in some respects similar to expectations for a future European currency: force East German firms to compete in the same currency, without recourse to devaluation, and they will quickly rationalize production and improve productivity. But this proved a major miscalculation: the Eastern firms were so much less productive that the requirement to pay wages and other costs in marks proved a catastrophe rather than a tonic. Such skeptics as Pöhl wondered aloud whether a similar experience might be in store for, say, Italian firms when pushed against the wall of a European currency, and whether the requirement for Germany might also be similar: vast transfers to bail them out.

The September 1992 currency crisis shattered some complacent illusions about harmonious, uninterrupted progress toward European unity. It showed that Germany was unwilling to exercise its monetary hegemony in the benign fashion that Britain, and other EMS partners with weaker currencies, expected. The Bundesbank had effectively served notice that, during a period of internal difficulties occasioned by the costs of reunification, German monetary policy would be guided by German national interests.[62]

CONCLUSION

The Franco–German partnership long ago achieved its historic goals. Economically, Germany and France became the driving motor of a European trading area that now constitutes the richest continental economy in the world. Politically, the Germans and French were able to turn bitter enmity into lasting peace; although historical pessimists will remind us that, in Aristotle's words what has happened can happen, the prospect of a renewed Franco–German war hardly ranks at the top of the world's problems.

Yet for champions of the Franco–German partnership, and the more general European project, this very implausibility of war has a curious and somewhat perverse consequence. I previously referred to a difference in generations vis-à-vis Germany's eastern and western orientation. But there is, as Guenter Nonnenmacher observes, a third generation coming along for which the memories of Franco–German war are so remote as to be incomprehensible. For these post–baby–boom Germans born after 1965, the creation of Europe cannot have the same urgency. It tends to be somewhat faddish, offering perhaps a more fashionable identity than the German national one. But it is not driven by their elders' same close knowledge of the midcentury horrors. Like all fads, it might easily be abandoned.

The challenge for future German statecraft, then, may be to make future progress in the partnership with France and Europe less dependent on fashion or ideology and more manifestly a matter of German national interest. Developing a vocabulary of German interests will be a delicate business, of course. But self–interest need not be unenlightened. History'shows that it is not in Germany's interest to let its size, dynamism, or past frighten its neighbors.

At the same time, a European policy that denies the existence of German national interests courts only grief. To take the most salient example, Germany will likely give up the mark only if it makes economic sense for Germany—not merely to appease the French. That economic case can be made, as argued above, but it is hardly self–evident. Likewise, in a dispute that erupted once more as this chapter was being written, German exporters were asking why they must forgo the trade benefits of a new GATT deal for the sake of French farmers.[63] And calling the Franco–German corps a "Euro–corps" will not relieve the Germans of the burden of deciding what kind of military presence they should have in the world.

When Germany looks at France, it sees a reflection of its own hopes and fears about its place in Europe and the world. That has been true since at least the time of Adenauer. That it will continue to be true is one of the few near–certainties of the post–Cold War world.

NOTES

1. Horst Teltschik, *329 Tage: Innenansichten der Einigung* (Berlin: Siedler Verlag, 1991), p. 61.

2. Julius Friend recently observed that consideration of Germany's relations with France often starts from a fallacy: that France and Germany were "hereditary enemies." But in fact, the German Holy Roman Empire was "interested in Italy, not in Western expansion," while "France's hereditary enemy was England, not Germany." Through the nineteenth century, well after the awakening of modern German nationalism, there was a climate of mutual admiration and cultural cross–fertilization. *The Linchpin: French–German Relations, 1950–1990* (New York: Praeger, 1991), p. 7. See also Patrick McCarthy's chapter 1 of this volume.

3. Richard Barnett, *The Alliance: America–Europe–Japan: Makers of the Postwar World* (New York: Simon and Schuster, 1983), chapter 1.

4. Ibid. See also Patrick McCarthy's chapter 1 of this volume.

5. Terence Prittie, *Konrad Adenauer, 1876–1967* (London: Cowles Book Company, 1972), p. 312.

6. For a historical discussion of Germany and European equilibrium, see David P. Calleo, *The German Problem Reconsidered: Germany and the World Order, 1870 to the Present* (Cambridge: Cambridge University Press, 1978).

7. Zbigniew Brzezinski, *Power and Principle: Memoirs of a National Security Advisor, 1977–1981* (London: Weidenfeld and Nicolson, 1983), pp. 287–311, 461–463; Helmut Schmidt, *Menschen und Maechte* (Berlin: Goldman Verlag, 1987), pp. 222–264; Schmidt, *Die Deutschen und ihre Nachbarn* (Berlin: Siedler Verlag, 1990), pp. 164–241.

8. See Patrick McCarthy's discussion in chapter 3 of this volume.

9. P. Armstrong, A.J. Glyn, and J. Harrison, *Capitalism Since World War II* (London: Fontana, 1984), p. 433.

10. Cobham, "French Macroeconomic Policy Under President Mitterrand: An Assessment," *National Westminster Bank Quarterly Review* (February 1984), p. 43.

11. U.S. Bureau of the Census, *Statistical Abstract of the United States, 1991,* 111th Edition (Washington D.C., 1991), p. 848; Patrick McCarthy, "France Faces Reality: Rigeur and the Germans," in David P. Calleo and Claudia Morgenstern (eds.), *Recasting Europe's Economies: National Strategies in the 1980s* (Washington D.C: Washington Foundation for European Studies, 1990), p. 53.

12. "Privatisierung bietet Anreiz fuer auslaendische Investoren," *Handelsblatt* 16 October 1992; Tom Redburn, "Eastern Europe Piques Appetite of U.S. Firms," *International Herald Tribune,* 28 July 1992.

13. Schmidt, *Die Deutschen und ihre Nachbarn,* pp. 219–241; Tom De Vries, *On the Meaning and Future of the European Monetary System* (Princeton Essays in International Finance no.138). On American exchange rate fluctuations in the 1980s, *OECD Economic Outlook, Historical Statistics: 1960–1986* (Paris: Organization for Economic Cooperation and Development, 1988), p. 19.

14. "Chronik der europäischen Währungsintegration," *Frankfurter Allgemeine Zeitung,* 22 September 1992.

15. Interviews with Bundesbank officials, September 1990.

16. Interview, Peter–Rüdiger Puf, Verband der deutschen Industrie, Köln, September 1990.

17. McCarthy, "France Faces Reality," p. 47.

18. Christian Deubner, *Die Bundesregierung vor der "sozialen Herausforderung" des einheitlichen Binnenmarktes* (Ebenhausen Germany: Stiftung Wissenschaft und Politik, 1989).

19. Carl E. Schorske, *German Social Democracy, 1905–1918: The Development of the Great Schism* (Cambridge: Harvard University Press, 1983).

20. Brandt, *People and Politics,* p. 318.

21. Helmut Schmidt, "The 1977 Alastair Buchan Memorial Lecture," London, 28 October 1977. Reprinted in *Survival* 20, no. 1 (January/February 1978) pp. 3–4.

22. Brzezinski, *Power and Principle,* pp. 287–311.

23. Dana H. Allin, "Understanding the Soviet Threat to Western Europe: American Views, 1973–1985" (Ph.D. diss., The Johns Hopkins University Paul H. Nitze School of Advanced International Studies, 1990), chapters 3–5.

24. Henry A. Kissinger, "Strategy and the Atlantic Alliance," *Survival* 24, no. 5 (September/October 1982), p. 194.

25. Irving Kristol, "Does NATO Exist?" in Kenneth A Meyers (ed.), *NATO: The Next Thirty Years* (Boulder: Westview Press, 1980); Richard Pipes, "How to Cope with the Soviet Threat: A Long–Term Strategy for the West," *Commentary* 78, no. 2 (August 1984), p. 24.

26. "Les Socialistes allemands se demarquent des thèses de M. Mitterrand sur la sécurité européenne," *Le Monde,* 3–4 January 1983. For Egon Bahr, long–time confidant to Willy Brandt and a leader of the SPD's left wing, Mitterrand was exercising unwelcome nuclear hegemony over the West Germans: see "Atomare Klassenunterschied," *Der Spiegel,* 14 February 1984.

27. See Philip Gordon's chapter 7 of this book.

28. Bruce W. Jentleson, *Pipeline Politics: The Complex Political Economy of East–West Energy Trade* (Ithaca: Cornell University Press, 1984).

29. For a comprehensive account, see Simon Head, "The Battle Inside NATO," *The New York Review of Books,* 18 May 1989, pp. 41–46.

30. Paul H. Nitze, "What Bush Should Do To Solve the NATO Flap," *Washington Post,* 14 May 1989, p. C1.

31. Horst Teltschik's subsequently published account makes clear that, whatever the pressures of westward emigration, the Bonn chancellery was strongly motivated by its own enthusiasm for German reunification. *329 Tage.*

32. Teltschik, *329 Tage,* pp. 26, 46, 71–73.

33. Friend, *The Linchpin,* p. 82.

34. John Newhouse, "Sweeping Change," *The New Yorker,* 27 August 1990, pp. 78–79.

35. Teltschik, *329 Tage,* pp. 42-44.

36. Ibid., pp. 37–38.

37. At a September 1990 meeting with Kohl in Munich, Mitterrand agreed to divide the withdrawal into two stages, thus allowing the German government to claim that some French troops would remain indefinitely. The concession was clearly cosmetic, however, and German press commentary was bitter. See "In der Sicherheitpolitik kein Fortschritt," *Frankfurter Allgemeine Zeitung,* 22 September 1990; "Zurueck zu Maginot," *Die Zeit,* 28 September 1990.

38. For reaction of German security community, "Die deutsch–franzoesiche Sicherheitskooperation im Zeichen osteuropaeischer Transformation und westeuropaeischer Integration," Protocoll, Deutsch–Franzoesisches Kolloquium, 6./7. December 1990, Stiftung Wissenschaft und Politik, Ebenhausen Germany.

39. Interview, Rüdiger Stephan, Bonn, July 1992.

40. Confidential interview, Bonn, July 1992.

41. On German reaction to the Gulf War, see Dana H. Allin, "Neue Balance im Bündnis?" *Frankfurter Allgemeine Zeitung,* 1 March 1991.

42. Alfred Grosser interview, Paris, April 1991.

43. "Germany: The Shock of Unity," *The Economist,* 23 May 1992. In the year ending December 1991, (West) German consumer prices rose 4.2 percent, compared to 3.1 percent in France. In the year ending October 1992, the consumer inflation rates were 3.8 percent for Germany and 2.6 percent for France. *The Economist,* 25 January 1992, p. 103 and 7 November 1992, p. 131.

44. On German interest rates, see *Financial Market Trends* no. 53, October 1992 (Paris: Organization for Economic Cooperation and Development, 1992), pp. 11, 110.

45. "Privatisierung bietet Anreiz fuer auslaendische Investoren," *Handelsblatt* 16 October 1992; Tom Redburn, "Eastern Europe Piques Appetite of U.S. Firms," *International Herald Tribune* 28 July 1992.

46. "Genscher will einheitliche EG–Politik: Die Frage der Anerkennung Sloveniens und Kroatiens," *Frankfurter Allgemeine Zeitung,* 5 July 1991. On the German ultimatum, see *Le Monde,* 30 July 1992.

47. Conor Cruise O'Brien, *The Siege: The Story of Israel and Zionism* (London: Paladin Books, 1988), pp. 331, 438.

48. *Frankfurter Allgemeine Zeitung,* 13 March 1990.

49. Alfred Grosser, *The Western Alliance: European–American Relations Since 1945* (New York: Vintage Books, 1982), p. 107.

50. Teltschik, *329 Tage,* p. 61 (Author's translation).

51. Ibid., p. 208.

52. On Germany's efforts to avoid choosing between France and America, see Günter Nonnenmacher, "Ambiguités franco–allemandes," *Le Monde,* 23 June 1992.

53. For a skeptical German view, Wolfgang Krieger, "Die deutsche Integrationspolitik im postsowjetischen Europa," *Europa–Archiv,* Folge 18, 25 September 1992, pp. 515–526.

54. A January 1992 survey by the respected Institut fuer Demoskopie Allensbach found that 62 percent of Germans worried that a European currency would be less stable than the mark, as opposed to only 18 percent who expected comparable stability. "Der lange Schatten nach Maastricht: Die Bevoelkerung rechnet mit dem Verlust der Waehrungsstabilitaet bei Einfuehrung des ECU," p. 2.

55. On the manifesto of 60 German economists opposing the monetary union, *Frankfurter Allgemeine Zeitung,* 11 June 1992.

56. Interview with *Bundesbank* press spokesman Christoph Lindemann, Frankfurt, July 1992.

57. "Lamont: Deutsche Politik erzeugt Spannungen," *Frankfurter Allgemeine Zeitung,* 19 September 1992; "Bonn: Britische Anschuldigungen 'unhaltbar'," *Frankfurter Allgemeine Zeitung,* 29 September 1992; "Waigel: Deutschland ist an der Währungsunruhe nicht schuld," *Suddeutsche Zeitung,* 24 September 1992.

58. "La solidarité allemande à l'épreuve," *Le Monde,* 23 September 1992. The Bundesbank in fact spent roughly DM 33 billion to support the pound during this crisis, "substantially more, by any measure, than Germany laid out to defend the franc the following week," according to unnamed German officials quoted by *The Economist.* On the other hand, as *The Economist* also noted, "In the battle to save the franc, the Bundesbank staked its reputation; it promised there would be no realignment. In the case of sterling, it called for one." "Some are more EMU than others," *The Economist,* 3 October 1992.

59. "Doch Alleingang zur Währungsunion?" *Die Welt,* 28 September 1992; "Die Banken schlagen eine 'kleine Union' vor," *Frankfurter Allgemeine Zeitung,* 22 September 1992.

60. "Gegen EG der zwei Geschwindigkeiten," *Frankfurter Allgemeine Zeitung,* 30 September 1992.

61. "Pöhl: Währungsunion zwischen Deutschland und Frankreich möglich," *Frankfurter Allgemeine Zeitung,* 22 September 1992.

62. *Frankfurter Allgemeine Zeitung* economics editor Hans Barbier, a consistent critic of the monetary union, judged the crisis to be the "consequence of a system in

which political speculation outpaces economic realities." See "Währungsdämmerung," *Frankfurter Allgemeine Zeitung,* 18 September 1992.

63. "Structurally Unsound," *The Economist,* 14 November 1992, pp. 33–34.

Chapter 3

France Looks at Germany, or How to Become German (and European) while Remaining French

Patrick McCarthy

France's relationship with Germany has been so intense over the last decade that one is tempted to consider this a new period. Even the most convinced believer in continuity must admit that the mid–1980s reorientation of French policy, both domestic and foreign, around a renewed friendship with Germany marks an important date in postwar French history. To quote only two specific examples, the French drive for Economic and Monetary Union (EMU), which is essentially a fusion of the franc and the mark, presupposes the disappearance of the national currency which de Gaulle fought so hard to rehabilitate. Similarly, Mitterrand's bid to invent a Europe that could provide a structure for the Franco–German relationship led him to weaken de Gaulle's policy of maintaining national sovereignty by insisting on the right of veto in the European Council.

However, the notion of a complete break with the past is erroneous. When Mitterrand and Kohl set up the joint Defense Council and Economic and Finance Council in January 1988, they were implementing the provisions of the 1963 de Gaulle–Adenauer Treaty. Indeed, Mitterrand was continuing the policy that had begun with the Coal and Steel Pool, namely, that of embracing Germany in order to control her and using her strength in order to strengthen France. The EMU may be seen in this context: Schuman sought to use the German steel industry; Mitterrand wished to gain some control over the mark. If reunification caused such trauma for France, the reason is that it threatened the goals she had been pursuing for forty years. Continuity is clear in another strand of France's policy: the attempt to use the German connection in order to increase her independence from the U.S. The Franco–German army corps, announced in October 1991, is a very Gaullist challenge to U.S. dominance in NATO.

If Mitterrand has gambled more on Germany than his predecessors, the reason goes back to the oil crisis. Between 1970 and 1985 the French energy bill was multiplied by seventeen. At home, France needed to deflate and increase the percentage of value added going to business; abroad, she needed to export more to the developed world, especially after the erosion of OPEC wealth in the early 1980s. Meanwhile, West Germany had emerged stronger from the oil crisis so that cooperation with her was crucial. Giscard d'Estaing had pointed the way and, after an interlude from 1981 to 1983, Mitterrand has marched down the same path of emulation and competition.

He could not, however, merely follow his predecessors, because his is a left–wing government. The Parti socialiste (PS) had to discard much of its cultural baggage in order to become a credible partner for Germany. In 1983 it renounced its beliefs both in rapid redistribution of wealth and in the ability of the French state to defy the market. Then the Socialists had to show that Franco–German cooperation made a more modern brand of leftism possible. This task was entrusted to Jacques Delors, who tried—not always successfully—to build an EC which would intervene in the economy and conduct a social dialogue.

This chapter is divided into four parts. The first deals with the 1983–84 reorientation of French policy, and the second with the development of the revived Franco–German alliance. Since cooperation encountered problems before reunification, the third part begins in 1987 and runs to 1990, when Kohl united Germany on his terms. The last section describes how France confronts the new Germany and ends with some reflections on the Maastricht referendum and its aftermath.

1983–84: A SHIFT IN NATIONAL STRATEGY

It has been argued that the break in Franco–German cooperation when the Socialists came to power in 1981 was more rhetoric than reality.[1] Talks on defense were held between Mitterrand and Schmidt in February 1982, while Germany had offered support for the franc when it went down after the 1981 elections. If this is true, it is a sign that cooperation had become so necessary to both countries that the old pattern of spurts and lapses was changing.

However, cooperation could not flourish until each country decided its national priorities and undertook the domestic policies to pursue them.

So if agreement on defense moved most quickly, it was because the Socialists knew what they wanted. On coming to power, they abandoned the neutralist elements in the 1972 Common Program and took a Gaullist stance. They endorsed the *force de frappe* and the commitment to a policy of national defense. For this there are several reasons, but the issue here is the link between domestic politics and the French view of Germany.

The Socialists could not afford the luxury of a neutralist security policy when they were undertaking sweeping nationalizations. To arouse further opposition both at home and abroad would have been folly. Nor was there any great support for a policy that was associated with an earlier period of close alliance with the Communists. The PS contained its own anti–nuclear, deterrence–criticizing elements, often ex–militants of the Parti socialiste unifié. But it also had Atlanticists from the old SFIO, while its left, the Cérès, believed that a socialist France must be able to defend itself. In general the dovish tendencies of a Socialist party, eager to cut spending on rockets in order to build hospitals, were balanced by the republican tradition of national defense. For this conglomerate of forces the Gaullist stance provided the perfect rallying point.

Having asserted her resolution to defend herself, France could now call upon others to do the same. In particular, she could combat the German drift towards what she perceived as pacificism. In part, France was genuinely alarmed by the vast peace demonstrations held in Germany in October 1981 and June 1982, by the rise of the Greens, and by the role of the Protestant churches. In its hostility to the installation of the INF missiles, Germany seemed to be heading down a new *Sonderweg*. Reassuming the role she had played in the Brandt years, France sought to bind Germany to the West.

It was Mitterrand's good fortune that such a role suited France in two other ways. It gave her influence over the forces in Germany which favored the INF installation, namely, the new Kohl government. Mitterrand continued the discussions on defense cooperation in his October 1982 meeting with Kohl, and in January 1983 he made his Bundestag speech in support of installation. The military implications of this initiative are discussed in chapter 7, but the part which defense was coming to play in the Franco–German relationship was bound to favor France as the stronger military power. This strength could be traded in for concessions in the economic area.

By a reversal of the 1960s situation France had also become for her allies the more reliable power. The Bundestag speech had an Atlanticist dimension and it pleased the U.S. In the long run this proved less important than the European dimension, but it serves as another example of how France was able to use her American connection to strengthen her position vis–à–vis Germany. The backing she received from the U.S. could then be used to lure Germany into a series of initiatives, such as the relaunching of the WEU, which would increase French autonomy of the U.S.

In this undertaking Mitterrand's natural partner was Kohl rather than the SPD. The French and German lefts were undergoing opposing evolutions. Whereas the SPD was pushed to the left by pressure from its base, which sought to fight unemployment by Keynesian job creation and to oppose the INF installation, its French comrades were embracing Gaullism. Nor was this coincidental. The SPD, like the British Labor Party, was trapped in a declining social–democratic tradition, but the French Socialists, whose roots in that tradition went less deep, could modernize their thinking.

In the area of economics the revision took place in 1983. For the previous two years the countries had pursued antithetical policies. Even before Schmidt left power the German government had, as explained in chapter 4, begun cutting social expenditure; the CDU–led coalition continued the cuts and instituted investment incentives for industry. The result was an export–led recovery which owed part of its success to French policy. In 1981 the Socialists had gambled on a demand–side expansion through increased social spending and job creation in the public sector. Import penetration increased, the trade balance with Germany worsened and the inflation differential was high—in 1983 French inflation was 7.6 percent higher than Germany's.

In 1983 renewed pressure on the franc provoked a crisis which Prime Minister Pierre Mauroy formulated as a choice between Europe and expansion.[2] France could remain within the EMS only by deflating her economy; her alternative was to leave the EMS, to impose at least temporary measures of protectionism, and continue her dash for growth. This presentation of the situation was, however, wrong, because leaving the EMS would cause the franc to plummet and create a siege economy—the so–called Albanian option. In reality deflation was the only possible course.

Politically, this realization had profound effects on the Parti socialiste and its leadership. After a brief debate where the Cérès left the government, the party accepted the need for deflation. This in turn allowed it to become a party of government and the exponent of the alliance with Germany. For its leaders, 1983 renewed the shock of 1973: the French economy had not adapted to the harsher international climate, and a new strategy had to be devised. This turned out to be a harsher version of Giscard d'Estaing's austerity. The government gave priority to shifting resources towards business: it held down wages, reduced the inflation differential with Germany to 0.6 percent by 1989, and liberated financial markets in order to promote investment.

This was a national strategy which had as one of its components a renewal of cooperation with Germany. Like Giscard d'Estaing, Mitterrand borrowed the authority of the Bundesbank in order to impose rigor. However, the EMS could not in itself bring French inflation down to the German level; the French government must pursue the same macroeconomic policy as the German government. It could also use its strength in the security area to win economic concessions from Germany. The 505 percent revaluation of the mark in April 1983 made it possible to limit the devaluation of the franc to 2.5 percent and may be seen as a trade–off for the Bundestag speech.

The adoption of rigor made possible a grand European policy, but here again Mauroy's formulation was incorrect. Europe was not a constraint but a way to lighten a self–imposed constraint. Delors puts it provocatively: "Creating Europe is a way of regaining that margin of liberty necessary for 'a certain idea of France.' "[3] Via the EC, the French state would acquire an influence over the international economic order that had defeated the Socialist experiment. By keeping a strong franc in the EMS and moving on to EMU, France would gain some leverage over the mark—the application of the Basel–Nyborg agreement in late 1987 is an example. This in turn would allow her to influence forces outside the EC. Another supposed reason for the failure of the 1981 policy was high U.S. interest rates; perhaps an EC endowed with a common currency would have imposed order on the dollar.

So Mitterrand's opening to Europe in 1984 was a renewal of France's traditional policy of seeking to expand her margin of sovereignty through embracing Germany. Or at least that was the gamble. It was just as likely that Germany would impose a monetary order which would condemn France to permanently high unemployment. The intertwining process between France and Germany was more extensive than ever before, at a time when Germany was stronger than ever before. But Mitterrand, cultivating the modesty that has marked de Gaulle's successors, and adding to it the new modesty born of the failed socialist experiment, set off to conquer Europe.

1984–87: THE BENEFITS OF FRIENDSHIP WITH GERMANY

During the French presidency of the European Council, the first half of 1984, Mitterrand worked to get the EC moving again, and at the Fontainebleau summit he managed to resolve the problem of the British rebate and to make progress on Spanish and Portuguese entry. That he was willing to risk the fury of French farmers by accepting milk quotas in order to reduce spending on the CAP is a sign of his determination.[4]

The relaunched EC was to be the theater of the Franco–German friendship. As in the whole postwar period, Europe was to offer Germany a space while France found allies to help her indicate to Germany the limits of that space. Italy often played this role: during reunification she supported French attempts to remind the Germans of their commitment to EMU. Conversely, France and Germany would be the leaders of the EC, making joint proposals to the European Council. A French fear was that Britain, which enjoyed good relations with Germany in NATO, might carry them over into the EC. This happened in 1985 when the two agreed to keep monetary union out of the Single Europe Act, and the threat was revived after Thatcher's departure in 1990. In general, however, Britain's minimalist stance has prevented her from challenging the Franco–German axis, as her withdrawal from the EMS in September 1992 confirmed.

Mitterrand adhered to Gaullist standards in resisting federalism and made no more than symbolic gestures in increasing the power of the European Parliament, yet he pushed for political integration via the Council of Ministers. Aware that he could not play the solitary role which de Gaulle tried to play after 1963, Mitterrand was willing to risk being out–voted in the Council. So during the debates about the Single Europe Act, France pressed for qualified majority voting. Indeed, in 1985 the French press was outraged when Germany used her right of veto to block the fixing of the corn price at too low a level.[5] Collective amnesia had descended on the "empty chair"! The Single Europe Act duly extended majority voting into certain areas, including all legislation that affected the internal market, and it also strengthened political cooperation, which was designed to improve foreign policy coordination among member states. This too pleased France, which sought to turn the EC into a confederation.

Mitterrand supported the Internal Market because it continued at the Community level the economic changes the Socialists were making at home. The decision to run the nationalized companies as profit–making concerns and the law on labor flexibility, landmarks of 1984–86, led naturally to the acceptance of increased competition imposed by the 1992 process. Yet Mitterrand believed in an active political center that would both regulate the market and strengthen European industries in worldwide competition. He came up with the ESPRIT and EUREKA programs, which he perceived as the seeds of an EC industrial policy.

In this, one rediscovers not merely the *dirigiste* tradition, present in France's European policy since Monnet, but also a Socialist president's attempt to turn the failure of old–fashioned leftism at home into the success of a newer leftism in the EC. According to socialists like Michel Rocard and

Jacques Delors, the state still had a role to play, but it should concert rather than coerce. The best example of such action in the EC was Delors's inauguration of the Val Duchesse process where, instead of the commission's legislating in the area of labor relations, management and unions were to meet and produce joint proposals that could then be passed into law. However, in its early years Val Duchesse achieved little.[6]

In general, France found support from Germany in her attempt to develop the EC. She grumbled that Kohl was unhelpful and compared him with Erhard,[7] and alternatively the Germans remained sporadically faithful to their federalist tradition, which she did not share. But Mitterrand's conversion to Europeanism succeeded, as it was designed to do, in improving Franco–German relations. The Val Duchesse initiative could find favor in Bonn since its conciliatory attitude towards labor relations was akin to the German concept of codetermination. Meanwhile defense cooperation went ahead on a bilateral basis, leading to the formation of the Franco–German brigade and the Bold Sparrow exercises in 1987.

The greatest success of this period, however, was domestic. The inflation rate, which stood at 13.6 percent in 1980, had been reduced to 2.9 percent by March 1986. Industrial investment, which had declined by 7 percent in 1982 and by 4 percent in 1983, rose by 10 percent in 1984. Wages had been de–indexed and company profits were rising. The shift of value added to business was taking place: in 1981 the share of salaries and social security in companies' output was 57.6 percent, whereas in 1987 it was 53 percent. This was a consequence not of the decision to remain within the EMS but of the decision to make the EMS work. *Modell Deutschland* was being reinvented by Mitterrand.[8]

Aside from its opposition role as critic, the right did not offer alternatives to Mitterrand's German policy, and the Single Europe Act was signed after Jacques Chirac became prime minister. The strains in the alliance appeared during cohabitation, 1986–88, in the monetary and defense fields. The first was a consequence of the very success of deflation, and the second was provoked by a change in the East–West situation.

1987–90: COPING WITH GERMAN POWER

Since inflation was low the Chirac government could legitimately bid for growth, but it did not enjoy much success in its attempts. Increase in GNP went from 1.7 percent in 1985 to 2.1 percent in 1986 and 2.3 percent in 1987. One reason for this was supposedly the high interest rates which were caused by the need to maintain the franc within its EMS band. Moreover, France's

interest rates were higher than Germany's, which penalized French businesses that were competing with their counterparts. When Chirac took office
the prime rate was 3 percent higher and two years later it was 3.5 percent
higher. This was the risk penalty factor investors demanded for keeping their
funds in francs and which the policy of the strong franc was supposed, in
time, to eliminate.

However, the franc was threatened by France's trade deficit. French
trade was shifting more towards the EC, as it was supposed to do: in 1985,
54 percent of exports went to Europe, whereas by 1990 the figure was 63
percent, and the trade deficit with Europe had been reduced from FF 77
billion to FF 40 billion. But the deficit with Germany grew from FF 39
billion in 1986 to FF 50 billion in 1988. Moreover, since much of this
deficit was in Germany's key area of capital goods, which industry buys
when expanding, France seemed caught in a trap. To grow she needed
price–inelastic capital goods imports, which caused a trade deficit that in
turn triggered a run on the franc, which had to be defended with high
interest rates that cut off growth.

And the erratic movements of the dollar did not help. When the dollar
went down, as in 1987, the flood of speculative funds into Germany drove
up the mark. This meant that France had to raise interest rates in order to
protect a franc which was then too high for her exports to the dollar zone.
When the dollar went up, as in 1989, the Bundesbank, ever worried about
inflation, raised interest rates to protect the mark, compelling France to do
the same. This perverse German–American collaboration represented precisely what the Franco–German relationship was designed to prevent.

In January 1987 Edouard Balladur, guiding Chirac's bid for growth, was
faced with a 3 percent revaluation of the mark as the dollar went down. At
the Louvre meeting of the Group of Seven, Balladur thought he had a
commitment from the Reagan administration to maintain the level of the
dollar, but in autumn it slid again. This engendered in French elites a sense
of their own powerlessness—two years before reunification.

However, the success of the Nyborg agreement, by which countries would
make short–term resources available to one another in order to keep currencies within their prescribed bands, suggested a solution to Balladur. The EMS
should be reformed "to prevent one country from determining the objectives
of economic and monetary policy for the group as a whole. On the contrary,
such objectives should be fixed by all the countries involved."[9] The absence
of such concertation explains why "the European currencies tend at present
to rise against the dollar and associated currencies, which works against the
fundamental interests of the European economies."

In simpler language, France should gain some control over the level of the mark, which in turn would allow the Europeans some control over the dollar. It is hard to imagine a better restatement of the original purpose of the Franco–German relationship as France envisaged it.

Meanwhile the relationship was losing one of its props as Gorbachev took away the need for the two partners to unite in self–defense against the Soviet threat. After inveighing against German pacifism in the early eighties, France was obliged to discover that Brezhnev's departure had made possible a second and more justified German wave of sympathy for the East. This posed a new problem: the decline of the Soviet threat meant a decline in the value of France's defense capacity as a means to exert influence over Germany. This probably explains why France was so slow to recognize the Gorbachev phenomenon. Still worse, the Reykjavik meeting in autumn 1986 revived Pompidou's fear of a détente where the superpowers would come to an agreement over Europe's head, while adding the fear that such an agreement would pave the way for Genscher's West Germany to expand her influence in the East.

This prospect provoked two reactions and divided right and left. Chirac, who was developing Giscard's defense thinking in a very different international context, opposed the INF agreement and promised to defend Germany "immediately and without reservations."[10] The offer contained both an order and a threat: Germany must accept French nuclear protection along with the continued exposure to Soviet missiles and the dependence on France which it implied. Or, if she refused, she would be abandoned to the vagaries of an unreliable Gorbachev. One of Chirac's supporters made the threat explicit: "France might even consider separating herself from the Federal Republic."[11]

But the threat lacked all credibility. How could France set herself against the doubly perverse collaboration of Germany, the U.S., and the USSR? As argued in chapter 7, Mitterrand saw that the correct course was to support the INF agreement, thus earning the gratitude of the German government. He gained doubly since German gratitude took the form of a preference for him over Chirac in the '88 presidential race, and since his stand appealed to his own left–wing electorate.

The Socialists had once more demonstrated that they were the best exponents of the Franco–German relationship, which Mitterrand could re-launch after his victory. However, the discomfort of the right revived old animosities towards Germany which would surface in the Maastricht referendum. Nor was it lost on the political class in general that German gratitude had been won not, as in 1983, by a bold initiative, but rather by an act of acquiescence. Alain Minc's *La grande illusion*, while proposing an unrealistic alternative to Franco–German cooperation in the shape of a French alliance with the Mediterranean countries, contains the more insidious message that France was too weak to hold her own with West Germany.

After his 1988 presidential victory Mitterrand sought to dispel such criticism by simultaneously relaunching cooperation with Germany in the EC, using the EC to win concessions from Germany, and competing with her outside the EC. The first policy was announced in his election manifesto where he calls for a Community "with a common defense, political unity and a social dimension."[12] During the French presidency of the Council in 1989 Mitterrand pressed all the more eagerly for social measures because Rocard was pursuing rigor at home. With German support and British opposition, the Social Action Program was drawn up and the Health and Safety Directive was passed, while the Val Duchesse discussions were steered towards topics like worker training, where there was more chance of union–employer agreement.

Competition with Germany took the form of a new French *Ostpolitik* which found expression in Mitterrand's visit to Moscow in the autumn of 1988. However, while France could not leave West Germany as Gorbachev's only continental European interlocutor, there was scant chance that she could compete on this terrain. Once more the security issue was working against France because Gorbachev needed cuts in Western arms deployment to which Germany could more easily agree.

This dilemma emerged in the debate about the renewal of the Lance missile, which took place in April–May 1989. Germany wanted to negotiate with the USSR before modernizing the Lance, whereas the U.S. and Britain wanted to proceed with modernization at once. Mitterrand adopted an intermediary position, advocating delay. Within France the battle over the INF agreement was fought again, while Anglo–Saxon observers did not fail to point out that Franco–German cooperation was turning into German domination.[13]

Nor, despite the formation of the Economic and Finance Council, was economic harmonization working. Even as it pursued rigor, the Rocard government was trying to nudge down interest rates in order to create growth. The dollar was now going up, however, so between July 1988 and August 1989 the Bundesbank increased the discount rate four times in order to protect the mark and block imported inflation. Although the French government protested, the Bundesbank remained impervious and did not conceal its suspicion of the Economic and Finance Council.[14]

Since the bilateral approach was not working, France tried to use the EC. The German trade surplus was becoming a burden to the European countries:

in 1985 it had been DM 73.4 billion, of which DM 31.6 billion was with the EC, but in 1989 the respective figures were DM 135 billion and DM 94.2 billion. The solution, in the eyes of the French authorities, was for the Germans to expand their domestic market, thus diverting to it some of their own exports while increasing imports from abroad. This in turn would require a change in German monetary policy.

In this lay the French use of the EC to bring pressure on Germany. Balladur had argued that monetary policy for the EC should not be set by the strongest country; the way to achieve this end was EMU. Monetary union offered the promise of eliminating the risk penalty factor, but its real goal was to enable France to regain a measure of control over monetary growth and interest rates by influencing German policy in such matters. EMU represented a national strategy: it was a bid to increase sovereignty by increasing interdependence. As such, it was a gamble because it offered Germany the chance to extend her control over France. All would depend on how unity was to be reached.

France had won a victory by succeeding in bringing EMU onto the EC agenda. The Delors report, commissioned in 1988 and published in 1989, broke through the silence imposed by Germany during the Single Europe Act debate. It went, however, in a German direction, in both its aims and its methods, when it declared that the goal of the European Central Bank would be price stability and that the Bank would be independent of political authorities. Not without contradiction, it made concessions to France by affirming that growth should be a secondary goal and that "a common overall assessment of the short–term and medium–term economic development in the Community would need to be agreed periodically."[15] So it remained unclear whether the Bundesbank model of tight money, tolerance of high interest rates, and a high exchange rate vis–à–vis the dollar would prevail over French hopes of more rapid growth, lower rates, and a bid to force the U.S. to stabilize the dollar.

Although the French government was strong in 1989 with Mitterrand's ratings high in the polls and with economic growth at 3.7 percent, there was at that same time a malaise about the relationship with Germany. Reunification and the way it came about transformed this malaise into a crisis. While paying lip service to reunification, French elites had relegated it to a distant future. They also thought that, if it were to happen, it would be part of an East–West settlement in which France, as de Gaulle had envisaged, would be the guarantor of German good behavior. Instead, reunification took place rapidly and the West German government was the dominant actor.

Mitterrand tried in two ways to insert himself into the reunification process. He led the EC countries in a campaign to convince Kohl that the Adenauer–Schuman model was still binding and that Germany must pay for reunification with a renewed commitment to Western Europe; he also reasserted France's role as a victor in the Second World War and tried to revive the wartime alliance with the USSR. As argued in chapter 1, his Kiev meeting with Gorbachev in December 1989 was a failure because Gorbachev preferred to deal with the U.S. as the leader of the Western bloc or directly with West Germany. Mitterrand did succeed in forging a bond with the Polish government, which was worried about Kohl's hesitations over the recognition of the Oder–Neisse border, but Poland was not strong enough to be a satisfactory ally. Nor did Mitterrand help his cause by a visit to the DDR in December 1989 during which he flirted with the groups who were opposed to reunification.[16]

There remained the other front of the EC where Mitterrand saw an opportunity to extract from the West Germans a commitment to EMU. This would have represented a happy reconciliation of French economic interest and the EC's role as anchoring Germany to the West, but Kohl wanted first to resolve the question of German monetary union and to win the DDR elections of 18 March 1990. So, despite pressure from France and Italy, he refused to fix a date for the intergovernmental conference on monetary union. Mitterrand was left making overtures to the SPD leader, Oscar Lafontaine, whose party was thrashed in the DDR elections.

By now, domestic and foreign issues were overlapping. That the Rennes congress, which exposed the Parti socialiste as idea–less and faction-ridden, should occur at the moment when Mitterrand's German policy was faltering, was not entirely a coincidence. Since 1988 Mitterrand had concentrated on Europe and Rocard on rigor. Both had been successful but neither had given to his project a left–wing content capable of rallying the PS. Fragments of what might be called a "post–labor" vision[17] may be seen in Delors' social dialogue and in Rocard's introduction of a minimum salary for unemployed persons who entered job training programs, but these were not enough. Seemingly secure in power but devoid of any mission, the party abandoned itself to a struggle among rival leaders.

The question posed here is to what extent the choice of cooperation with Germany damaged Mitterrand and the Socialists. By weakening the party's sense of itself as a left–wing party, it exposed the Socialists to such problems as factionalism and corruption, the latter becoming a crucial issue when they complacently granted themselves an amnesty for illegal campaign financing in January 1990. However, neither problem was created by the German connection, and a more serious issue is whether the decision to tie the franc to the mark was the cause of the persistently high unemployment that has brought the Socialists much unpopularity. Even in the good year of 1989 unemployment was 9.5 percent, down only 1 percent from 1987, and it has been argued that "there was a large margin of maneuver for non–inflationary expansion of the economy."[18] If the government did not try this strategy, the reason was the need to maintain high interest rates in order to preserve the franc's position in an EMS, designed to answer German needs.

The orthodox view, however, is that French unemployment is caused by structural problems such as the weakness of key sectors like the machine–tool industry, inadequate job–training programs, and a demographic profile which sees the labor force increasing in number until around 2005. The strong franc and the link with Germany were designed to help correct some of these weaknesses, although it could be argued that the Mitterrand government was guilty of not persuading the Germans to be more helpful in redesigning the EMS to suit French needs. This in turn leads back to March 1990 and the demonstration of Mitterrand's inability to shape the process of reunification.

Here again one might distinguish between perception and reality. The pressure exerted by France was at least one reason for Kohl's decision, after his victory in the DDR elections, to reroot Germany in Western Europe by moving towards the political and monetary unity of the EC. Moreover, in his television interview of 25 March, Mitterrand reiterated the concept of a national strategy and stated that reunification offered France an opportunity to catch up with Germany, on condition that "we have confidence in ourselves and produce more."[19]

He was reflecting the view associated with the now–Minister of European Affairs, Elisabeth Guigou, that reunification would compel the Kohl government to pursue an expansionist economic policy, which would help solve the problem of the French trade deficit with Germany. However, since this would require yet more rigor of the French, it could not arouse popular enthusiasm. And it was obvious to elites that Kohl's decision to resume close cooperation with France was very much his decision and was made only when the moment suited him.

French public opinion was kind to reunification: 61 percent supported it and only 15 percent were opposed, whereas the figures in Britain were 45 and 30 percent, respectively.[20] But elite opinion was critical of the way Mitterrand handled the crisis, and the impression of weakness spilled over into the more explosive question of the way he was handling unemployment. However unfair such judgements may be, Mitterrand's government was never as strong after November 1989.

1990—AND YET THERE IS LIFE AFTER REUNIFICATION

Although this weakness complicated Franco–German cooperation in the early nineties, the striking feature of this period is the way in which Mitterrand has continued his previous policies. Even as he has sought to adapt them to the new situation in Eastern Europe or to the changed role of the U.S., he has followed the historic patterns of Franco–German cooperation. The "new European architecture" is curiously familiar.

As his 25 March 1990 statement indicated, Mitterrand has reaffirmed the national economic strategy begun in 1983. The Cresson interlude, 1991–92, which marked a rhetorical shift to the left, did not change the decision to give priority to the strength of the franc. As Finance Minister, Pierre Bérégovoy tried sporadically to convince the markets that increases in German interest rates reflected the economic fragility which stemmed from reunification and that France need not follow them.[21] In October 1990, when the Bundesbank raised the Lombard rate by 0.5 percent, the Banque de France cut its rates by 0.25 percent. France has indeed benefited from reunification in that the risk penalty factor has been subsumed: in July 1992 the prime rate in France stood at 9.85 percent compared with 11.0 percent in Germany, although the yield on long–term government bonds remained higher in France, at 8.72 percent as compared with 8.35 percent.[22] Similarly the French trade deficit with Germany was reduced from FF 58.6 billion in 1989 to FF 42 billion in 1990.

However, French interest rates were still forced up by the interplay of the dollar and the mark, exacerbated by the Bush administration's willingness to let the dollar go down and the Bundesbank's resolution that the cost of reunification would not trigger domestic inflation. In November 1991 the dollar slumped and the concomitant rise of the mark forced France to raise interest rates by 0.5 percent. The EMS had still not, as France had hoped, split the alliance of Germany and the U.S. Moreover, since the number of French jobless had risen to 9.7 percent, the fear that the EMS was perpetuating high unemployment returned. In a shift of loyalties, the French government's ally in Germany had become the Bundesbank. Whereas in the late 1980s French politicians sided with their German counterparts against the bankers' mania for raising interest rates, in the early 1990s they supported the bankers in railing against the politicians' refusal to finance reunification by raising taxes. Since French complaints made no greater impact now than then, the malaise about Franco–German cooperation persisted despite the economic benefits France had derived from reunification.

Mitterrand's European policy was designed, as before, to dispel such malaise by demonstrating French strength, and he was greatly assisted in this by Saddam

Hussein. The Gulf War gave the lie to the notion that military power counted for nothing after the end of the East–West struggle. France seized the opportunity to send forces to the Gulf all the more readily because it fit with her postwar attempt to assert her military might against German economic might, and it allowed her to reverse the defeat she had suffered during the previous year.

This was another case where France was able to establish a privileged relationship with the U.S., which she could flaunt against a Germany that incurred American displeasure by her inaction and her noisy antiwar movement. Yet France also sought to maintain her independence of the U.S. by taking, insofar as Saddam Hussein's intransigence permitted, a more flexible line. Mitterrand's UN speech of September 1990 implied, for example, that a promise to withdraw from Kuwait would be sufficient to bring about discussions with Iraq, whereas the U.S. was insisting on an actual withdrawal. Had Saddam Hussein been less intractable, this could have become the position of an EC led by France.[23]

As it was, the combination of French boldness, German hesitation, and EC impotence set the stage for Mitterrand to make a fresh bid to conquer Europe. In December 1990 he won Kohl's support for a joint statement which called for "confirming and broadening the role and tasks of the European Council" and for the EC to adopt "a genuine security policy which would lead in time to a common defense."[24] Set alongside the commitment to EMU made by Kohl after his victory in the DDR elections, this represented a long step forward down the road Mitterrand had taken in the mid–eighties.

All these victories, however, were flawed. At the Maastricht summit of 9 December 1991, qualified majority voting in the Council of Ministers was extended to such areas as research, the environment, and social policy. Other innovations in social policy included an agreement that the social dialogue was an explicit objective of EC policy. Yet this did not constitute—even had Britain signed on—a left–wing vision of Europe. The extension of QMV was riddled with ambiguities, and employers retain much power to delay the progress of dialogue.

France gained a plan for EMU, but Germany imposed a delay until 1997 as well as tough conditions of entry. Like the Delors report, the Maastricht document insists on price stability as the main goal and on an independent European central bank as the main agent. This seems far removed from Balladur's demand that monetary policy should be decided by all the countries in the group, and he was opposed to EMU. However, the president of the embryo Eurofed is to be appointed by the Council of Ministers and its decisions are to be taken by majority voting. This leaves room for input by politicians, who are more likely than bankers to be sensitive to unemployment, and it

weakens German control. So both the French bid to influence German monetary policy and German resistance to French interference are, as Roger Morgan
explains in chapter 5, continuing.

Progress towards a common foreign policy has been slight and rifts have
appeared between France and Germany over particular issues. Two are significant: the Eastern Europe–EC relationship and Yugoslavia. In the former case
France, unlike Germany, has opposed the admission of Poland, Hungary, and
Czechoslovakia for fear that their entry would weaken the structure of the EC
and hence reduce the Community's importance as an arena where France can
exert influence over Germany. Obliged to propose some organization to link
East and West Europe, Mitterrand has come up with the notion of a European
Confederation. In French eyes this presents two advantages: it would be too
loose to interfere with the unifying process of the EC, and it would exclude
the U.S. Unsurprisingly, James Baker has pressed instead for a confederation
from Vancouver to Vladivostok, while Vaclav Havel has criticized Mitterrand
for suggesting that Czechoslovakia must wait "decades" before joining the EC.
In general this latest version of *Ostpolitik* has not helped France counter
German influence in Eastern Europe.[25]

France's struggle to control Germany, compete with her, and limit American influence in Europe emerged in her reaction to the break up of Yugoslavia. Her reluctance in 1991 to recognize Slovenia and Croatia arose in part
from the fear that the two new republics would at once fall under German
domination. However, when the issue of EC intervention arose in September
1991, France was in favor because she wished to expand the EC's role in the
area of security. That Germany was in favor of but unable to participate in
such an intervention would reinforce French leadership.

Similarly, in 1992 France was less harsh than Germany in her criticism
of Serbia's role in the Bosnian fighting. Yet after the EC summit in June,
Mitterrand undertook his theatrical visit to Sarajevo and offered to send
French troops to help bring about a cease–fire. His action sprang not only
from his desire for an activist, French–led EC, but also from fear that the
U.S. might take charge of an intervention. The daytrip to Sarajevo seemed
a media stunt, however, and France has been unable to organize an international intervention of her own.[26]

It is no coincidence that clashes between France and the U.S. have grown
more frequent since the twin events of reunification and the end of the Cold
War. As de Gaulle foresaw, the removal of the Soviet threat reduces Europe's
dependence on America. Yet the Bush administration, while cutting the cost
of hegemony, wishes to preserve as much power as it can. Since Mitterrand
is free to launch his challenge, Franco–American conflict is inevitable.

Moreover, the increase in Germany's potential economic strength and the reduction of France's influence over her make it more necessary for Mitterrand to assert France's political might.

In the early 1990s France has sought above all to establish a Franco–German military presence. As always, she has combined a direct approach to Germany with a bid to involve the EC. In 1990, Minister of Defense Jean–Pierre Chevènement outlined a proposal for a European pillar of NATO, based on the French and British nuclear deterrents and led by a High Command which would be linked to, but not subordinate to, the American SACEUR.[27]

In May 1991 a meeting of NATO defense ministers drew up plans for a leaner, cheaper NATO with a new Rapid Reaction Force composed of European units and led by a British commander.[28] France was not consulted, U.S. power in NATO would remain intact, and the power of America's traditional European ally would be increased. If the situation was reminiscent of the early 1960s when de Gaulle sought a greater role within NATO and was rebuffed by the Anglo–Saxons, there were significant differences. Mitterrand did not break with NATO but instead sought allies to change the balance of power from within.

He pressed for a greater role for the Western European Union (WEU), which was to be organically tied to the EC. This produced ambiguous statements at the NATO summit of November 1991, as well as at Maastricht, which left the WEU poised in a void between the rival organizations. Aware of the difficulty of annexing the WEU, originally created as a fig leaf to hide West Germany's entry into NATO, Mitterrand turned directly to Germany. Not that this was easy, and Elisabeth Guigou complained loudly that Germany was "apathetic" about European defense.[29] But in October 1991 the Franco–German army corps was announced. Logically, Mitterrand spoke in January 1992 of a "European nuclear doctrine," following Giscard in emphasizing the European aspect of the Gaullist legacy.[30] As Philip Gordon notes in chapter 7, however, there are obstacles to this latest attempt at Franco–German defense cooperation.

Such subtle tensions seemed trivial in August 1992 when the Maastricht referendum, called by Mitterrand primarily to win an easy victory which would boost his domestic position, turned into a battle over France's role in Europe. The "no" camp (although a politically motley band of Communists, some Greens, a Socialist splinter led by Chevènement, an RPR majority rallied behind Philippe Séguin and Charles Pasqua, and the Front national) had an economic and sociological coherence. It won 61 percent of workers—especially in areas of smokestack industries like the Pas–de–Calais where unemployment is high— and 63 percent of farmers worried about cuts in the Common Agricultural Policy.

The able Séguin called into question precisely the notion that France strengthened her autonomy by increasing her interdependence. True to his brand of
popular Gaullism, he noted the Maastricht Treaty's weak industrial and social
chapters and attacked the expansion of the WEU.[31]

It is difficult to estimate in the "no" vote the role of opposition to Franco–
German cooperation. It did not emerge as a major theme until the last bitter
stage of the campaign. Then Séguin and Chevènement hammered at the theme
that EMU would mean rule by the Bundesbank and stunted economic growth.
Chevènement, who had been an Albanian in 1983, spoke of "turning over the
keys of French industry to German banks."[32] Already Marie–France Garaud,
who had witnessed Pompidou's doubts about Brandt, had criticized the extension of QMV because "all the qualified majorities will be German."[33] However, that Kohl's appearance on Mitterrand's 3 September television debate
could raise, albeit briefly, the "yes" vote to 56 percent in the polls, is a sign
that crude anti–German feeling was not widespread.

During the troubles that afflicted the EMS in September, the Franco–
German monetary connection held, and the Bundesbank extended greater
help to the franc than to the pound or the lira. Yet the impression of a superior
Germany benevolently assisting a struggling friend may well make it difficult for France to pursue closer—or at least more public—monetary ties. Jörg
Boche's depiction in chapter 4 of a Franco–German–Benelux monetary
union is not what France has been seeking for the last several years.

Not that German superiority is necessarily an economic, much less a
political, reality. If French elites—Giscard and Chirac as well as Mitterrand—were weakened by their narrow referendum victory, the Kohl
government—plagued by irate Ossis, Naziskins, and its own economic
mistakes—needs French support. But the French government, of whatever
political ilk, will have to make a fresh effort to convince the population that
embracing Germany really does produce greater autonomy. The right–wing
government that seems likely to emerge from the March elections may not
be inclined to make such an effort.

CONCLUSION

It has been suggested that France might seek closer ties with the Anglo–
Saxons in order to counterbalance the increased weight which reunification
has awarded Germany.[34] Whatever the value of this as a prescription, it does
not appear to be happening. Rather, France continues to feel that it has no
choice but to continue working with Germany.

Evidence is provided by the cultural interest in things German which has increased since the late 1970s. Like Giscard, recent commentators have written of "the long, patient compromises between social partners" which distinguish German labor relations and which supposedly contrast with the conflicts that damage the French economy. Michel Albert's *Capitalisme contre capitalisme* contrasts the alliance between banks and industry, which permits long–term investment in Germany, with the emphasis on quick profits in Anglo–Saxon capitalism. The seemingly chauvinistic Edith Cresson flaunted her admiration for the German apprenticeship system.[35]

At times the admiration seems uncritical. When a contributor to *Esprit* argues that the well–trained, well–informed German working class is a model for the French left, one wonders whether repentance for the left's traditional anti–German stance has not gone too far. When the head of the employers association regrets that France did not adopt *Modell Deutschland* forty years earlier, one cannot but remember the surging French growth of the 1950s and 1960s.[36]

Exaggerated fear is the flip side of this praise. Even before the referendum, French observers had pored over the *Historikerstreit* and discovered the seeds of future German nationalisms. A much–read book on reunification is entitled *The Return of Bismarck,* while the compliments heaped on the East German writer Christa Wolf are inversely proportionate to the scorn with which West German intellectuals have greeted her.[37]

Yet Mitterrand's gamble has not proved wrong, and the benefits of a decade of renewed cooperation outweigh the drawbacks. By choosing to link the franc to the mark, France has repaired her economy and, allied with Germany, she has become the hard core of a nowadays bewildered EC. She can take a certain amount of credit for the orderly way in which the political process of reunification has come about. Since 1989 her foreign policy has been characterized by a desperate need to demonstrate influence, but the supposed weakness of the French state is very much a matter of French perception.[38] As a left–winger Mitterrand may be disappointed that he has not given a left–wing slant to cooperation, and he will certainly be displeased that it has contributed, albeit in a minor way, to his and his party's unpopularity.[39]

The second goal of the Franco–German relationship, namely, achieving a more equal partnership with the U.S., had only partially been achieved before the referendum and now seems more remote than ever. France's influence over Germany and Europe probably gives her greater independence of the U.S. than at any time in the postwar period. But in key areas such as monetary and security policy she and Germany have not put together convincing shared proposals which could be presented amicably yet firmly to the U.S. The new balance of power, which seemed possible in the Schmidt–Giscard years, is proving elusive.

NOTES

1. Alfred Frisch, "Convergences et divergences: l'entente franco–allemande reste un acquis fondamental," *Documents,* March 1982, pp. 21–30.

2. Pierre Mauroy, "Choisir l'Europe, c'est choisir la rigueur," *Express,* 8 April 1983, p. 36. The best account of this decision in English is Julius W. Friend, *Seven Years in France: François Mitterrand and the Unintended Revolution* (Boulder: Westview, 1989), pp. 64–69. In French, see Pierre Favier and Michel Martin–Roland, *La Décennie Mitterrand* vol. 1, (Paris: Seuil, 1990) pp. 465–493. For the effect on the Socialist Party, see my "The Parti socialiste in 1986" in Patrick McCarthy (ed.), *The French Socialists in Power* (Westport: Greenwood Press, 1987), pp. 175–180.

3. Jacques Delors et Clisthène, *La France par l'Europe* (Paris: Grasset, 1988), p. 60.

4. On Mitterrand's European policy in the mid–eighties, see Haig Simonian, *The Privileged Partnership: Franco–German Relations in the EC 1969–1984* (Oxford: Clarendon Press, 1985), pp. 313–336.

5. André Fontaine, "L'Europe sans la foi," *Le Monde,* 2 July 1985.

6. For information on EC social policy I have drawn on Adrian Westlake, "European Collective Bargaining: Dream or Reality?" M.A. thesis, Johns Hopkins University Bologna Center, 1992.

7. Alfred Grosser, "Surmonter la défaillance allemande," *Le Monde,* 3 July 1985. On the roles played by France and Germany in the creation of the Single Europe Act, see Juliet Lodge, "The Single Europe Act," *Journal of Common Market Studies* 3 (1986), pp. 203–223.

8. On French economic policy and the concept of national choice, see my "France Faces Reality: *Rigueur* and the Germans," in David Calleo and Claudia Morgenstern (eds.), *Recasting Europe's Economies* (New York: University Press of America, 1990), pp. 48–64.

9. Edouard Balladur, "Mémorandum sur la construction monétaire européenne", . *Ecu* 3 (1988), pp. 19, 18.

10. Jacques Chirac's speech of 12 December 1987, at the Institut des hautes études de la défense nationale, printed in *La Politique étrangère de la France* November–December 1987, p. 21. For defense issues during cohabitation see Philip

Gordon, *A Certain Idea of France: French Security Policy and the Gaullist Legacy* (Princeton: Princeton University Press, 1993), pp. 139–157.

11. François Fillon, "D'un anniversaire à l'autre," *Politique étrangère* 4 (1988), p. 838.

12. François Mitterrand, *Lettre à tous les Français,* published as a supplement, paid for by the Parti socialiste, to several French newspapers, 7 April 1988, p. 14.

13. Joseph Fitchett, "French Diplomacy Taking a Back Seat to Bonn," *International Herald Tribune* 28 April 1989.

14. Karl–Otto Poehl described it as "not indispensable," quoted in Xavier Gautier, "Visite à l'antre des voleurs," *Documents* (October 1988), p. 39.

15. Committee for the Study of Economic and Monetary Union, *Report on Economic and Monetary Union in the EC* (Brussels: EC Publications, 1989), p. 20.

16. For a German view of Mitterrand's policy towards reunification, see Robert Picht, "Deutsch–franzoesische Beziehungen nach dem Fall der Mauer" in Robert Picht and Wolfgang Wessels (eds.), *Motor fuer Europea? Deutsch–franzoesischer Bilateralismus und europaeische Integration* (Bonn: Europa Union Verlag, 1990), pp. 47–68.

17. For the concept of "post–labor" policies, see Frances Fox Piven (ed.), *Labor Parties in Postindustrial Societies* (New York: Oxford University Press, 1992).

18. J.–P. Fitoussi and P.–A. Muet, "French Economic Policy in the Eighties," *Rivista di politica economica* (April 1989), p. 252.

19. François Mitterrand, *Le Monde* 27 March 1990.

20. Georges Valance, *France–Allemagne: le Retour de Bismarck* (Paris: Flammarion, 1990), p. 264.

21. Pierre Bérégovoy, *Le Monde* 8 April 1990.

22. *The Economist* 11 July 1992.

23. François Mitterrand, *Le Monde* 26 September 1990. For a longer account of how Mitterrand dealt with the Gulf War see my "France and the EC: Can a Gaullist World Power Find Happiness in a Regional Bloc?" *Johns Hopkins University Bologna Center Occasional Papers,* 1992, pp. 32–37.

24. "Lettre commune de MM. Kohl et Mitterrand," *Le Monde* 9 December 1990.

25. François Mitterrand, *Libération* 18 June 1991. Havel stated that the confederation project should not be a "brake" on the Eastern countries' entry to the EC. For Baker's proposal, see *Le Monde* 20 June 1991. A *Le Monde* editorial critical of Mitterrand appeared on 25 June.

26. In his Bastille Day address Mitterrand stated that France could not send troops unless other countries did so. See *Le Figaro* of 15 July 1992.

27. J.–P. Chevènement, "La France et la sécurité de l'Europe," *Politique Etrangère* 3 (1990), p. 529.

28. *Financial Times* 30 May 1991.

29. Elisabeth Guigou, *Libération* 24 June 1991.

30. François Mitterrand, *Le Monde* 12 January 1992.

31. For Séguin's commentary on the Maastricht Treaty see *Libération* 31 August 1992.

32. J.–P. Chevènement, *Libération* 31 August 1992.

33. Marie–France Garaud, *Le Monde* 15 April 1992. See also her and Philippe Séguin's *De l'Europe en général et de la France en particulier* (Paris: Le Pré aux clercs, 1992). On the cover is a picture of a fifty mark note! German opponents of EMU take the view that the French will subvert the mark: see Rudolf Augstein, "Naïv oder tükisch?" *Der Spiegel* 8 (1992), p. 20.

34. David Yost, "France and the New Europe," *Foreign Affairs* (Winter 1990–91), pp. 107–128.

35. For the superiority of German industrial relations see Benjamin Coriat, "Dans le cercle vertueux de la qualité du travail," *Le Monde diplomatique: Allemagne, Japon, les deux titans* (Paris: Le Monde, 1991), p. 29. For Cresson see *Le Monde* 3 April 1992. She was another believer in emulation and competition.

36. Gérard Collomb, "Rennes: affrontement des hommes ou congrès des idées?" *Esprit* 1 (1990), p. 48. For the views of François Perigot, president of the employers association, see *Die Zeit* April 1992, no.15–3.

37. On the *Historikerstreit* see André Gisselbrecht, "Les inquiétants arguments du néopatriotisme allemand," *Le Monde diplomatique: Allemagne, Japon, les deux titans*, pp. 13–14. This collection of articles illustrates the fascinated anxiety with which French commentators view Germany. It also shows how fear of Germany overlaps with fear of Japan. For Christa Wolf see Jean–Michel Palmier, "Christa Wolf et la mémoire de la RDA," in *Allemagne, Japon, les deux titans*, pp. 89–93. For "the return of Bismarck" see note 20 above.

38. For the domestic ramifications of the state's interdependence–autonomy, see my "The State's Will to Survive and the Discontents of its Citizens: A Reading of Domestic French Politics," paper presented to the Washington Foundation for European Studies, 17 November 1992.

39. In the month of Maastricht, December 1991, Mitterrand's approval rating was 31 percent, the lowest since he took office in 1981.

Chapter 4

Franco–German Economic Relations

Jörg Boche

INTRODUCTION

This chapter describes Franco–German economic relations with a focus on the evolution of their macroeconomic compatibility over the past ten years. It argues that French and German policy–makers could reinforce their national economic strategies by cooperating with each other. In the course of the 1980s, Franco–German economic cooperation led to a far–reaching convergence of economic policies and trends in the two countries. This convergence, in turn, made possible the development of regimes and institutional structures in the Community for the coordination of economic policies. The stability of the European Monetary System (EMS) in the 1980s and the Single European Act of 1986 are examples of the success and dynamics of European integration in the past decade. Both the EMS and the Single Market project incorporate a new consensus among French and German policy–makers about how their economies should be governed, a consensus that seems to encompass several of the major aspects of economic policy.

First, monetary policy in the European Community has become increasingly stability–oriented. Within the EMS, and under the leadership of the German Bundesbank, anti–inflation policies have become the European norm in the 1980s. Member countries—with the arguable exception of Germany—have given up their national independence with regard to monetary policy. Moreover, the general macroeconomic affairs of EMS member countries are also subject to international coordination. The Maastricht Treaty has only confirmed and formalized already existing trends in this general direction. The need for concerted macroeconomic policies of those EMS countries that are willing to accept a single currency significantly increases the chances that formerly profligate governments will make every effort to meet the rather severe stability criteria laid down in Maastricht. And even if the Maastricht Treaty will not be ratified by all current EMS members, those countries that intend to move toward a single currency are likely to apply the Maastricht rules to themselves.

Second, the trend toward concerted Community–wide macroeconomic management is paralleled by the construction of a Europe–wide regulatory framework for the governance of markets. Most of the framework conditions that are going to apply to the governance of Community–wide markets are embodied in the move toward the Single Market of 1993. The general idea of this initiative is to increase market competition and, at the same time, set minimum standards for product quality, capital–labor relations, and environmental safety. Certainly the harmonization of market regulations in the Community will be far from perfect, but it still constitutes a relatively unified approach to market regulation and creates a level playing field for Community companies.

Third, Europe's new economic consensus of the 1980s has also led to the creation of what might be called a European technological identity. In the worldwide battle among economic "blocks," technology is the key to independence and self–assertion.[1] Having joined forces successfully in "mission–oriented" technological projects (like the Airbus and the European Space program), EC nations discovered in the course of the 1980s that they needed to create "diffusion–oriented" European networks for developing and applying high technology.[2] French and German firms in particular have emerged as major participants in various programs such as ESPRIT, EUREKA, and BRITE. The sums involved in these technology networks and the tangible successes may still be modest, but the point is that structures are evolving which have already become an important element of the framework conditions under which European firms operate.

Why did France and Germany (and other EC countries) intensify their cooperation in the 1980s? What moved them to create Community–wide regimes and institutional structures within which the macroeconomic affairs of member–states, the control over EC–wide markets, and the technological strategies of European industry could be coordinated? Answers to these questions may start with the major economic challenges which confronted the French and German governments during the 1970s and 1980s.

Probably the most difficult challenge they (and other European governments) had to wrestle with was rebalancing the financing of the welfare state.

They also had to balance, on the one hand, the growing claims of organized labor on the economy's resources and, on the other hand, the financial equilibrium of private industry. Overregulated and burdened by the exploding costs of generous entitlement programs, French and German industrial investment patterns seriously deteriorated in the 1970s. The profit shares in national income were severely squeezed and the returns on capital investment (as opposed to financial placements) declined. The precondition for higher rates of investment, job-creation, and faster growth was a prolonged period of income redistribution towards private business. And, as the 1980s showed, monetary policies focused on the fight against inflation could help reverse the distributive disequilibrium of the 1970s.

Further challenges came from the disruptive conditions of the world economy: American macroeconomic management repeatedly undermined French and German policy–makers' efforts to bring back stability and growth after the turbulence of the 1970s. As Patrick McCarthy points out in his introduction, the EMS was both a way for Giscard d'Estaing to impose monetary discipline on the French economy and an attempt by French and German policy–makers to protect themselves against U.S. monetary and exchange rate policies. The EMS was the earliest step toward the creation of a sort of European economic superpower that could negotiate international economic affairs from a position of equals with the United States. A common European currency, for example, is the only way in which the French and German governments can hope to end the hegemonic position of the dollar in world finance. At the same time, of course, it is also the only way in which the French government can hope to put an end to the Bundesbank's hegemonic position in European financial and monetary affairs.

Another challenge for France and Germany was to adapt to the rapid pace of technological change in the world economy. Europe's well–tested technologies and established industrial structures of the postwar period came under growing competition from low–cost producers in the Third World, particularly Asia. The appropriate response was to move up–market with more sophisticated products and better quality. This, however, required considerable effort and restructuring. Not only was it necessary to develop new technologies, but these technologies also had to be applied in improved production methods and converted into marketable products. This involved high rates of capital investment and improvements in work organization and labor training. As the examples of the French automobile and the German electronics industries show, many European business firms had serious problems with the growing demands placed on their innovativeness and technological sophistication.

There are many examples of how greater Franco–German economic cooperation served both countries' vital interests in the sometimes difficult economic circumstances of the 1970s and 1980s. In 1983, for instance, the French government used the exchange rate constraint of the EMS to introduce its successful anti–inflation strategy of *rigueur*. In "borrowing" the credibility of the Bundesbank as an inflation fighter, the government succeeded in de–indexing wages and prices and thus was able to begin redistributing national income to profits.[3] This was the precondition for the investment boom that occurred in France in the late 1980s. Many French firms used their growing share of national income to upgrade their products and productive resources, and thus laid the ground for the strong improvement in the French trade balance in the early 1990s.[4]

For Germany, the EMS has become an important shelter for its international price competitiveness when the United States uses the dollar to promote its own exports. It is true that German industry did not lobby for the EMS with the argument of exchange rate protection, and it is also true that many German exporters have trade interests that go beyond the EMS area, but it is nevertheless clear that improved German price competitiveness with other EMS countries in the late 1980s brought about a welcome reorientation of German exports, precisely when the dollar began to depreciate. The importance of the EC market for German export surpluses has grown very quickly in the course of the 1980s. In 1979 the German trade surplus with other EC countries amounted to 59 percent of the total German trade surplus; by 1989 this share had risen to 72 percent.[5] The importance of European exchange rate stability for German prosperity has also been highlighted by the EMS crisis in September, 1992. The depreciation of the pound and the lira directly touched approximately 16 percent of German exports and around 62 percent of German export surpluses.[6] Following the monetary crisis, banks and brokerages cut their earnings forecasts for export–oriented German firms in the automobile, chemical and machine–tools industries and sent the Frankfurt stock market to a new low for the year.

The evolving European regulatory framework for continental–scale markets allowed French and German governments in the 1980s to counter the growing overregulation of their domestic economies. Deregulation in the name of European unity was a welcome catalyst for the introduction of greater market competition and flexibility in France and Germany. But the Common Market also strengthens Europe's position in international trade negotiations. In an international economy that seems to be moving toward a system of "managed trade" among major economic blocks, the French and German governments have come to appreciate the additional clout they can gain vis–à–vis the United States and Japan by cooperating with each other. The defense of French agricultural interests in the Uruguay Round, for instance, heavily relies on the closing of ranks among EC nations in these negotiations.

French and German efforts to boost the technological competitiveness of their industries have also been aided by cooperation in the name of Europe. In Germany, well–developed networks for generating and diffusing technologies already exist. These networks, however, are very heavily geared to the needs of three sectors: automobiles, mechanical engineering, and chemicals. Other industries, particularly those in the electronics sector, do not benefit from the same attention.[7]

Their technology tends to be mediocre by international standards. European diffusion–oriented technology networks provide an escape for these firms. The example of ESPRIT shows how German and other European electronics firms can join forces in designing a research and development strategy for their needs, and then apply for Community funding.

In France, on the other hand, the generation of technology is very highly geared to state–sponsored projects with limited applicability for general industry. And for all the successes of the TGV, the French nuclear program, or the aircraft industry, French firms in other important industrial sectors such as automobiles get relatively little state support for their technological development.[8] As in Germany, European networks provide an escape from the insufficiencies of the national technological infrastructure.

GERMAN MACROECONOMIC TRENDS

The difficulties with economic growth and stability in the 1970s and 1980s were rather similar in France and Germany. The worldwide inflation in the last years of the Bretton Woods system was reinforced by the first oil shock and coincided with a period of renewed labor militancy and a buildup of the welfare state. Profit rates and investment declined and slow growth coexisted with continuing inflation. After the second oil shock, a deep recession and intensive industrial restructuring led to very high rates of unemployment in France and Germany.

However, even though the same set of problems challenged policy–makers in both countries, the crisis was less severe in Germany than in France. Therefore, Germany could appear as an economically, and to some extent socially, successful model in the mid–1970s and 1980s. In my view the critical difference between the two countries was that Germany possessed the institutional prerequisite to effectively fight the two principal evils of the period: distributive conflict and inflation. This institutional feature of the German political economy was, of course, the political independence of the Bundesbank. With hindsight, policy–makers from the center–left coalition under Helmut Schmidt pointed out that they were quite happy to see the Bundesbank turning against the cost–push inflation after the oil shock and disciplining labor unions and employers in their wage– and price–setting behavior.[9] By abruptly reducing the expansion of the money supply as early as March 1973, the Bundesbank limited the scope for price increases and precipitated a stability recession by 1974. Unemployment, sanctioning excessive wage demands, rose rapidly and brought about moderation in the 1975 wage negotiations. Beginning in 1975, labor costs were under control and the profit share in national income could begin to recover.[10] Thus the use of what could be called the "regulatory power" of monetary policy by the Bundesbank was the key to Germany's relatively successful reaction to the oil shock and the distributive struggles of the early 1970s.

After the first oil shock and the recession of 1975, the Bundesbank's monetary policy continued to dominate German macroeconomic policy. In the period between 1975 and 1979 fiscal policy oscillated between efforts to reduce the budget deficit (1975–76) and attempts to boost growth and reduce unemployment through spending programs (1977–79). The government's understanding of the role of fiscal policy was clearly Keynesian. Until 1978, fiscal and monetary policy, as well as income distribution trends, worked in relative harmony. Growth accelerated quickly after the recession of 1974–75 and helped reduce the enormous budget deficit of 1975 (5.6 percent of GDP). When growth stalled by 1977, fiscal policy turned expansionary. This stance was reinforced at the Bonn summit of July 1978. By 1979, growth had reached 4 percent and unemployment was falling. With declining rates of inflation and a rapidly depreciating dollar, the Bundesbank allowed the overshooting of its monetary targets in 1977–79.

Things began to go wrong when the rapid growth of the German economy in 1979 collided with the second oil shock. Strong growth of domestic demand, the long period of the mark's appreciation (particularly against the dollar), and the abrupt deterioration of Germany's terms of trade due to the oil shock combined to send Germany's current account into deficit and weaken the mark. By 1980, the German economy had slid into the second oil–shock–induced recession within less than a decade. Despite the recession, the Bundesbank tightened monetary policy and followed the high interest rates set by the Federal Reserve. In 1980–82 the Bank was not inclined to accommodate a more expansionary fiscal policy and speed up economic recovery for fear of undermining the international confidence in the mark. In the early years of the EMS the mark was relatively weak and did not become the anchor currency of the system until 1982–83.

In 1983 the center–left coalition of Helmut Schmidt was replaced by Helmut Kohl's center–right government, which abandoned the former Keynesian–type fiscal strategy in favor of long–term budget consolidation. Triggered first by a fall of the savings rate and a rise in domestic demand, then pulled along by strong exports, the economy began to recover. At the same time, inflation declined steadily and the budget deficit was reduced. In the years 1984–89 the German current account surpluses rose to record levels and the mark was firmly established as the key currency in the EMS. As the profit shares in national income climbed back to the levels of the boom years of the 1960s and beyond, the profitability of private enterprise recovered. In 1988–89 the economy, pulled along by strong investment and exports, moved to an even higher growth path, creating new jobs and bringing with it the long–awaited reduction in unemployment.

This growth pattern was changed as a result of German reunification. The massive transfers to the former GDR translated into large budget deficits which in turn led to a strong reflation of the economy. What had been investment– and export–led growth was transformed into a demand–induced boom. The excessive current account surpluses of the late 1980s were quickly eliminated. Unfortunately, however, the need to transfer resources from western Germany to eastern Germany provoked an angry refusal of wage–earners in the West to acquiesce in real pay cuts for the benefit of the East. In the spring of 1992 labor unrest erupted and strikes were called during the wage round. As in 1974, when internal monetary stability was threatened by distributive conflict and excessive government deficits, the Bundesbank kept monetary policy tight and interest rates high. Determined not to accommodate the government's enormous borrowing and not to underwrite excessive pay increases, the Bank once again insisted upon macroeconomic stability.

Germany's position with regard to the coordination of macroeconomic policies in the EC is very much related to its own experience with macro-economic stabilization in the years since the oil shock. German policy–makers have learned that high rates of growth and investment together with low inflation only come as the result of a continuing struggle against the two principal ills of modern welfare capitalism: distributive conflict and undis-ciplined government borrowing. Germany herself has been plagued by these two problems during the past two decades much more seriously than foreign analysts usually realize.

FRENCH MACROECONOMIC TRENDS

The period of the first oil shock marks the end of France's successful postwar macroeconomic strategy. Based on a highly specific institutional structure in which considerable power was concentrated in the Ministry of Finance, the French formula of the 1950s, 1960s, and 1970s blended state–led economic development with Keynesian macroeconomic policies. Both monetary and fiscal policy were controlled by politicians in the ministry of finance and strongly influenced by growth–oriented technocrats from the Commissariat du Plan. The macroeconomic pattern that evolved was characterized by state–directed (and subsidized) credit supply for industry, discretionary fiscal policy, and, in times of need, adjustments of the French franc's exchange rate to restore the external competitiveness of French industry.[11] Under this macroeconomic regime, French industry benefitted from generally strong pressure of demand, cheap credit for investment, and a relatively stable cost structure that made a high and predictable self–financing ratio possible. French labor was pacified by an "implicit pact" made with capital and the state, based on growing real wages and welfare benefits in exchange for productivity advances and industrial modernization.[12] The positive results of this growth formula are obvious: in the postwar period France quickly overtook Britain and became Europe's second largest and, in some respects, most sophisticated economy. The growth rates of the 1960s were higher than Germany's and the accumulation of investment capital was rapid. It was only in the 1970s that the limitations of France's postwar growth formula became apparent. Under the impact of the oil crisis and the already existing distributive conflicts of the early 1970s, French industrial production collapsed in 1974 and inflation rose rapidly. Although Germany had the same problems in principle, the depth of the crisis in France was different. First, in France the oil shock coincided with a period of quickly growing domestic demand and rapid expansion of the money supply, which brought about a large balance of payments deficit together with a franc crisis. In Germany, both a mark crisis and external deficits were avoided because of restrictive monetary and fiscal policies in 1973. Second, the fall in the profit share of national income was much more serious in France than in Germany.[13] Therefore, I would argue somewhat differently from Patrick McCarthy in his introduction that the drawbacks of the growth–oriented French reaction to the first oil shock became apparent much earlier than the late 1970s.

After the first oil shock, the macroeconomic disorder and the sclerosis of the supply side of the French economy proved very tenacious. In

1975–76 Jacques Chirac attempted to reflate the economy out of the recession and to put the country back on its former growth path. The results were disappointing. Inflation soared, the current account moved into deficit, and the franc had to be taken out of the European Currency Snake. At the same time, investment and growth remained sluggish. The lessons from Chirac's failure were drawn by his successor, Raymond Barre. Barre, who became prime minister in late 1976, attempted to hold domestic demand in check in order to eliminate France's external deficits and keep the franc stable. He also attempted to bring down inflation and the growth of labor costs in order to improve the financial position of France's industry. As it turned out, Barre was successful in controlling domestic demand and in rebalancing the current account. Moreover, during his tenure as prime minister the franc never had to be devalued.

He did not, however, succeed in bringing down inflation, and the growth of real labor costs rose to a level where industry's profit margins could not be durably improved. The reason for this failure was his unwillingness or incapacity to eliminate the excess liquidity in the French economy inherited from his predecessors. Under Barre the growth rate of the French money supply was stabilized at a level which allowed ample room for inflationary price and wage increases.[14] In my view, this failure was rooted in the institutional setup of the French economy, where elected politicians are responsible for monetary policy. With a central bank dependent on political decisions, politicians are reluctant to assume responsibility for tough policies even though they are economically desirable: monetary policy follows economic trends instead of regulating them.[15] With the establishment of the EMS in 1978, Raymond Barre and Giscard d'Estaing hoped to be able to use a fixed exchange rate with the mark to follow the more restrictive policies of the German Bundesbank, but, as mentioned, between 1979 and 1982–83 the mark itself was weakened by German current account deficits.

After March 1983, when the French Socialists jettisoned their demand–oriented policy of redistributionary Keynesianism, the franc/mark link in the EMS worked in the sense that Giscard and Barre had anticipated. The evolution of the French money supply was aligned with developments in Germany; thus, the newly acquired credibility of the French government's deflationary policies brought with it lower wage increases and a redistribution of national income towards business firms. At the same time, the French government embarked on a process of successful budget consolidation which continued into the early 1990s, when the deficit–reduction process in Germany was interrupted by the economic consequences of reunification. Other than Germany, France (together with Luxembourg and Denmark) today stands as one of the few countries of the EC that already fulfills all the macroeconomic requirements for entry into the final stage of Monetary Union. By 1992 France had one of the lowest rates of inflation in Europe, a positive trade account, a strong currency, and an above–average rate of growth. These are the results of the revolution of French macroeconomic policy which occurred in the 1980s, intimately linked to the progress of Franco–German macroeconomic cooperation in that decade.

FRANCO–GERMAN ECONOMIC CONVERGENCE IN THE 1980s

Franco–German economic convergence in the 1980s began with the need to align monetary policies in the EMS. This was complemented in both countries by efforts at fiscal consolidation. By the late 1980s both the French and the German government budget deficits were very much under control and did not exceed 1 percent of GDP. As with monetary policy, the crucial year for this fiscal change of heart was 1983. In Germany, budget consolidation became one of the principal policy goals for the new center–right government under Helmut Kohl. In France, the negotiations leading up to the EMS realignment of March 1983 proved to be of lasting impact for the country's subsequent macroeconomic strategy.

Nominally, these negotiations were only supposed to determine the rate of devaluation of the franc. In fact, however, the bargaining between Jacques Delors, then minister of finance, and his German counterpart, Gerhard Stoltenberg, produced a complicated package deal in which the mark was revalued by 5.5 percent, while the franc's devaluation was limited to only 2.5 percent. Thus, the larger share of the exchange rate adjustment was transferréd to the German currency. In exchange, the Germans obtained guarantees about the future conduct of French fiscal policy.[16]

This outcome suggests some interesting conclusions about the workings of Franco–German macroeconomic cooperation in the 1980s. First, although nominally only concerned with monetary policy, the EMS has become just as important for other stability–relevant policy areas. Second, even the theoretically more influential country, Germany, cannot easily adopt an attitude of benign neglect with respect to the impact of its own policies on other countries. Instead of provoking a breakup of the negotiations, the Germans preferred to make a face–saving concession to the

French with regard to the franc in order to assure that fiscal policy in France would follow a stability–oriented path.[17] Obviously, the Germans did not invent *rigueur* for the French, but they provided political leverage for those members of the French government who—like Delors—wanted to change course anyway. According to one source, the details about future French fiscal policy negotiated between Stoltenberg and Delors had a significant impact on the budget consolidation plan put together after the devaluation.[18]

After March 1983, the macroeconomic profiles of France and Germany began to converge while France progressively eliminated controls on prices and capital movements. The budget deficits were reduced, inflation and interest rates moved towards the same levels, and investment (long the Achilles' heel of both economies) began to rise again. Conflicts of interest remained, of course. In January 1987, for example, the Germans had to agree to a three percent revaluation of the mark, while the French minister of finance, Edouard Balladur, refused to consider a devaluation of the franc. Although this realignment was caused primarily by the decline in the dollar, the episode suggests again that Germany could not easily ignore the impact on other EMS countries of the mark's position in international currency markets. Rather than risk an open clash with the French and endanger the future of the EMS, German policy–makers again preferred to make a concession about the exchange rate while simultaneously insisting on the continuation of stability–oriented macroeconomic policies; hence the rejection of domestic and foreign calls for a more expansionary macroeconomic policy that coincided with the mark's revaluation.[19]

European ministers of finance took steps to strengthen the EMS at the Nyborg meeting in September 1987. The discussions were essentially about the distribution of the burden of adjustment between strong and weak currencies in the EMS. The result of these negotiations was a strengthening of the crisis mechanisms of the EMS through an extension of the credit facilities available for intra–marginal interventions.[20] Although the Bundesbank refused to agree to an automatic extension of ecu–denominated credit in case of a currency crisis, the Nyborg Accord did improve the solidarity of EMS mechanisms.

Following the compromise at Nyborg, the old debate about more expansionary German macroeconomic policy resurfaced in 1988. This time, however, Pierre Bérégovoy, the new French minister of finance, came up with the idea to "recycle" the German current account surpluses via a sort of intra–EC mini–Marshall plan that would finance infrastructure projects in the Community.[21] Needless to say, the plan got nowhere and

German policy–makers argued that if France wished to attract the German funds flowing to the United States, it could do so by choosing the appropriate monetary policy.

Another critical episode in the evolution of Franco–German economic relations in the 1980s was triggered by growing German concerns about the sustainability of a fixed franc/mark exchange rate because of growing German trade surpluses with France. In the second half of 1989, German policy–makers and economists multiplied their calls for a revaluation of the mark with respect to other European currencies, particularly the franc: they justified their case by the need to use the exchange rate as a shield against imported inflation. The French government, however, was at the time attempting to establish the franc as one of the hard currencies within the EMS and therefore was determined to build up confidence in the French currency's stability. Given this objective, nothing was more unwelcome than a German debate about a coming devaluation of the franc. Following intense political pressure from the French, the Germans gave up their intention to change exchange rates.[22]

Another reason for the quick denouement of the crisis was of course German reunification, which was becoming increasingly possible in late 1989 and early 1990. The financial burden of reunification immediately reversed the results of several years of budget consolidation, leading to strong growth in domestic demand and deteriorating external accounts. In particular, the French trade deficit with Germany began to decline quickly. In 1990–91, the economic consequences of reunification and the continuation of stability–oriented macroeconomic policies in France brought about further convergence between the two countries. In fact, by mid–1991 France's rate of inflation had fallen below Germany's, and in October 1991 French short–term interest rates were slightly lower than the corresponding German rates. All this happened under conditions of perfectly liberalized capital markets and a fixed franc/mark exchange rate.[23] The convergence of French and German macroeconomic trends, begun in 1983, was practically complete.

Thus, in the period between 1983 and 1990 a set of formal rules and informal norms developed around the EMS, guiding Franco–German macroeconomic convergence. Neither of the two countries "opted out" by choosing a policy of benign neglect with respect to its European partner. Indeed, as I have argued, even Germany, the most likely candidate for such a policy, has repeatedly shown that it would rather compromise than risk the survival of the system. German reunification runs the danger of changing this pattern, but for the 1980s it seems clear that macroeconomic convergence and the EMS served both countries' national interests well.

GERMAN REUNIFICATION AND THE FUTURE OF
FRANCO–GERMAN CONVERGENCE

Naturally, the task of reunification came to dominate German economic policy after 1990. In particular, the need to finance the transition from a command economy to a market economy in East Germany strongly influenced fiscal trends. Early estimates of the magnitude of the challenge proved optimistic. West Germany's public finances in 1989 were healthy and the total government financial balance even showed a small surplus of 0.2 percent of GNP. The budget plan for 1990 foresaw a small general government deficit of one percent of GNP, caused by the implementation of the third stage of the 1986–90 tax reform. However, as the reunification process unfolded in the course of 1990, three supplementary budgets were added to cover the quickly rising outlays. The first came as early as February, the second in May, and the last—by far the largest—in October.[24]

Under the terms of German Monetary Union, the federal government agreed to cover two–thirds of the former GDR's government deficit. Bonn would also provide temporary finance for the East's social security system. In addition, the federal government established a "Unity Fund" with the mandate to borrow up to DM 95 billion from 1990 to 1994 in order to cover part of the eastern authorities' deficits. In May 1990, unemployment was expected to average only 430,000 during 1990–1991 after the introduction of the mark in the East. Output was expected to contract for only a short time and by a limited amount, and a vigorous recovery of the East German economy was expected to follow quickly. Reflecting these optimistic assumptions, total transfers to the East were projected at DM 25 billion in 1990 and DM 38 billion in 1991. In the end, they rose to DM 45 billion in fiscal 1990, and far exceeded DM 100 billion in both 1991 and 1992. On the other hand, the general government financial deficit of 1990 was DM 20 billion less than budgeted, thanks to strong economic activity in West Germany and delays in appropriations spending in the East.[25]

Estimates in November 1990 indicated that the federal deficit in 1991 would amount to about DM 100 billion in the absence of restraining measures.[26] Alarmed by these projections, the government proceeded to lower its planned 1991 deficit to around DM 67 billion. This was to be achieved by sharp reductions both in defense spending and in transfers to the Federal Labor Office. In addition, policy–makers cut subsidies, redirected spending to the East, and increased the transfers from the postal services.[27] In March 1991, however, the government adopted the *Aufschwung Ost* program which made DM 24 billion available for additional infrastructure investment in East Germany in 1991 and 1992. When outlays thus continued to rise much more quickly than projected, Helmut Kohl used the German Gulf War contribution of another DM 17 billion as an excuse to break his election pledge of no new taxes. His tax package of early 1991 included a 7.5 percent "solidarity surcharge," an average 35 percent increase in fuel and energy taxes, a 25 percent increase in tobacco taxation, and an increase in the tax on insurance premiums.[28]

Thanks to strong revenue growth and continued underspending of appropriations in the East, the outcome for public finances in 1991 was much better than expected. Instead of rising to DM 67 billion as planned, the federal deficit amounted to only DM 52.2 billion. Overall, the general government financial deficit rose to 2.8 percent of GNP, up from 1.9 percent in 1990. This included a 50 percent increase of the Unity Fund's borrowing requirement. Although the general government financial deficit in 1992 is projected to reach only 2.8 percent of all–German GNP (the same as 1991), the total borrowing requirement of Germany's public sector will be much higher than that. The public sector recourse to the capital market also covers such items as public financing of subsidized loans, which are extended by the European Recovery Program, for example. Moreover, according to projected estimates, the Treuhand, the public body charged with the privatization of East German businesses, will have a deficit of DM 30 billion by the end of 1992. All told, the borrowing requirement of Germany's public authorities could reach 5.2 percent of GNP in 1992.[29]

The Bundesbank had already tightened its policy in 1988 and 1989, and, given the low rate of inflation, saw no need for further measures in the first quarter of 1990. The money supply (M3) target for 1990 had been established at 4 to 6 percent, and the actual outcome was 5.6 percent.[30] Initially, German Monetary Union seemed to pose little threat to price stability. In December 1990, the Bundesbank announced that it would hold to its 1990 target range for M3 in 1991, but extended it to the entire currency area. Following a sharp increase in M3 in late 1990, the Bundesbank raised its Lombard rate by 0.5 percentage points to 8.5 percent in November 1990, and its Lombard and discount rates by another 0.5 percent in February 1991. Thereafter, the growth rate of all–German M3 came back to the target range of 4 to 6 percent.

However, as a consequence of German Monetary Union, the all–German money supply in the first quarter of 1991 was about 20 percent higher than the West German money supply a year earlier. When the Bundesbank derived its M3 target for 1991, the first year after monetary union, it originally calculated that the integration of the GDR would add about 10 percent to the all–German GDP. The Bank also projected the nominal growth of Germany's production potential at 5 percent. Given these estimates, a 20 percent jump in M3 was clearly too much and had to be seen as a potential danger for future price stability.[31]

In the second half of 1991 the Bundesbank was again forced to raise interest rates. A very sharp acceleration in the growth rate of M3 made this necessary.[32] To some extent, the increased use of the mark as parallel currency in Eastern Europe caused this sharp acceleration. Other factors were portfolio shifts resulting from the inverse yield curve in Germany and the planned introduction of a withholding tax on interest income. Moreover, demand for credit in East Germany was very strong and did not respond to higher Bundesbank interest rates since most of it was heavily subsidized.[33] In December 1991, the Bundesbank set its target range for M3 in 1992 at 3.5–5.5 percent. With M3 growing at almost 10 percent in late 1991, prominent German economists argued that this target range was too low and that it was based on wrong assumptions about the growth of Germany's production potential, the demand for marks in Germany and Eastern Europe, and other factors like the inflationary impact of the gradual decontrol of rents in East Germany.[34] The Bundesbank's intention was to warn the government and the trade unions that it no longer accepted behavior that threatened stability. Unfortunately, however, the wage settlements reached in early 1992 after weeks of strikes still added up to an average increase of 5.75 percent, and in September 1992 the growth rate of M3 was still as high as 9.1 percent. At the same time, German inflation was running at about 4 percent, and the Bundesbank risked losing its credibility.

When the Bundesbank council met in July of 1992 to consider whether it was appropriate to change the M3 target for 1992, or whether measures should be taken to bring the growth rate of M3 at least somewhat closer to its projected 5.5 percent maximum, it opted for the latter and raised the discount rate from 8 to 8.75 percent. The Bank confirmed its original M3 target for 1992 and insisted that money supply trends in Germany continued to threaten stability.[35] Thus, given the gradual loss of control over the evolution of the German money supply in 1991 and 1992 as well as the strong cost pressure from high wage settlements in 1992, the Bundesbank concluded in July 1992 that it had no other choice but to continue fighting inflation if it wanted to preserve its national and international credibility.

Since reunification, Germany's high interest rates have aroused increasing international criticism. The pressure for EMS countries to follow German rates clearly slowed down their economic recovery, particularly since late 1991. In 1991, some EMS countries, including France, had lower growth and less inflation than Germany, but still could not bring interest rates down.

To some extent, the Bundesbank accepted this criticism in July 1992, when it decided not to raise the Lombard rate, which would have had a much more direct effect on foreign interests rates than the discount rate alone. But the Bundesbank also argued that the stimulation from Germany's high level of demand in 1990 and 1991 overcompensated for the contractionary international impact of tight money. According to the Bundesbank, growing exports to Germany added 0.4 percentage points to French GNP in 1990 and 0.7 percentage points in 1991.[36] The Franco–German trade balance improved by 21.6 percent in 1990 and by 40.8 percent in 1991. Between 1989 and 1991 French car exports to Germany doubled.

In September 1992, the Bundesbank finally began to lower its Lombard and discount rates. The move was part of a package deal in the EMS where German interest rates were cut in exchange for a devaluation of the Italian lira and the Spanish peseta. The British government did not participate in the realignment and rejected calls for a devaluation of the overvalued pound sterling. Triggered by statements from Helmut Schlesinger, the head of the Bundesbank, a dramatic pound crisis began and on 16 September the British currency together with the lira left the exchange rate mechanism of the EMS and depreciated by more than 20 percent with respect to the mark.

After the timid approval of the Maastricht Treaty in the French referendum on 20 September, foreign exchange dealers also began to speculate against the franc. The French currency was pushed toward its lower intervention point against the mark and markets were heavily betting on an impending franc devaluation. However, the speculators who had successfully gambled on the devaluation of the pound and the lira overlooked the fact that in the French case there was no economic justification for a devaluation vis-à-vis the mark. A devaluation based purely on speculative, and hence short–term capital flows, contradicts the very idea of the EMS, which is to create a zone of relative monetary stability in Europe. France has successfully used the EMS to pursue stability policy since 1983 and to build confidence in the franc as one of Europe's stronger currencies. By mid–1992 French inflation was running at about 2.5 percent, which compares favorably with Germany's 4.0 percent, and the French trade and current account balances continued to improve. Therefore, a devaluation at this point would also have destroyed a decade–long effort at macroeconomic stabilization in France. It would have contradicted the economic logic of the EMS and erased the results of Franco–German macroeconomic cooperation since 1983.

Thus, the German government and the Bundesbank had many reasons to side with the Banque de France in the September "battle for the franc."[37] German support for the franc was unconditional: Finance Minister Waigel and the Bundesbank issued statements pointing out that there was no need to change the franc's EMS parity, and the German central bank carried out heavy intra–marginal interventions selling marks for francs. In the end, the franc was not devalued and the speculators walked away with heavy losses. By mid–October, the Banque de France felt that the franc's position in the EMS was strong enough to bring down interest rates. Short–term money market rates were lowered in two steps from 9.6 percent to 9.1 percent. In Germany, interest rates fell quickly as well, after the denouement of the September crisis. Although the Bundesbank did not change its intervention rates, short–term money–market rates plummeted by one percentage point to 8.75 percent and 10–year bond yields fell to around 7.2 percent. At the same time, the diminishing interest rate gap between Germany and the United States led to a rising dollar, which in turn helped ease tensions in the EMS.

CONCLUSION

Since 1990, the economic consequences of German reunification have put other European economies, particularly France, under enormous strain, and there is the danger that Germany's current fiscal crisis and continuing contradictions between German wage and monetary policy will undermine the Community's further integration as well as the results of Franco–German macroeconomic convergence over the past ten years. On the other hand, the process of interest rate reduction appears to have begun in Germany and throughout Europe, and German policy–makers have announced that they were preparing future tax increases and spending cuts to help consolidate government finances. Furthermore, as the September monetary crisis seems to suggest, both the French and the German governments remain strongly committed to the continuation of economic convergence between the two countries.

Thus, whether or not the Maastricht Treaty will finally be ratified by all EC countries (including Britain and Denmark), the continuation of the European integration process at present depends heavily on the compatibility of economic trends in Germany and the rest of Europe. If the Maastricht Treaty fails, but Germany and France can return to their economic convergence of the late 1980s, further integration continues to be likely. One possibility would be to reduce the fluctuation bands for the franc/mark exchange rate and slowly work toward a de facto Monetary Union (with or without a single currency) among the core EMS countries. This would result in a two–speed Europe revolving around a monetary center with France, Germany, and the Benelux countries.

Although the idea is at present a political taboo in the Community, it seems a much more realistic outlook than the ratification and application of the Maastricht Treaty by all twelve EC countries.

NOTES

1. Peter W. Schulze, "Bridging the Technology Gap: The Role of National and Regional Research and Development Programs in Europe," in Beverly Crawford and Peter W. Schulze (eds.), *The New Europe Asserts Itself* (Berkeley: University of California at Berkeley, 1990), pp. 197–210.

2. For the origin of the distinction between "mission–oriented" and "diffusion–oriented" technology policies see Henry Ergas, "Does Technology Policy Matter?" (Brussels: Center for European Policy Studies, 1986), CEPS Papers no. 29.

3. Pierre Poret, "The 'Puzzle' of Wage Moderation in the 1980s," OECD Working Paper no. 87 (November 1990), pp. 13–14.

4. Kamal Abd–El–Rahman, "Stratégies des Firmes et Résultats du Commerce Extérieur Français," *Economie Prospective Internationale,* (2e Trimestre 1990), pp. 95–109.

5. Calculated from OECD, *Economic Survey of Germany, 1989–90* (Paris: OECD, 1990), Table G, pp. 110–11.

6. The calculation is based on 1991 figures from OECD, *Economic Survey of Germany, 1991–92,* (Paris: OECD, 1992), Table G, pp. 118–19.

7. INSEE, *Rapport sur les Comptes de la Nation* (Paris: INSEE, 1990), p. 87.

8. Ibid.

9. Fritz W. Scharpf, *Sozialdemokratische Krisenpolitik in Europa* (Frankfurt/New York: Campus Verlag, 1987), p. 171.

10. Thomas Mayer et al., "Economic Developments in the Federal Republic of Germany," in Leslie Lipschitz and Donough McDonald (eds.), *German Reunification: Economic Issues* (Washington: International Monetary Fund, 1990), pp. 17–49.

11. Peter Hall, *Governing the Economy* (New York/Oxford: Oxford University Press, 1986), pp. 243–46.

12. Robert Boyer, "The Current Economic Crisis," in George Ross, Stanley Hoffmann, and Sylvia Malzacher (eds.), *The Mitterrand Experiment: Continuity and Change in Modern France* (New York: Oxford University Press, 1987), p. 34.

13. OECD, *Economic Survey of France, 1989–90* (Paris: OECD, 1990), p. 28.

14. OECD, *Economic Survey of France, 1980–81* (Paris: OECD, 1982), p. 40.

15. Consider the following statement by John R. Hicks: "So long as wages are being determined within a *given* monetary framework, there was some sense in saying

that there was an 'equilibrium wage,' a wage that was in line with the monetary conditions that were laid down from outside. But the world we now live in is one in which the monetary system has become relatively elastic, so that it can accommodate itself to changes in wages, rather than the other way about. Instead of actual wages having to adjust themselves to an equilibrium level, monetary policy adjusts the equilibrium level of money wages so as to make it conform to the actual level. It is hardly an exaggeration to say that instead of being on a Gold Standard, we are on a Labor Standard." John R. Hicks, "Economic Foundations of Wage Policy," *The Economic Journal* (September 1955), pp. 389–404, p. 391.

16. Franz–Olivier Giesbert, *Le Président* (Paris: Seuil, 1990), p. 180.
17. Henrik Uterwedde, *Die Wirtschaftspolitik der Linken in Frankreich. Programme und Praxis 1974–86* (Frankfurt/New York: Campus Verlag, 1988), pp. 194–95.
18. Serge July, "Mitterrand dans l'oeil du cyclone," in *Libération,* 21 March 1983, p. 6.
19. Elke Thiel, "Macroeconomic Policy Preferences and Co–ordination: A View from Germany," in Paolo Guerrieri and Pier Carlo Padoan, *The Political Economy of European Integration,* (Savage: Barnes & Noble Books, 1989), p. 221.
20. Ibid., p. 223.
21. George Valance, *France–Allemagne. Le Retour de Bismarck* (Paris: Flammarion, 1990), pp. 218–19.
22. Ibid., pp. 280–81.
23. François Renard, "La France profite de la désinflation pour baisser ses taux," *Le Monde,* 19 October 1991, p. 25.
24. OECD, *Economic Survey of Germany, 1991* (Paris: OECD, 1991), p. 64.
25. Ibid., pp. 62–63.
26. Ibid., p. 65.
27. Ibid.
28. Ibid., pp. 66–67.
29. OECD, *Economic Outlook, 51* (Paris: OECD, June 1992), p. 64. Also OECD, *Economic Survey of Germany, 1991,* pp. 67–68.
30. OECD, *Economic Survey of Germany, 1991,* pp. 73–81.
31. Ibid., pp. 74–79.
32. OECD, *Economic Outlook, 51,* p. 62.
33. Ibid., p. 65.
34. See, for example, Norbert Walter, "The Bundesbank Should Raise Its Monetary Targets," *The Wall Street Journal,* 12 November 1992, p. 8.
35. "Bundesbank wirbt im EWS fur ihre Zinspolitik," *Borsen–Zeitung,* 15 July 1992, p. 5.
36. Ibid.
37. Jean–Claude Casanova, "Du bon usage d'une crise," *L'Express,* 9 October 1992, p. 17.

Chapter 5

France and Germany as Partners in the European Community

Roger Morgan

THE CRISIS OF 1992:
WILL FRANCE AND GERMANY SAVE THE EC?

In late September 1992 the European Community seemed to be faced with a serious threat of disintegration: specifically, a threat that some member–states would refuse to ratify the Treaty on European Union which their twelve governments had signed the previous December in the Dutch city of Maastricht. Such a refusal would mean that the entire intricate package of commitments to build such a Union—the development of the unified internal market of "1992" into an economic and monetary union with, one day, a single currency and a European central bank; the attempt to achieve common policies in diplomacy and international security; and the strengthening of the European Parliament along with other Community institutions—would all be swept away, and that even the integrationist advances made by the 1986 Single European Act would themselves be at risk.

The situation was indeed critical. The British and Italian currencies had dropped out of the Exchange Rate Mechanism; the Danish government seemed to have little chance of inducing its voters to reverse the "no" to the Maastricht Treaty they had expressed in the referendum three months earlier; and finally, on 20 September, the French people only voted "yes" on the same issue by the smallest of margins.

In this alarming situation, as so often before in the Community's history, the clearest message of continued commitment to the goal of European Union came from the united voices of Paris and Bonn. President Mitterrand and Chancellor Kohl, meeting in Paris two days after the French vote, launched a hard campaign to revive the momentum towards the program of political and economic union embodied in the Maastricht Treaty. It is true that, for the first time on such an occasion, the two leaders refrained from issuing a formal joint communiqué. Commentators suggested that they were unwilling to create additional complications between themselves and the United Kingdom, which was trying to combine the formal presidency of the EC with a policy of "wait for Denmark" as far as the British ratification of Maastricht was concerned.

The Franco–German message, however, was clear enough. As Kohl expressed it in an interview before leaving Paris, "for me and for the president, it is clear: we want the ratification of Maastricht. The process must not be stopped. We want to expand but also deepen the Community."[1] It may be noted in passing that on the last point mentioned by Kohl—the problem of widening the Community as distinct from deepening it—the French and German positions are far from identical.

Yet the overall message from Paris was unambiguous: whatever hesitations and obstacles might be preoccupying London, Copenhagen or Rome, the Franco–German "tandem" was bent on proceeding towards European Union with the same determination that Kohl and Mitterrand had expressed on countless occasions over the previous ten years.

At one level, this commitment seemed to have become a personal obsession for the two leaders, fuelled by the sense of a desperate race against time. Kohl, it was reported, had confided to a member of his staff: "while we are both alive, François and I have to make Europe's unification irreversible . . . our successors will never manage it."[2]

At a more technical level, however, French and German spokespeople were at pains to tell the world that the manifest and systematic pursuit of cooperation between Paris and Bonn was not based on a political commitment to give their partnership priority over all else. Rather, it had a solid basis in the existence of common objective characteristics, as well as shared views on policy issues. On the monetary front, for instance, when the Bundesbank governor and his staff were accused of favoritism in giving all-out support to the French franc (while they had allowed the pound and the lira to be devalued), their answer was to deny any inconsistency. As a correspondent of *The London Times* reported:

> Herr Schlesinger's public support for the franc, which stood in contrast to the
> Bundesbank's frequently expressed skepticism about the pound and the lira,

was explained by German bank officials as a matter of economics, not politics. The franc could not be described as unstable or overvalued against the mark, said one, since France had a current account surplus and lower inflation than Germany.[3]

Over and beyond technical arguments of this kind, however, the peoples and the governments of Europe received from the Mitterrand–Kohl meeting the message they were intended to receive: the president and the chancellor were reaffirming their oft–declared resolve to proceed, despite all difficulties, and despite some differences in perspectives between their two countries, towards the goal of European union. In the days after their meeting, there were press reports that they had agreed on firm plans for a "two–speed Europe" in which a hard core of countries under Franco–German leadership would proceed rapidly towards further integration, leaving the peripheric laggards to catch up as and when they could. The German magazine *Der Spiegel* even announced that plans had been agreed for a Franco–German central bank, to be headed by a French citizen and located in Frankfurt, as a financial nucleus for this "Carolingian Europe."[4] Reports of this kind were officially denied, but the overall reaffirmation of the French and German commitment to European union, as well as further statements by Bundesbank officials and others about the possibility of pursuing monetary integration among a group of less than all twelve EC states if necessary, confirmed the general impression that Paris and Bonn still saw themselves in late 1992 as leading the EC into the next phase of its creation of an ever–closer union among the peoples of Europe.

How close, in reality, were French and German views on the precise form this union should take? On the power relations, for instance, between the projected European Central Bank and the political directors of Europe's macroeconomic policy? On the powers of the European Parliament, Commission, European Council, and other Community organs? On the ways in which the union should develop its diplomatic and external security policies? On whether it should give a strong priority to "deepening" the degree of integration between its existing twelve members or work urgently to "widen" itself by bringing in the EFTA countries and some of the new democracies to the East?

To understand the role of such issues in French and German attitudes towards the EC in the 1990s, it is necessary to look back at the situation which developed between the Single European Act in the mid–1980s and the profoundly revolutionary changes which swept across Europe at the end of that decade. The issues were drastically affected and the debate transformed.

FROM THE SINGLE EUROPEAN ACT
TO THE FALL OF THE BERLIN WALL

The Single Act, negotiated in 1985, signed in 1986, and implemented in 1987, had much in common with other significant steps in the EC's long process of integration. Like the European Monetary System established at the end of the 1970s, for instance, it contained elements that suited the interests of some member–states more than those of others. It had institutional features as well as substantive ones, and it reflected, in many of its more important provisions, a trade–off between the interests of France and those of Germany, the two countries which had done the most to bring it about.[5]

More specifically, the Single Act enshrined the commitment of the EC to complete the liberalization of its internal market by 1 January 1993. This "1992" program comprised in principle the achievement of the so–called four freedoms: free movement throughout the EC of goods, capital, persons, and services. The Act gave the Community a bigger share of authority in policy areas related to the internal market, including environmental, competition, and fiscal policy. It also substantially increased the powers of the European Parliament (directly elected since 1979) in the EC's legislative process, in external relations, and in the admission of new members. Perhaps the most revolutionary of all the changes detailed in the Act was in giving the EC's Council of Ministers the possibility of taking certain decisions on matters related to the liberalization of the internal market by majority vote, rather than as hitherto by unanimity, thus reducing the veto power of the member–states.

This package of reforms can readily be seen to contain certain items which some member–states only accepted as the price they had to pay in order to obtain certain other concessions. Britain's Prime Minister Margaret Thatcher, for instance, keenly interested in the opening–up of the internal market in goods and services to free competition, accepted some institutional strengthening of the EC which, she was advised, would facilitate this opening–up (but which she later regretted). Our main concern here is to identify parts of the package which were of particular interest to Germany and to France.

Germany's fundamental interests in European integration could very briefly, and obviously too crudely, be summarized as the following:[6]

- Economically, the achievement of the maximum degree of trade liberalization within the internal market (and between the EC and its external trading partners), to allow German exporters to maximize their competitive advantages in manufactures, if not always in services.
- Politically, the development of fairly strong EC institutions of a democratic and federal type, so that German citizens could readily identify with a developing European Union as part of their general, but not absolutely automatic, commitment to Western liberal democracy.
- And, underlying these specific desiderata, a wish to develop a political framework around Germany—the thing that Chancellor Willy Brandt once called "a sensible government for Europe"—which would help the Germans to exorcise their historic "demons" of nationalism and expansionism.

Subordinate to these essential concerns, one could of course list a whole range of other German objectives:

- A Community–wide area secure for investment as well as trade, to allow German manufacturers to locate their productive plant, and investors their capital, throughout Europe.
- The maintenance of the basic idea of the EC's Common Agricultural Policy, which, despite complaints from German consumers and taxpayers about the heavy cost, brought direct benefits to hundreds of thousands of full–time and part–time German farmers.
- The development of European Political Cooperation, the EC member–states' network of diplomatic coordination, redefined in the Maastricht Treaty as a "Common Foreign and Security Policy," which has helped Germany's international influence to grow without forcing her, for instance, to take the controversial step of deploying military forces outside the NATO area.
- And, deriving from the general German wish to see a federal–type constitution for the future European Union, an interest in giving the individual states of the Federal Republic of Germany more direct links with the central institutions in Brussels and greater influence in shaping Community legislation.

This is obviously by no means a complete list of the priorities of German *Europa–Politik* (policy on Europe). On the other hand, some of the elements in the list were latent rather than active during the period 1985–89. The list, however, gives a broad indication of what Germany wanted to gain from the EC, which will be analyzed in more detail below. How does this list compare with a similar one of the concerns of France? France's view of what she wanted to achieve from European integration included the following:[7]

- Politically, the development of European institutions which would allow France and other states to keep the economic potential of their German neighbor under collective control (corresponding to one of the objectives in the German list, although for the French it often came first).
- Economically, the maintenance of the CAP and the general benefits of an open European market, which to France meant something rather different from the "pure" market economy espoused (though in very different ways) by German "neo–liberals" or Thatcherite Conservatives. For France, the EC was expected to have some of the characteristics of France's national economic planning commission, including an interventionist stance towards industrial policy and regional development.
- Monetarily, the pursuit of European "economic and monetary union" through active concentration on its monetary aspects: the fixing of currency exchange rates was expected to permit the weaker French franc to gain support from the stronger German mark, while strengthening the anti–inflationary discipline imposed on France's economy by the national policies adopted since 1983.
- And finally, in the diplomatic framework of European political cooperation, a system which would help France mobilize European support (not least the resources of Germany) for her pursuit of French interests in the world, including the bid to establish a "European identity" less dependent on the United States.

Like the underlying orientations of Germany, those of France tended to be reflected in a number of more specific concerns, such as the following:[8]

- Emphasis on the idea that the EC should be more than just a common market or free–trade area. It should, in French eyes, systematically develop common policies, with the necessary common resources, not only for agriculture but also for energy, industrial concentration, research and development, and EC regulation of the services sector and public procurement.

- In institutional matters, a general view that the main authority should remain with the national governments of the member–states, rather than passing to the institutions of the Community. Thus a reluctance, in principle, to concede greater powers to the Commission—even after its president from 1985 on was Jacques Delors, formerly a French minister under President Mitterrand—or to the European Parliament, and a preference for upgrading the role of the European Council of national government leaders, a body initiated by Mitterrand's predecessor Valéry Giscard d'Estaing in 1974.

- In the EC's foreign relations, a concern not to allow collective decision–making, either in the EC's trade negotiations or in the diplomacy of European political cooperation, to impede the pursuit of national interests and to resist European concessions to the United States both in the GATT (where a degree of protectionism is legitimate to defend Europe's identity) and in NATO (where Western Europe should concentrate on promoting its own military defense structures, including Western European Union and bilateral Franco–German cooperation, as part of the concept of "European Union").

Again, as with the German "shopping list" sketched earlier, not all of these French objectives were matters of active debate in the EC in 1985–89, nor is this list complete, but the general orientation of France's EC policy was along these lines.

The actual process of interaction between these French and German positions, and the process of finding common ground on specific points between them while integrating the positions taken by the EC's other ten member–states, proceeded relatively slowly in the first years after the Single Act came into force. This was partly because the Community's institutions and its national capitals were preoccupied with processing the huge volume of legislation which was now needed to complete the liberalization of the internal market by the end of 1992, and partly because for some important governments in the Community, the agreement to carry out this 1992 program was a substantial achievement in its own right. They were not convinced of the need to look beyond it to new tasks and new goals for the Community. This was certainly the view of the British government under Margaret Thatcher, who saw 1992 as a means of achieving throughout Western Europe the program of liberalization and deregulation by which she expected to achieve the salvation of the United Kingdom. What further development of the EC, beyond this, could be needed or even wished for?

While it would be a great exaggeration to portray the attitude of Helmut Kohl's Bonn as being close to that of Margaret Thatcher's London, the two did have some features in common. Whereas many of France's objectives in the EC, as sketched above, entailed changes, innovations, and increased expenditure—more EC intervention in industrial policy, more resources for development in the Community's Mediterranean regions, big research programs such as EUREKA—German wishes were more likely to be met by the consolidation of existing policies, accompanied by a concerted drive to make a success of the 1992 program.

There were, of course, some areas in which Germany wanted change and development. On some of these, notably Franco–German military cooperation, France and Germany moved forward together although, strictly speaking, this had nothing to do with the EC or with European Political Cooperation. On other issues, however, such as the continued commitment to making the EC's institutions more democratic as well as more effective, there was more interest in Bonn than in Paris.

In contrast, on some of the big issues which were beginning to be defined in the late 1980s, and which would dominate Western Europe in the early 1990s, France's interest at this stage appeared to be stronger than Germany's. The biggest of these issues was the renewed prospect of economic and monetary union: this was by no means a new issue since it had been on the EC's agenda since the Werner Plan of 1970, but it now became acutely topical once more as the European Commission under Jacques Delors began to reflect on the further implications of the liberalization of the internal market through the carrying–out of the "1992" program.

There were several reasons why French minds were more attracted than German ones to the logic of Delors's argument, developed in a series of studies and documents published from 1988 onward, that the "1992" program in itself would not leave the European economy in a steady or sustainable state.[9] Part of the argument was that the maintenance of the single market might itself be compromised if Europe's systems of currency management were left essentially in national hands; the already existing European Monetary System must therefore be developed, in parallel with the program of market liberalization, into a full Economic and Monetary Union, involving progress towards a single currency managed by a European Central Bank. It is immediately apparent that one of the reasons why this logic was less appealing in Germany than in France was that Germany was indubitably the strongest member of the EC in terms of the stability and influence of its currency, and that any transfer of authority from the German Bundesbank to the putative European bank would have to be managed very carefully, to put it mildly.

The specific problems of Economic and Monetary Union, and the difficulties of reconciling French and German views on them, especially in the context of a European Community divided by multiple cleavages, were only to become fully visible during the negotiations of 1990–91 and their aftermath. However, in retrospect, they can be seen to have underlain the period of uncertainty—as far as the longer–term prospects for the EC were concerned—which followed the coming into force of the Single Act. As noted above, the act produced a massive outburst of negotiating activity in the EC, directed towards completing the legislation necessary for "1992," but at the level of high politics and long–term designs there was much less going on, and this suspension of activity masked some important incongruities between French and German thinking.

When President Mitterrand and Chancellor Kohl met in Paris on 22 January 1988, to celebrate the twenty–fifth anniversary of the Elysée Treaty signed by de Gaulle and Adenauer, their stirring speeches called on the EC to overcome its current short–term preoccupations (including major disagreements about the budget, which were indeed resolved at a special summit in Brussels a few days later), and to respond, as Mitterrand put it, to the "strong will in Paris and in Bonn to unite our objectives and our possibilities in order to take Europe forward." Kohl, in reply, went further:

> The Germans and French must together build the hard core of a European Union—a Union that sees itself not merely as a common market, but as a community of the values of democracy based on freedom, the rule of law, and the social responsibility of the state. We must . . . step forth as a Community of action. We warmly invite our European partners to collaborate in this work—but we will not let ourselves be diverted from carrying this Union forward and completing it, together with those who want to work at it.[10]

In the period of less than five years which elapsed between these declarations and the two leaders' reaffirmation of the same message in September 1992, Europe was to go through convulsions—political, economic, and psychological—which were to produce a pressurized rerun of all the arguments about European unification of the preceding four decades and shed a sharp light on some elements of Franco–German divergence.

THE IMPACT OF 1989 ON FRANCO–GERMAN
RELATIONS IN THE EC

As far as Western Europe was concerned, there were two principal effects, as well as a host of lesser ones, of the collapse of the Soviet Empire: it made the reunification of Germany possible, and it gave a new urgency to the debates about European Union whose previous leisurely course we have followed. There was much talk in 1989–90 to the effect that the two processes of German unification and (West) European unification were intimately linked. Chancellor Kohl frequently called them "the two sides of the same coin," and many commentators argued that Germany, now at last given a chance to carry out the task of national unification laid down by Article 23 of the 1949 Basic Law, was likely to proceed with similar fervor to the task of "transferring sovereign powers to intergovernmental organizations," pre-scribed by Article 24 of the same document.[11] We have already noted Kohl's apparently deep commitment to the idea that European unification is an urgent task to be irreversibly advanced before he and "François" leave the scene, since their successors cannot be trusted to do it. Similar thoughts may be plausibly attributed to President Mitterrand, whose reactions to German unification certainly included the view that the tighter integration of Western Europe, already desirable in order to contain the power of the pre–1989 Federal Republic, was an absolute necessity now that its size was being drastically increased.

At one level, the Franco–German dialogue on European Union, as it proceeded under the pressures of the dramatic events of 1989–90, had certain essential features in common with some earlier versions. In the late 1920s, for instance, when the French and German foreign ministers Aristide Briand and Gustav Stresemann were jointly awarded the Nobel Peace Prize for their efforts at European reconciliation, the "Europes" for which they worked, although similar, were not identical. While Briand's idea of a United States of Europe was essentially that of a static construction in which the basic features of the Versailles settlement (including Germany's subordinate sta-tus) would be preserved, Stresemann saw European unity as a dynamic, revisionist process which would allow German influence to revive and grow. In the memorable words of Stresemann's biographer, "their two Europes mutually excluded one other."[12] In the 1950s, when Konrad Adenauer cooperated with the leaders of the Fourth Republic to create the European Community, there was a similar difference in perspectives, as the French desire to control the rising power of the Federal Republic coexisted with Adenauer's drive first for equality of status and then for a degree of leadership. The Giscard–Schmidt partnership of the 1970s had some similar features, as Giscard tried through the European Council and the EMS to harness some of Germany's political and economic dynamism to French purposes, and Schmidt saw the EC partly as a structure in which Germany's economic dynamism would give Bonn a position of leadership.

It makes some sense to view the interaction between Kohl's Europe and Mitterrand's, circa 1990, in a similar light. For Kohl the EC was a valuable framework in which to make Germany's enhanced power and newly–won sovereignty acceptable to her neighbors, and one of the Community's next tasks had to be its extension, entailing the extension of German economic and political influence, to Eastern Europe as well. For Mitterrand, on the other hand, one of the EC's functions was to keep the new Germany under collective control, and the idea of enlarging the Community to the East must be firmly resisted, partly because a wider Europe of this kind would enhance Germany's influence and leave France marginalized in its Western corner.

These schematic portrayals of strategic objectives, of course, grossly oversimplify the extremely complex realities. The efforts of Kohl and Mitterrand to pursue the policies these objectives might dictate, tempered by all the conflicting cross–pressures of their countries' other interests in various aspects of European integration, add up to a highly confused and ambiguous pattern of events. Before attempting to analyze the unfolding of France and Germany's EC policies during the period since 1989—which will be divided, artificially but probably usefully, into their political and their economic aspects—it is worth underlining one fundamental fact: German unification was a fait accompli, at least in the legal and institutional sense, before the debate about the further unification of Community Europe was even formally started. It is not in fact surprising that the two German states were able to carry through the formal act of unification as early as 3 October 1990—supported, however grudgingly, by the four Great Powers who joined them in the "two–plus–four" negotiations—a full two months before the EC's twelve governments even held the formal opening of their intergovern-mental conferences on European Union in Rome.[13] This meant that these conferences proceeded, during the twelve months leading up to the signature of the Maastricht Treaty in December 1991, against the background of the fact that Chancellor Kohl already represented a Germany "united" in a formal sense, although profoundly riven by the social and economic consequences of what it had done. France, like the EC's other member–states, could do no more than react to the revolution that had already occurred.

A further complication was that the Franco–German interaction during these intergovernmental conferences, and the interactions involving their ten

EC partners, were carried out under the changing oversight of the Community's six–month rotating presidency. The Italian presidency of late 1990, following that of Ireland, was succeeded in January 1991 by a low–profile Luxembourg presidency, and in July by a more ambitious Dutch one, whose original high–flown designs had to be radically scaled down to produce the consensus which the Twelve finally achieved at Maastricht in December.

It is convenient to distinguish between Franco–German interactions on the "economic" and on the "political" aspects of European Union, because Brussels during 1991 was in fact the scene of two quasi–permanent intergovernmental conferences (IGCs), each devoted to one of these two branches of the subject. In the conference on Economic and Monetary Union (IGC–EMU), the leading role was taken by the member–states' ministries of finance (for France and Germany, the Ministère des Finances and the Bundesfinanzministerium). The conference on Political Union (IGC–POL) was in the hands of the ministries of foreign affairs (including the Quai d'Orsay and the Auswärtiges Amt). The necessary linkage between the two sets of negotiations was maintained by the member–states' permanent missions (quasi–embassies) to the EC, and by the usual interministerial coordinating machinery in the national capitals during the later stages, before the final meeting of the European Council of heads of state and government at Maastricht.[14]

FRENCH AND GERMAN VIEWS OF ECONOMIC AND MONETARY UNION

The work of IGC–EMU, from beginning to end, was more systematic and coherent than that of the parallel IGC–POL, which had the task of processing a highly disparate collection of institutional, diplomatic, and other issues grouped under the general title of "Political Union." IGC–EMU, in contrast, was able to base itself on years of preparatory work—as already noted, the question of Economic and Monetary Union had been on the EC's agenda since the early 1970s—and notably on the reports produced since the late 1980s by a series of EC Commission expert groups. In particular, the so–called Delors Report of April 1989 on the general principles of EMU, and the more specific document of November 1990, containing proposals for a European Central Bank, gave the conference a solid basis for its deliberations.[15]

The French and German negotiators in this conference were themselves highly expert specialists, many of whom had been working on the issue for years. They had no difficulty in accepting, at least in principle, the logic of the Delors Commission's argument that consolidation of the free internal market, accepted by the Twelve in the Single European Act, required a move towards monetary union and entailed, in the long run, a common currency managed by a European Central Bank. The central element of this argument was that the free movement of goods and services through the liberalized internal market would be hampered if national governments retained the right to decide on currency parities, since unilateral changes in these would segment the market.

Starting from this premise, the IGC–EMU, including its German and French members, reached agreement on an elaborate timetable for the successive stages of progress towards full Economic and Monetary Union. The plan involved gradual progress from the European Monetary System as it already functioned—including the Exchange Rate Mechanism, or ERM, to which all the major members of the EMS belonged once Britain joined it in October 1990—through ever–closer cooperation between the EC's central banks in the European System of Central Banks, to the final stages of permanently locked and then unified currencies managed by a single European Central Bank.

By the end of 1991, this scheme was duly included as one of the central elements of the Maastricht Treaty. It is not possible here to go into all the details of the intricate negotiations which led to this result. It is enough, in an account of Franco–German interactions, to highlight two points of disagreement between Paris and Bonn which emerged during the year and which indicated fairly serious divergences within the context of a broad agreement on the general goal.

The first concerned the timetable for the progressive linking and ultimate merger of the national currencies of the Twelve. At the beginning of the negotiations, France, Germany, and others agreed that the European Central Bank should be established in 1994, in Stage II of the plan. However, in February 1991 Chancellor Kohl, reflecting a German view that progress towards EMU should not be hurried, put forward a revised treaty draft in which the Central Bank would only be set up in 1997, at the beginning of Stage III.[16] This deceleration of the timetable was unwelcome to France, which was interested in the quickest possible progress towards the unification of the French franc with the much stronger German mark. As was mentioned earlier, France's approach to EMU had always been a "monetarist" one, in the sense that France believed in the capacity of monetary integration to bring economic convergence in its train, whereas the German view was basically that monetary integration could only succeed once a substantial degree of genuine economic convergence had already taken place.[17] The Maastricht Treaty registered an uneasy compromise between these conflicting viewpoints, partly by laying down a very stringent list of economic criteria as conditions for membership of EMU, but underlying Franco–German differences still remained.

The second major disagreement was on the institutional question of whether the proposed European Central Bank should be independent of political control or should be subject to instructions from the ruling authorities of the proposed European Union. This issue, which divided France and Germany throughout the duration of the IGC and has continued to divide them ever since, reflects deep–seated historical differences between French and German ideas about the proper relationship between governments and central banks. Whereas the Banque de France is regarded as an agency of governmental economic policy and receives instructions from the political authorities, the Bundesbank has a statute which guarantees its autonomy and is in principle able to have the last word on monetary policy in the name of its paramount duty to prevent inflation. In practice, the Bundesbank's autonomy is less than perfect—its former governor, Karl Otto Pöhl, was forced to accept Chancellor Kohl's policy on the terms of the monetary union between the two German states in summer 1990—but in German minds the principle of a politically independent central bank remains a vital ideal. France, on the other hand, may leave the central bank a certain margin of maneuver, yet remains committed to the view that it should be subject to political direction in the interests of the government's economic strategy; to put the argument in terms of democratic accountability, the state's bankers should be responsible to the elected representatives of the people.

Although the wording of the relevant passage of the Maastricht Treaty appeared to lay down the clear principle that the governors of the European Central Bank should not accept political directives, thus accepting the German view, French spokespeople from President Mitterrand downward continued to repeat their interpretation of the text during 1992, namely that the Bank should execute the financial policy decided by the European Union's political leadership.[18] Even though the determined Franco–German solidarity of the autumn of 1992 looked as though it might in time produce a modus vivendi between these conflicting viewpoints, it was not at all clear how this might be done. Meanwhile, however, France and Germany, in stoutly maintaining their determination to ratify the Maastricht Treaty and carry it into effect, continued to proclaim their shared belief in the desirability and the feasibility of the EMU project contained in it.

FRANCE, GERMANY, AND POLITICAL UNION

As noted above, the contrast between IGC–EMU and IGC–POL was very marked: while the finance ministry officials in the former were working their way systematically through an agenda predetermined by years of expert preliminary work, the diplomats in the latter were striving to produce an orderly result from a jumble of national proposals on a miscellany of topics all deemed to be "political." Under this heading, as has so often occurred in the history of the EC, the topics varied from institutional matters such as the future powers of the European Parliament and the numbers of commissioners, to "human rights" questions like the creation of an EC ombudsman to receive citizens' complaints. Also included was "European Political Cooperation" as formally defined in the EC, namely the system of policy coordination between the foreign ministries of the Twelve (and now perhaps their defense ministries, too, if the proposed new "Common Foreign and Security Policy" acquired any substance). It is no wonder that one of the participants, after comparing the IGC–EMU to an elite military unit advancing with well–drilled precision towards its objective, likened the IGC–POL to a disorderly rabble streaming in confusion over a wild hillside.

In the vast and disparate agenda of IGC–POL, it is possible to identify many points on which the French and German positions were very close. For instance, on the project for the development of "European Political Cooperation" into a "Common Foreign and Security Policy," the French and German negotiators appear to have agreed without difficulty, at least on the principles guiding the new system. It remains to be seen how close French and German positions will be on the substance of the foreign policy which it is designed to produce (as Philip Gordon argues in chapter 7). In the military dimension of European unification, there were also numerous declarations of Franco–German solidarity, for instance in a joint Franco–German draft for part of what became the Maastricht Treaty which Kohl and Mitterrand submitted to the Dutch government shortly before the European Council meeting in Maastricht.[19] Military cooperation, although strictly outside the domain of the EC so far, in fact remains an area which has been exceptionally productive of joint Franco–German statements, and even of action in the form of the creation of joint military forces.

There are, however, a number of important issues, mainly institutional ones, on which French and German statements during 1991 indicated a wide degree of divergence. On some of them the absence of any agreed decision in the Maastricht Treaty indicates that the differences were never overcome. One of the biggest issues concerned the very question of how closely the economic aspect of European Union (i.e., EMU) should be linked with the political aspect. Chancellor Kohl took a clear and strong line on this point, declaring on several occasions that, despite the importance of EMU for Germany, he would only be willing to submit an economic treaty for parliamentary ratification if it was accompanied by equally decisive steps in the political dimension. On 30 January 1991, for instance, he told the Federal Parliament:

> For us Germans and for the Federal Government, the parallelism of the two intergovernmental conferences is of fundamental significance. The link between the two projects is both intrinsically and politically overwhelming. However important the achievement of the economic and monetary union may be, it would remain only a fragment if we did not achieve political union at the same time. To put it clearly and simply: as I see it, the only possibility for the Federal Republic is to agree to both at the same time. Both projects are indissolubly linked to each other.[20]

On 29 May, speaking in Edinburgh, he again stated:

> For me, these conferences (i.e., the IGCs) form a single whole: the treaty on Political Union must not fall behind the Economic and Monetary Union either in its capacity for action or in its basic objectives.[21]

From the French side, despite rhetorical affirmations of the need "to develop, strengthen and accelerate the structures of the Community," as President Mitterrand put it after the Strasbourg European Council meeting of December 1989,[22] there were fewer concrete proposals for political or institutional reforms than from Germany. Whereas Chancellor Kohl, in numerous speeches throughout the year, continued to propose greater decision–making powers for the European Parliament, a larger role for regional and local authorities in European affairs, and other means to bring Europe "nearer to the citizens," proposals from the French side were less far–reaching. They included a number of specific suggestions regarding, for instance, European cooperation against terrorists and other criminals (France had pioneered the idea of making the EC into "a single legal area"), but no very innovative ideas of an institutional kind. Whereas German thinking, based on federalist principles, produced arguments in favor of the strengthening of the European Parliament or enhancement of the powers of regional governments in the name of "subsidiarity," French thinking about "the construction of Europe" concentrated more on enhancing cooperation between sovereign states. During the debates of IGC–POL, French proposals thus tended to concentrate on strengthening the parts of the Community's decision–making machinery in which the member–states played the decisive role, notably the European Council composed of the heads of state (for France) and of government (for the other eleven members). There were also French suggestions for a European "Senate" of delegates from national parliaments and proposals that the new European Union should be given strong and consistent leadership through the replacement of the EC's rotating presidency by a president elected directly by the citizens of Europe, to serve—like the President of France—for a term of several years. Such suggestions did not appeal to France's partners (including Germany) and thus made no mark on the text finally agreed to at Maastricht.

We may thus conclude that, on the institutional front, French and German positions remained fairly far apart. There was no French echo of Chancellor Kohl's insistence on the need for political and economic union to go hand in hand—at least no echo in terms of institutional proposals along the lines of those he made himself. The institutional reforms contained in the Maastricht Treaty are not far–reaching: in part this is certainly because anything more radical would have been unwelcome to the representatives of other member–states, notably Britain and Denmark, but it can also partly be explained by the fact that here was an area where France and Germany failed to agree.

CONCLUSION:
FRANCE, GERMANY, AND THE EC AFTER MAASTRICHT

The Treaty on European Union probably represents the maximum of consensus on the subject that is attainable in the circumstances of the early 1990s: for some member–states it may not go far enough, while for others it goes too far. France and Germany, despite the differences in their positions which have been explored here, are certainly committed to going forward in the direction represented by Maastricht, and they appear likely to do this, even if they are accompanied by a group of less than all ten of the EC's other member–states.

One reason why a degree of consolidation of the Community appears urgent both in Paris and in Bonn is that the question of enlarging its membership will become increasingly hard to postpone. Here again, French and German views are not identical: while France feels more comfortable in a West European Community with limited membership (perhaps combined with a loose "confederation" embracing the eastern part of the continent, as proposed by President Mitterrand since 1989), Germany is increasingly preoccupied with building solid structures including the EC's eastern neighbors. The German interest in bringing the "reform countries" of the East into closer association with the EC—and preferably one day into membership of it—is very strong and stems from a variety of sources. These include, apart from Germany's historic links with Central and Eastern Europe, a positive hope, the hope of more economic dealings with a changing Eastern Europe, and a negative fear, the fear that continuing stagnation and frustration to the East will bring unwelcome immigration and other pressures and instabilities for Germany as the economic magnet and the eastern outpost of the EC.

This German concern with developing the EC's links with the East, going in a direction in which *Europa–Politik* means no longer just "policy towards the EC" but increasingly "policy towards Europe as a whole,"[23] is clearly disturbing to France and indicates a future in which the justly celebrated "Franco–German couple" of recent years may find it harder to maintain its harmonious relationship. However, the numerous links of common (or common enough) interest which have led to many years of successful Franco–German cooperation are likely to keep them fairly close together.

The question of whether the Franco–German partnership will be able to lead the EC towards much closer integration, in view of their own divergences and the recalcitrance of other member–states, is hard to answer. What is certain is that they are still trying harder to do this than any of the EC's other major member–states, and that if they fail, no one else is likely to succeed.

NOTES

1. "Bonn and Paris Pile On Pressure," *Guardian,* 23 September 1992.
2. As reported in *Der Spiegel,* 28 September 1992, p. 18.
3. *The London Times,* 22 September 1992.
4. *Der Spiegel,* 28 September 1992, pp. 18–23, and the interview with Karl Otto Pöhl, ibid., pp. 23–28, which includes arguments going in this direction.
5. See Andrew Moravcsik, "Negotiating the Single European Act: National Interests and Conventional Statecraft in the European Community," *International Organization,* 45, no. 1 (Winter 1991), pp. 19–56, and the same author's contribution to R. O. Keohane and S. Hoffmann (eds.), *The New European Community: Decision–making and Institutional Change,* (Boulder: Westview, 1991).
6. For a fuller account, see the author's chapter "The Federal Republic of Germany" in C. & K. Twitchett (eds.), *Building Europe,* (London: Europa, 1981).
7. See Annette Morgan, "France," in Twitchett, *Building Europe.*

8. Jean–Pierre Landau, "France and European Economic Integration," paper presented to the Washington Foundation for European Studies, December 1991.

9. See Michael Emerson et al., *One Market, One Money* (Oxford: Oxford University Press, 1992), and the earlier EC reports and studies cited therein. For a useful survey, see Dennis Swann (ed.), *The Single European Market and Beyond. A Study of the Wider Implications of the Single European Act,* (London/New York: Routledge, 1992).

10. Declarations reprinted in Hans–Peter Schwarz, *Eine Entente Elémentaire. Das Deutsch–französisches Verhaltnis im 25. Jahr des Elysée–Vertrags,* 2nd ed., Bonn, 1990: quotations on pp. 62, 69. See also on this period the useful report *Franco–German Relations and the Future of Europe* (Berlin: Aspen Institute, 1988).

11. See my "Germany in Europe," *The Washington Quarterly* 13, no. 4 (Autumn 1990), especially p. 157.

12. Anneliese Thimme, "Gustav Stresemann. Legende und Wirklichkeit," in *Historische Zeitschrift* 181 (1956), p. 324. For the contemporary parallels, see my "French Perspectives on the New Germany," in *Government and Opposition* 26, no. 1 (Winter 1991), pp. 108–114.

13. On the implications of these differences in timetable, see Roger Morgan, "Political and Institutional Implications for the EC," in Wolfgang Heisenberg (ed.), *German Unification in European Perspective* (London: Brassey's, 1991), especially pp. 89–91.

14. The progress of the IGCs may best be followed in the well–informed daily bulletins of *Agence Europe*. In what follows, information not otherwise attributed is often based on this source.

15. See Emerson, *One Market,* and sources quoted therein. Also Wilhelm Nölling, *Good–bye to the Deutsche Mark? The Future of the German Currency following the Maastricht Resolutions* (Hamburg: Landeszentralbank, 1992).

16. *Agence Europe,* Brussels, 27 February 1991.

17. See Hans Tietmeyer, *Economic and Monetary Union. A German Perspective* (Ludwig Erhard Memorial Lecture), (London: Konrad Adenauer Foundation and London School of Economics, 1992); and Françoise Nicolas & Hans Stark, *L'Allemagne. Une nouvelle hégémonie?* (Paris: Dunod, 1992), pp. 94–112.

18. *Der Spiegel,* 28 September 1992, p. 24.

19. *Bulletin,* Presse–und Informationsamt der Bundesregierung, Bonn, 18 October 1991, pp. 929–931.

20. Ibid., 13 January 1991, p. 73.

21. Ibid., 29 May 1991, p. 475.

22. Quoted in Renata Fritsch–Bournazel, *Europe and German Unification,* (New York/Oxford: Berg, 1992), p. 174.

23. The implications of this are explored in Roger Morgan, "Germany in the New Europe," in Colin Crouch and David Marquand (eds.), *Towards Greater Europe?* (Oxford: Blackwell, 1992), pp. 105–117.

Chapter 6

Small Countries and the Franco–German Relationship

Erik Jones

It is difficult to imagine that the Franco–German relationship would thrive in a vacuum. If France and Germany were the only two countries in Europe would they now be striving to patch together the empire of Charlemagne? It is doubtful. Certainly, when the smaller countries in Europe were neutral, and pretended to be anywhere except between two rival powers, their pretensions were not enough to ward off the ravages of several World Wars. Put another way, it is a short drive from Ypres through Waterloo to Bastogne.

Of course it is possible that the Second World War finally ended the historic animosity between the French and Germans. Having learned their lesson, they are now resigned to working out their problems in a less bellicose fashion. A quick read of most of the literature written about the Franco–German relationship would support this assertion. Nevertheless, as a description of the dynamic involved in that relationship, it is incomplete.

The other states in Europe do have influence, and although they do not play a central role, their influence transcends the technical formulation of the latest Commission directive on transport—at least potentially. More importantly, the role played by the small countries is an essential one to the relatively smooth functioning of the Franco–German locomotive.

That said, the question of small–country influence really concerns the proper context for Franco–German reconciliation. As Patrick McCarthy pointed out in his introduction, it is sometimes necessary for third powers to intervene in order to mediate between France and Germany. The examples he uses are the United States and Great Britain, and his assumptions are largely geopolitical, concerning the necessity of strengthening the European middle in the conflict between East and West.

The purpose of this chapter is to broaden those assumptions.[1] If it is to endure, the Franco–German relationship cannot be strong only from the outside looking in—it must also be strong from the inside out. But how can the United States, or possibly even Great Britain, be invoked to resolve purely domestic disputes? The short answer is that they cannot. The domestic political experience of the Anglo–Saxon world is in many ways too different from the continental to allow for useful mediation. In this sense there is some truth to de Gaulle's assertion that the Anglo–Saxons are made from a different wood than either the Germans or the Gauls[2]—an interpretation supported by the less–than–expected influence of the British within the Community after 1973.[3] Such mediation, I would contend, must come from the smaller countries of Europe. If the empires of the Gauls and Franks are to reunite, they must include the middle kingdom of Lothar.[4]

In keeping with that theme, the focus of this chapter is on relations between the Franco–German couple and Belgium, the Netherlands, Luxembourg (Benelux), and Denmark. It is an interaction that has developed over time and largely within the context of the European Community. The chapter is organized in four parts: the first section looks at the 1960s and the Fouchet Plan for European political union; the second focuses on the 1970s and 1980s and more particularly on the relaunching of Europe; the third deals with the most recent drive for political union, culminating in the Maastricht Treaty; and the fourth concludes with the debates surrounding the ratification of the Maastricht accords.

SMALL COUNTRIES AND A GAULLIST EUROPE

De Gaulle's reception of Adenauer at Colombey–les–deux–Eglises in September of 1958 was a dramatic illustration of the necessity of Franco–German reconciliation. With the benefit of hindsight it can also be described as a necessary first step in de Gaulle's four–tier strategy to revive the "old continent" as a power in its own right, equal in standing to the U.S. and USSR. Close French and German cooperation was the most important aspect of his strategy; more, it was the edifice he wanted to erect for posterity.[5]

The second part of de Gaulle's strategy was revealed only some weeks later through his ill–fated trip to Washington. There, he proposed a three–power directorate that would not only give the French some say in the use of American nuclear weapons, but would assure France a privileged role on the continent. As a fall–back position, de Gaulle encouraged the development of a French nuclear arsenal, building on the research initiated under Mendès France. That this was meant as a powerful symbol of French particularity was underscored by Michel Debré's assertion that nonnuclear states were only "satellites" of nuclear powers.[6]

The third element of de Gaulle's strategy was to change the nature of European integration to center on the nation–state. This also had the effect of maximizing French influence by reorienting it around bilateral relations, where the enormous presence of the general could have its fullest impact. This can be seen not only in de Gaulle's proposal for a confederated Europe—later called the "Fouchet Plan"—but also in the flurry of diplomatic activity that surrounded its negotiation. Another example can be found in France's insistence that each of the six members of the European Economic Community be represented in the handling of the British application.[7]

The fourth element of de Gaulle's design was to limit American, and, by extension, British, influence on the continent. Evidence for this is hardly lacking and includes both de Gaulle's suspicion of the British application to the EEC as well as his gradual withdrawal from NATO's military command, culminating in 1966 but originating in the removal of the French Mediterranean fleet in 1959.

For each of these elements, it is possible to reconstruct Adenauer's position as well. The long–time German chancellor strongly shared de Gaulle's belief in the need for Franco–German partnership, both as a means to strengthen Germany's position in the West and as a safeguard to prevent France from returning to "her old game with Russia."[8] While Adenauer must have been uncomfortable with de Gaulle's bid for French supremacy in the relationship, he clearly recognized it as a necessary aspect of the postwar situation. The Americans and British had shown signs of withdrawing from their staunch support of German interests—largely during the Berlin crisis—and the European Economic Community was proving to be a less–than–expected success.[9]

With only a little imagination, it is possible to see that these French and German perspectives on de Gaulle's strategy are closely interrelated, and that together they suggest a description of Europe that is not far from the British assertion that de Gaulle was trying to reconstruct the Holy Roman Empire. The Americans and British had to be kept out because their service to European interests (as de Gaulle, and indeed Adenauer, saw them) was untrustworthy. And it was this concern that drove Adenauer so deeply into the embrace of de Gaulle. This is not to imply that either was against Atlantic solidarity, only that they distinguished it from European continental interests. Nothing illustrates this more clearly than de Gaulle's hard–line position in the Berlin crisis, tempered by his later unswerving support of Kennedy in Cuba. For Adenauer, it is possible to contrast his early support of the American multilateral force concept, simultaneous to his negotiation of the Elysée accords.

A similar point can be made about the particular importance of France and the confederal Europe of states. On the one hand, France required a certain status in order to manipulate a Europe of states. And France's leadership of Europe would in turn offer that country a privileged position in world affairs. Notice, for example, de Gaulle's de facto representation of Germany in the second four–power summit to be held after the end of the war.[10]

It should also be conceded that France did have particular importance that made her uniquely suited to lead a Europe of states. As Patrick McCarthy suggests, the strategic location of France, and the virtue of that country's sovereign integrity vis–à–vis Germany, gave her a particular and often underestimated strength in European affairs. Moreover, a Europe of States would be without direction in the absence of French leadership.[11] To be sure, a man as aware of the importance of circumstance as General de Gaulle could not expect French leadership to endure forever. But at that time in history, it can be argued, it was an essential aspect of European political life.[12]

But where, in all this, were the small countries, namely Belgium, Luxembourg, and the Netherlands? Certainly, in the initial construction of this grand edifice they were largely absent. De Gaulle's proposals were made either in bilateral consultation, usually with Adenauer, or through his profoundly eloquent press conferences.[13] The smaller countries of Europe were wholly neglected in spite of the personal standing of their representatives or the official positions which they held at the time. Paul–Henri Spaak, for example, was secretary general of NATO when de Gaulle made his proposal for a European confederation in July 1960.

The situation did not get better, but worse. Small–country attempts to influence the unfolding of events were alternately regarded as disingenuous or impudent. Spaak relates one memorable instance where the difference between the success and failure of his intercession with de Gaulle rested on the choice of salutation in his correspondence: Spaak chose "Mon cher Général" instead of "Monsieur le Président," and was rebuffed.[14] De Gaulle describes the same letter as a willful—or worse, foolish—contradiction, supporting both supranationalism and British participation in the EEC.[15] Nothing speaks more profoundly of the powerlessness of small countries in traditional bilateral relations.

It is in his complete dismissal of the small countries of the Community, however, that de Gaulle laid the seeds for the destruction of his own designs. By refusing any compromise to Dutch concerns that the Fouchet Plan would undermine both NATO and the Commission of the European Economic Community, de Gaulle dramatically underscored small–country concerns about French hegemony within Europe. When de Gaulle repeated this gesture in front of the whole Community through the introduction of a personally revised draft of the Fouchet Plan in January 1962, he inadvertently broke the isolation of the Dutch (who had been in complete opposition from the start), and, for the first time, united the small countries against his own proposal.[16]

On this point, however, it is important to note that it was not Dutch intransigence that brought an end to de Gaulle's designs for Europe. On the basis of the minor concessions that had been made during the negotiations of the Fouchet Plan, the French representatives, and particularly Christian Fouchet himself, were convinced that Dutch opposition could be overcome in the end.[17] The Belgians, it should be remembered, were not inherently opposed to de Gaulle's designs. Although they were clearly apprehensive about the implicit threat posed to both NATO and the Commission, the Belgians preferred to adopt a conciliatory position to one of direct confrontation. In the words of one recent analyst, de Gaulle's submission of this revised proposal placed the Belgian negotiators in "a difficult position."[18]

Analysts of the Fouchet negotiations see de Gaulle's actions as somewhat of a mystery.[19] De Gaulle biographer Jean Lacouture suggests that the General had grown apprehensive about the necessity of having to consult closely with his German and Italian counterparts on all aspects of foreign affairs, and had submitted this draft in order to torpedo the negotiations.[20] Whether or not that is the case, it is incorrect to accredit the demise of the plan to the Dutch. Rather, it was the combination of Dutch and North German opposition to a Gaullist Europe—in the interests of common Hanseatic notions of free trade and northern Atlanticism—that proved decisive.[21] De Gaulle had not only undermined his own plans, he had also deepened the rift between the "Atlantic" and "Gaullist" elements of Adenauer's ruling coalition—a fact that would prove fatal to the General's larger designs.[22]

In this interpretation of events, German foreign minister Gerhard Schröder plays as important a role as Joseph Luns.[23] It was not small–country influence that tipped the scales, but small–country influence aligned with the rising elements in a changing German domestic balance of power. This point is underscored by the failure of de Gaulle's immediate attempts to revive the plan. Although he did succeed in enlisting the support of Adenauer, he could not rally German negotiators away from their opposition.[24]

Turning away from the Fouchet Plan (which de Gaulle did not again revive until his 1969 discussion with Soames),[25] the General focused his energies on the first and foremost element of his grand design—a formal alliance with Germany but within which France would hold the position of first among equals. This fact was assured by French possession, and German renunciation, of nuclear weapons. Once again, however, de Gaulle's insistence on bilateral, or indeed unilateral, action proved his undoing. De Gaulle's brutal rejection of the British application to join the Community forged anew the alliance of Low Country and North German forces.[26] This resulted in a poisoning of relations within the Community and led inevitably to the Bundestag's adoption of the "protocols of renunciation" to the Elysée accords.[27]

Before long, however, the coalition of small countries began to lose solidarity. Although the Netherlands remained closely aligned with North Germany, Belgium assumed a more conciliatory posture and began to move closer to France.[28] Luxembourg had already made a similar shift, creating a certain distance between itself and Belgium and the Netherlands. Foreign Minister Emile Schaus, described by Spaak as "torn between his pro–French sentiments and his allegiance to the Benelux,"[29] clearly chose the former.[30] This realignment of forces worked to mitigate the damage to Franco–German relations within the EC.

This gives rise to two important observations. The first has already been suggested and is that small–country influence has little chance of success at shaping matters between France and Germany unless supported by some powerful domestic political group operating within either of the two larger countries. The second is that the multiplicity of interests represented by either France or Germany makes it unlikely that the small countries will enlist themselves permanently in the service of one large country or the other.[31]

In a multilateral context, the range of interests represented at any given point in time is such that the small countries are free to make and change alliances frequently. This point is often made by analysts of small countries and explains, more than anything else, why these countries are such staunch advocates of supranationalism, whether in the context of the European Parliament or of the Commission.[32] Small countries are not eager to give up sovereignty, but they recognize in supranationalism the critical opportunity to enlist the large–country support they need in order to effectively pursue their national interest. They do not perceive this benefit in a close alliance with a single large country. Neither France nor Germany can be all things at all times to Belgium, the Netherlands, or Luxembourg. Faced with making a once–and–for–all commitment, the small countries have traditionally preferred neutralism. That is why, as Christian Franck explains, "Commitment to multilateralism was not the opposite to neutrality: it represented a search for the same objectives but within a completely different international system."[33]

Given the dependent nature of small–country influence, it is also logical that they would prefer a larger Community to a smaller one. The more countries involved in a multilateral framework, the more options there are available for interest alliances. And, as more countries are required to adhere to any given decision, the need for strong institutional procedures becomes imperative. In other words, there is a dynamic consistency in small–country support for both deepening and broadening the Community. That in mind, it is easy to recognize that by steering European integration back into the arena of bilateral diplomacy, de Gaulle represented a significant threat to the foreign policy objectives of small countries.

In the context of the Franco–German relationship, the policy actions of small countries serve a different function. As they align with domestic forces in France and Germany, small countries also effectively stabilize the relationship between their larger counterparts. In most cases, this ensures that neither France nor Germany is completely isolated in a conflict between them. It also suggests the potential for small countries to represent (albeit surreptitiously) the nongoverning interests of large countries in intergovernmental fora. The Belgians (and, indeed, the Commission itself!) went to the aid of the French in the Common Agricultural Policy debates during the crisis period surrounding the empty chair, and the Dutch represented rising north German opposition to Adenauer in the Fouchet negotiations.[34]

This Belgian example combines small–country impact in terms of alignment with large–country domestic interest and advocacy of multilateralism. Whether or not they agreed with French insistence that the financing of the Common Agricultural Policy be given first priority, the Belgians, at least, argued that vendetta-like tactics were antithetical to the stability of multilateral diplomacy.[35]

Consider now the alternatives. Had de Gaulle succeeded in implementing his Europe of States, he would still have been faced with the rising strength of the anti–Adenauer, anti–French, and pro–Atlantic interests in Germany. One possibility is that Adenauer would have failed to bring the Fouchet Treaty through parliament, just as he failed one year later to ratify the Elysée accords—at least in any meaningful form.[36] Another possibility is that latent German opposition to the treaty, once locked in a network of bilateral relationships, would have worked to bring the functioning of the Community of states to a stand-still, even as that organization undermined the more supranational functions of the Commission and the Parliament.[37]

In either event, the changing balance of domestic power in Germany could have been perceived as anti–European as well as anti–French. With the only remaining forum for Franco–German interaction being one from which France had already chosen to pull away (NATO), it is hard to imagine where and when a final reconciliation could take place. Certainly it is not too much to say that the strains between France and Germany would have been greater. Not to mention the larger tensions provoked by a perceived anti–European drift in German foreign policy.[38]

By pushing constantly against de Gaulle's Europe of States, the Dutch and Belgians preserved the supranational alternative for both France and Germany. They saved Germany from the necessity of turning away from the institutions meant to bind it to the West, and they provided France with unexpected, though welcome, support during a moment of crisis. While it is true that de Gaulle was not against the construction of Europe, it is also true that his vision for organizing the continent was not one with which Germany could live comfortably. De Gaulle's four–tier strategy necessarily collapsed, leaving intact only those elements which France could achieve unilaterally. In short, the Franco–German relationship could not survive in a confederation based on bilateral relations any more than it could survive in a Europe of the Two. In the early days of Franco–German reconciliation, the small countries played an essential cushioning role.

Going into the late 1960s, the relationship between de Gaulle and his German counterparts cooled and the process of European integration with it. Erhard, Kiesinger, and Brandt were more interested in affairs to the West and to the East than in the process of European construction. Although some decisions were reached—like the Werner plan for monetary union—these were greatly offset by events adverse to Europe, like de Gaulle's withdrawal from NATO in 1966 and his rejection of the second British application in 1967.

The stagnation of Europe did not last forever. By the end of the 1980s, the Community once again experienced a period of growth and renewal. In contrast to the 1960s, however, there were some substantial differences. A council of heads of state or government had the predominant say in European affairs, the Community was a power in many ways equal to any on the globe, and concern was more focused on American isolation than interference. The similarity with the 1960s was largely to be found in the Franco–German relationship. Although that partnership had suffered through great upheavals, it survived, and by the end of the 1980s it again formed the backbone of the drive for European union. Where, then, were the small countries?

This question shows the other side of small–country interaction with the Franco–German relationship. Cooperation between France and Germany is the motor for European integration. For the small countries it provides the leadership essential for consensus building in the construction of Europe. While it has been argued that small–country influence in many ways suggests the context for the Franco–German relationship, it is even more true that the cooperation of those two large countries defines the environment of their smaller neighbors. A Europe of the Two is unstable, but a Europe without the two is no Europe at all. Indeed, this can be seen in the renewed drive for European integration that started in the early 1980s.

SMALL COUNTRIES AND THE "RELAUNCHING OF EUROPE"

Before the start of the now famous *relance européenne,* the small countries fell victim to the combination of limited success and structural weakness. While they had been rewarded in their desires to broaden the Community— Great Britain, Ireland and Denmark gained admission in the early 1970s, Greece in 1981, and Spain and Portugal were well–advanced in their own bids for entry by 1983—progress toward European integration slowed, and the deepening of Community institutions took an unfavorable turn. Small– country influence within the Community declined as the birth of European Political Cooperation coincided with a growing emphasis on bilateral diplo- macy. This development can be at least partially attributed to the divergence of political interests in economic integration—a divergence which coincided with the collapse of postwar corporatist arrangements in northern Europe and was aggravated by the breakdown of the Bretton Woods system.[39]

The situation was further exacerbated by global economic circumstances. While the 1960s were a period of unprecedented prosperity for the small countries, the late 1970s, simply put, were not. Belgium and the Netherlands experienced deepening fiscal crises that undermined all attempts at domestic coalition building. Denmark was similarly pressed by rising public debt and falling international competitiveness; Ireland, Greece, and Portugal sank into an ever–deepening economic morass.

Within Europe, the great achievement of this period was the creation of the European Monetary System. Yet, far from being a "European" event, it should really be seen as the culmination of the new Franco–German entente—if not, more specifically, as the first real act of German economic leadership on the continent.[40] The election of a left–wing coalition in France, followed by Mitterrand's ill–timed bid for growth, renewed the division between French and German interests. And, as in the mid–1960s and the early 1970s, the small countries were deprived of leadership within Europe.

It was during this period that the European integration process suffered from "pessimism" and "sclerosis."

The year 1982 marked the turning point, as first Belgium, then the Netherlands and Denmark, adopted strong currency policies coupled with stringent austerity measures.[41] The leadership they had lacked was found in the German Bundesbank and in a slightly modified version of German economic theory. Although the krone and Belgian frank were devalued in February of 1982, they soon began to move upward, away from the French franc and toward the German mark.

As in Germany, terms of trade were kept high to hold down the cost of imported inputs to production, while inflation was kept low to provide a stable environment for investment. Moreover, old cooperative arrangements between workers and management were revived to put a tight squeeze on unit labor costs. The overall effect was a large real (cost–adjusted) devaluation of the Danish, Dutch, and Belgian currencies which was to be used as a springboard for export–led growth.[42]

It was the transformation in France, however, that augured the relaunching of the Community and the revival of close Franco–German cooperation.[43] As Patrick McCarthy points out, "the key choice of 1983 to remain in the EMS at the price of deflation was not merely presented as a bid by the nation to gain control over inflation, but was accompanied by a battery of other initiatives in European policy."[44] The link between Mitterrand's 1983 Bundestag speech, the revaluation of the German mark, and the gradual application of the 1963 Elysée agreements is widely discussed in this volume and elsewhere.[45] Although Low Country and North German Atlanticism might have been expected to oppose this development, three factors mitigated Atlanticist opposition: the recent popular protests against the installation of American cruise and Pershing missiles; the rapid escalation of defense costs coupled with American complaints about burden–sharing; and the perceived pro–NATO shift in French defense strategy. In this context, the small countries happily signed on to rhetoric about the creation of a European defense pillar. Belgium and the Netherlands took part in WEU exercises in the Persian Gulf, and they also participated in numerous joint weapons projects from the tri-partite minesweeper to the European fighter aircraft.[46]

For Europe, the French initiatives provided added support to growing business pressure for the completion of the "internal market." Whether France or European industry should be held responsible for the Single European Act is beyond the scope of the present discussion.[47] Suffice it to say that both were instrumental to agreement on the 1992 program—

providing an emphasis to intra–European trade that was wholly in line with small country interest in export–led growth. According to one Dutch political scientist, and former cabinet chief for EC Agricultural Commissioner Sicco Mansholt:

> The Single European Act, '1992,' the internal market, or whatever the catch-phrase people prefer to use to refer to the process of integration, adds no fundamentally new dimension to European cooperation as it exists at the moment. . . . [The] Single European Act was attractive to the Netherlands for the same reasons as the European Community itself thirty years earlier.[48]

If the program for completing the internal market was not different from small–country objectives, the process of its initiation was. More than anything else, the Single European Act was the product of the European Council. As one analyst recently commented, "the history of the internal market initiative is to a significant degree the history of those [European Council] meetings."[49]

For the small countries, reliance on intergovernmental negotiation implied a relative loss of influence—particularly in a widened Community. The result was very similar to the 1960s: the negotiation of the Single European Act was heavily influenced by the progress of Franco–German bilateral summits. The Ad Hoc Committee on Institutional Affairs, for example, was established on the basis of a Franco–German compromise.[50] Consequently, the small countries were more successful in their opposition to integration than in their advocacy of supranationalism, and only then when supported by one of the two larger powers. In discussion of monetary union, for example, the Belgians chose a conciliatory posture, sitting squarely on the fence between French arguments for closer monetary union and German insistence on the need for "real" (meaning structural) convergence.[51] By contrast, the Dutch aligned with Germany, and succeeded in separating the completion of the internal market from talks of economic and monetary union.[52] The Danes, credited with delaying the internal market program through their obligatory national referendum, seemed increasingly dubious about the value of their participation in Europe. And even though the referendum passed, the margin was somewhat narrower than in 1972, and analysts described Danish support for European integration as being more inevitable than enthusiastic.[53]

When the program outlined in the Single European Act began to go into effect, interest in Europe returned to the question of Economic and Monetary Union. From the small–country perspective, however, the pattern was much the same. A first crystallization of these discussions came in Hannover in June of 1988, where Delors was commissioned to study the challenges posed by monetary integration. And that summit had been preceded by a meeting between Kohl and Mitterrand (2 June) where the two leaders "simply exchanged some suggestions" regarding the future president of the commission as well as discussing the liberalization of capital movements and the prospects for a European central bank.[54]

Once again, however, the small countries held a strong interest in the drive for further integration. Because of the relatively small size of their respective currency markets, the small countries were forced to pay an interest premium over German rates in order to protect the value of their currencies relative to the mark. Financial market liberalization promised to bring much needed liquidity to small–country currency markets, raising their attractiveness as investment currencies and lowering the premium on interest rates. But financial market liberalization also threatened small–country currency markets with greater instability. The price for higher liquidity is paid for with the danger of speculation. A closer alignment of monetary policies would mitigate that danger by depriving financial speculators of the economic rationale to attack a small country currency. In other words, for the small countries, economic and monetary union seemed a "natural complement" to market liberalization.[55]

The period leading up to the autumn of 1989 was one of relative euphoria. Although the common market program posed many significant challenges, the small countries saw in close Franco–German cooperation the strong leadership necessary for success. On the same day that Margaret Thatcher was attacking the European Commission from Bruges, Danish Prime Minister Poul Schlüter was celebrating the imminent demise of the nation–state in London.[56] Within the week, the Belgian prime minister had also spoken out in favor of "economic unity" and an "economically and politically independent Europe."[57] ·

But in many ways, this Europe was too perfect. While the French and Germans worked more closely toward a harmonization of national interests, the small countries continued to press for ever more representative fora for interaction. And with growing support inside Germany, it was likely that the small countries would have succeeded in their desires to strengthen the democratic and supranational aspects of the Community. However, born in the economic crisis of the West, the relaunching of Europe began to founder on the political crisis of the East. As the French and Germans strove to assert themselves in the turbulent world environment, the Europe of the 1980s failed to satisfy either their needs or their ambitions.

SMALL COUNTRIES AND THE "EUROPE OF MAASTRICHT"

The fall of the Berlin Wall marked the turning point. By promising a substantial increase in the relative size and power of the Federal Republic, as well as by opening up Germany's traditional hinterland, the liberation of the Soviet–occupied Länder permanently altered the equilibrium of the Franco–German relationship. The euphoria of the 1980s gave way to delirium as both France, and to a lesser extent, Germany, began to question the possibility for and the utility of future privileged collaboration.

But the danger of a prolonged Franco–German split, though real, was small. Both countries realized the necessity, and indeed the inevitability, of their partnership. Although the established pattern of their relationship was strained by the dramatic change in the balance between them, Kohl and Mitterrand saw in Europe the means necessary to achieve a new balance. Nevertheless, in the final months of 1989, cooperation between the two large countries was hardly smooth. The separate visions of Europe initially proposed by Mitterrand and Kohl were not harmonious.[58] In very crude terms, Kohl wanted to strengthen the democratic component of the Community in order to more closely involve the political aspirations of the German people in Western Europe. Mitterrand, in contrast, wanted to strengthen the European Council—a forum wherein France, as the second European power, could better influence events in Germany.

With the rapid acceleration in the pace of German unification, the French president and the German chancellor again moved closer together. Their joint letter to the Irish presidency of the European Council in April 1990 represents a compromise between French concerns for "efficiency" and German desires for "democratic legitimation."[59] It also symbolizes an important shift in the nature of Franco–German leadership within Europe. Where before the French president might have equivocated in his meetings with Chancellor Kohl about "making decisions for the member–states of the Community,"[60] the two leaders began openly to set the agenda for the future.

Nevertheless, the "post–Wall" drive for European union was very different from the relaunching of Europe in the 1980s. The relationship between France and Germany was based less on a unity of purpose than on the necessity for reconciliation. The contrast can be found in comparing the failure of the 1985 Draft Treaty on Political Union with the success of the letter to the Irish presidency. The 1985 proposal collapsed around the completion of the internal market as a least common denominator for integration. The 1990 proposal did not envision such a minimalist compromise. In this sense, the post–1989 model for Franco–German cooperation more closely corresponded to de Gaulle and Adenauer than Giscard and Schmidt.

During 1990 and 1991, the agenda that Mitterrand and Kohl set forth bore a striking resemblance to the four–tier strategy of de Gaulle: the principal institution was the European Council of heads of state or government; the primary policy initiative concerned the coordination of foreign and security policy; and there was a strong conviction to proceed with the unification of Europe in spite of British reluctance. Although the completion of the internal market and progress toward monetary union were retained as strong objectives for European unification, they were negotiated parallel (and not prior) to the more political issues.

Also as in the 1960s, the interests of the larger and smaller countries diverged. While Kohl exercised, and Mitterrand tried to harness, Germany's newfound self–confidence, the small countries retreated toward supranationalism. The close cooperation between France and Germany was no longer perceived as a positive source of leadership. Rather it awoke old fears about large–country hegemony on the continent. Although the small countries were clearly still interested in the economic side of the discussions, their enthusiasm for Europe was tempered by a desire to see a strengthening of the more representative institutions of the Community. First Belgium, then Denmark, Luxembourg, and the Netherlands went on record in favor of a strengthening of the roles of the commission and the parliament.[61]

The inclusion of Denmark in the list of supranationalists is indicative of small–country concerns. Danish reception of the Single European Act had been skeptical, and Denmark had long expressed apprehension about the intrusive aspects of the Community. Nevertheless, the sudden rise of German power foreshadowed an even greater threat than the European Commission, and so "many politicians and intellectuals who had been against or sceptical [sic] of European integration now saw European integration as the only way to exert some influence on future German policies."[62]

The bilateral Franco–German consensus on defense issues also raised the opposition of the small countries. Here again, the line–up is very similar to the 1960s. The Dutch and the Danes came out in strong support of the Atlantic alliance. Their principal objection was that the incorporation of the West European Union—to which Denmark did not even belong—into the institutions of the Community would undermine North American commitment to Europe. The threat perceived in Denmark was particularly acute. Although often seen as conflictual members of NATO, the Danes clearly preferred that forum to one ostensibly dominated by France and Germany.

The Belgians and Luxembourgers assumed a more conciliatory posture toward the coordination of European security policy—but the nature of that conciliation should be understood in light of their participation in the Persian Gulf War. Although Belgium was able to send aircraft to Turkey, a NATO ally, their rules of engagement allowed only for self–defense in the event of invasion. Moreover, the Belgian domestic political situation was too delicate to allow the sale of munitions to Great Britain.[63] Luxembourg, then holding the presidency of the European Council, did try to achieve some coordination within Europe, but limited its own participation to providing financial resources.[64]

It is at this point, however, that the easy parallels between the Fouchet negotiations and the present drive toward European unity cease to operate. In response to the Luxembourg draft treaty, it was the Dutch and not the French who submitted a completely revised draft. As a last–ditch effort to "keep the spirit of Fouchet in the bottle," the Dutch departed from the three–pillar outline of the Luxembourgers—which yielded power to the European Council as the sole overarching institution—and suggested a unitary institutional framework to be jointly managed by the Council, Commission, and Parliament.[65]

This proposal immediately appealed to the Belgians and should have appealed to the Germans. However, given the growing crisis in Yugoslavia and the strongly perceived need within Germany to coordinate foreign policy with France, the Dutch draft was met, not with German support, but with a Franco–German initiative on foreign and defense policy. In an ironic twist, first opposition to the Dutch draft came not from France but from British Prime Minister John Major.[66] Rather than assuming a confrontational position, the French and the Germans chose instead to use their bilateral contexts to drive the negotiation of the draft in a favorable direction. And while Dutch Prime Minister Ruud Lubbers complained about this Franco–German strategy, he was virtually powerless to avert it.

In the run–up to the Inter–Governmental Council meeting in December of 1991, British opposition combined with specific complaints of other member–countries, particularly Denmark, and the Dutch draft was replaced with the older Luxembourg proposal. It is a development that confirms two observations made during the Fouchet negotiations: small countries have little decisive influence without the support of either France or Germany; and, as de Gaulle pointed out, small–country advocacy of supranationalism is inconsistent with active British participation in Europe. The final epitaph for the Belgo–Dutch effort to promote supranationalism was offered by John Major speaking before Commons: "In

September, a new Dutch text on political union appeared. That was quite unacceptable and we rejected it."[67]

In December of 1991 the final draft of the Treaty on Political Union was ratified, and in January of 1992 it was signed. By all accounts, the new Franco–German model for cooperation within Europe was a great success. The European Council was the primary beneficiary of the drive toward political union. Defense cooperation through the WEU survived the diplomatic recognition of Croatia and Slovenia, and even received the reluctant approval of the United States. And the British were given special "opt–out" clauses, enabling them to support the treaty without necessarily being bound by all of its proscriptions.

SMALL COUNTRIES AND THE FRANCO–GERMAN RELATIONSHIP

Mitterrand and Kohl succeeded where de Gaulle and Adenauer had failed. And Piet Dankert, Dutch state secretary for European Affairs, had failed where Joseph Luns "succeeded." But neither of these observations should be taken to imply that the small countries are any less important to the smooth functioning of the Franco–German relationship. To the contrary, it could be argued that Mitterrand and Kohl succeeded in their drive toward European Union because of their greater willingness to compromise, not just with each other, but with the smaller countries as well. By assuming a determined low profile and constructive position with regard to the Dutch proposals, the French and Germans succeeded in fulfilling their primary objectives. They also succeeded in underscoring the spirit of cooperation essential for further progress toward integration.

In addition, it is important to note that the Europe of the 1990s is very different from the Europe of the 1960s. From the small–country perspective, not only is there a strong recognition of the need for Franco–German leadership within the Community, there is also a highly sophisticated practice of interest representation, both public and private, within Community institutions. Looking only at the Netherlands, for example, there are about 50 public and 100 private actors represented in Brussels.[68] It should not be surprising that small countries have particular influence with respect to certain Community policies: the Dutch, given the importance of Rotterdam and Amsterdam with respect to shipping, have a powerful role in transport policy. Although the small countries may continue to press for greater supranationalism, they have significantly increased their abilities to form alliances through existing Community institutions with separate large–country interests over the past thirty years.

Yet in some ways, the Europe of the 1990s is not so different from the Europe of the 1960s. The Franco–German relationship is still based on reconciliation, and so there continue to be disputes that require the intercession of third parties. Small countries continue surreptitiously to represent the nongoverning interests of the large countries.

The Danish veto of the Treaty on European Union provides a striking example. Although part and parcel of Danish skepticism toward European integration, the popular rejection of the Maastricht accords was largely unexpected. The driving motivations behind the Danish veto were a distrust of political elites and a concern for the preservation of national sovereignty and democratic legitimacy. The Danish electorate perceived the Treaty on Political Union to be too subject to the hegemony of France and Germany, and they accused their ruling class of being too eager to sacrifice the national interest in negotiation with the larger countries of Europe. Nevertheless, Denmark was only one of the twelve signatory countries. If the other eleven continued to press on with the ratification of the treaty, the Danish veto would have been little more than a "highly regrettable nuisance."[69]

Indeed, in the first weeks of the summer, this seemed to be the case. Mitterrand and Kohl issued a joint declaration affirming "their determination to firmly pursue [*sic*] in a meaningful way the establishment of the European union,"[70] and defense ministers Pierre Joxe and Volker Rühe argued that "the future 'Eurocorps' would not be a 'new structure in competition with the WEU or NATO.' "[71] In a manner consistent with the post–1989 drive for European Union, "Chancellor Kohl and President Mitterrand . . . insisted on moving French–German cooperation ahead of the rest of the Community in the hope that others will catch up."[72]

The Danish veto did, however, have a significant impact—albeit indirectly. Within hours of the Danish polling, President Mitterrand announced that the Maastricht Treaty would also be the subject of a referendum in France. His motivations, it has been argued, were largely domestic. At the time, European integration enjoyed widespread popular support, and yet the right–wing opposition parties were clearly divided on the treaty of Maastricht. Thus, "the Maastricht Treaty [became] the central weapon in President Mitterrand's strategy to regain ground from his conservative opponents."[73]

The strategy backfired and the referendum barely passed. During the summer of 1992, opposition to Mitterrand and to the Maastricht Treaty grew to unexpected and, indeed, frightening proportions. By August, it looked even as if the referendum would fail. The timely intercession of Chancellor Kohl—whose speech before the French public evoked strong parallels to Mitterrand's 1983 speech to the Bundestag—assisted the proratification movement but was more than offset by the obstinate policies of the Bundesbank. And, although the German central bank relented a week prior to the referendum, the easing of monetary policy was too little too late. The currency markets went into a turmoil and the British pound and the Italian lire dropped out of the exchange rate mechanism. Many of the same business leaders that had rallied to Mitterrand in the early 1980s turned against him, and it looked as if the prospects for European integration were dimming.[74]

For the small countries, a loss of momentum within Europe was unacceptable. In Denmark, while more than a few citizens may have enjoyed their inadvertent influence on European affairs, the political leadership rallied again to the cause of European Union. In the October 1992 White Paper, Danish political elites tried again to explain the importance of Europe for Denmark. They described the French referendum as a positive result both for European integration and for "national identity" within Europe. Moreover, they concluded that "it is difficult to imagine how it could be practically/legally feasible to apply the new basis (the Maastricht Treaty) to some Member States and the old basis (the Treaty of Rome) to others."[75] And the final chapter of the White Paper suggests that the Danish and French referenda have "increased interest in concepts such as a higher degree of democratic control, more decentralization, a higher degree of subsidiarity, more openness, and transparency in the decision–making process."[76]

The paper explicitly refused to take a stand on the precise direction that Danish European policy would pursue. Nevertheless, it is evident that Danish elites would prefer to return to the more limited role of a small state within Europe, a fact underscored by Prime Minister Schlüter's Birmingham pronouncement in favor of a future ratification of the Maastricht Treaty.[77] Although the White Paper listed withdrawal from the European Community as a possibility for Denmark, that option clearly ranks among the least desirable alternatives. From the Danish perspective, the logic of the late 1980s still holds true. It is better to work within the Community than to be a satellite of the Franco–German couple.

Reactions within Belgium and the Netherlands were even more to the point. Voices were raised in both countries that whatever benefits were to be gained through the French referendum were more than outweighed by the risk of a "no" vote.[78] While the Belgian and Dutch governments continued to advocate the further democratization of the Community, both were also concerned that a slow–down in the integration process would undermine attempts at economic and monetary union. Throughout the Benelux there is a strong desire to maintain the pace of monetary integration, even if the other members of the union include only Germany and France. Nowhere was this more evident than in Belgium, where the budgetary debates were focused primarily on the convergence indicators for 1996. As in the 1980s, the rationale for monetary integration overshadowed the desire for greater supranationalism.

The struggle within the exchange rate mechanism offers a final display of the stabilizing influence of small countries within the Franco–German relationship. When the French franc came under pressure, Belgian and Dutch central banks offered their support. And when the Bundesbank came under criticism, the Belgian and Dutch press rallied to its defense.[79] From the small–country perspective, neither France nor Germany could be left isolated in the conflict. Though it would be difficult to argue that the small–country role in either of these issues was decisive, it would be equally difficult to deny that it helped.

The Franco–German relationship remains the motor for Europe. But it is still difficult to believe that their relationship would survive in a vacuum. Recent events have shown that the small countries of Europe recognize the importance of French and German leadership. These same events have also demonstrated that the small countries continue to play an important stabilizing role, whether as representatives or supporters. In that respect, the Europe of the 1990s is not so different from the Europe of the 1960s. What is different is the greater sensitivity of both France and Germany to small–country concerns. This greater sensitivity is important for the Franco–German relationship as well as for the small countries. Benefitting from a greater openness to small–country concerns, France and Germany are unlikely to repeat the mistakes of the 1960s. Although it will still take time, France and Germany will succeed in their reconciliation. But it will be within Europe, and within a Europe increasingly populated with small countries.

NOTES

1. Research for this chapter was made possible through the generous support of the Belgian–American Educational Foundation. Many thanks to Patrick McCarthy, Veerle Coignez, and the participants of the CEPS Junior Research Seminar for their many helpful comments and suggestions.

2. For much of the early history of the Franco–German relationship I have drawn heavily from Jean Lacouture's magisterial biography of de Gaulle. See Jean Lacouture, *De Gaulle 3: Le souverain, 1959–1970* (Paris: Seuil, 1986), chapters 11 and 12. The reference to the particular "wood" of the Anglo–Saxons comes from p. 318.

3. See William Wallace, "Introduction," in Roger Morgan and Caroline Bray (eds.), *Partners and Rivals in Western Europe: Britain, France and Germany* (Aldershot, U.K.: Gower, 1986), pp. 1–6.

4. The French may contend that the postwar world was decided at Yalta, but from the point of view of the Luxemburgers it is often asserted that the pivotal moment came in the division of Charlemagne's kingdom into three.

5. Lacouture, *De Gaulle*, p. 294.

6. Ibid., p. 298.

7. Paul–Henri Spaak, *Combats inachevés: De l'espoir aux déceptions, tome 2* (Paris: Fayard, 1969), pp. 398–99.

8. Franz Josef Strauß, *Die Erinnerungen* (Berlin: Siedler, 1989), p. 418. See also, Thomas Jansen, "Die Entstehung des deutche–französischen Vertrages vom 22. Januar 1963," in Dieter Blumenwitz et al. (eds.), *Konrad Adenauer und seine Zeit: Politik und Persönlichkeit des ersten Bundeskanzlers, Band II, Beiträge der Wissenschaft* (Stuttgart: Deutsche Verlags–Anstalt, 1976), pp. 249–71.

9. This argument is drawn largely from Lacouture, *De Gaulle*, chapter 11.

10. Ibid., p. 297.

11. As David Calleo pointed out in an early analysis of the Gaullist Europe of states: "Could a Gaullist believe that a coherent policy for Europe would ever be formulated from the six equal representatives of six separate states, each with its own interests to be achieved at the expense of others?" See David P. Calleo, *Europe's Future: The Grand Alternatives* (New York: Norton, 1967), p. 131.

12. My thanks to Professor David Calleo for pointing this out.

13. For a detailed historical account of the drafting of the Franco–German treaty, see Jansen, "Die Entstehung." For the Fouchet Plan, see Alessandro Silj, "Europe's Political Puzzle: A Study of the Fouchet Negotiations and the 1963 Veto," *Occasional Papers in International Affairs, Number 17* (Cambridge: Harvard Center for International Affairs, December 1967).

14. Spaak, *Combats inachevés*, p. 375.

15. Lacouture, *De Gaulle*, p. 324. Spaak's response to this criticism was to say that: "the essential argument of the Belgian position is that on entering the proposed political union, the small countries have two different possible safeguards: either the community procedures or the counterweight of Great Britain. . . . Certainly it is too optimistic in the actual state of affairs to hope to attain both objectives simultaneously. But Belgium feels it indispensable to obtain at least one of the two." Spaak, *Combats inachevés*, pp. 368–69.

16. Spaak, *Combats inachevés,* p. 363.

17. See Pierre Gerbet, "In Search of Political Union: The Fouchet Plan Negotiations (1960–62)," in Roy Price (ed.), *The Dynamics of European Union* (London: Croom Helm, 1987).

18. Sophie Vanhoonacker, "La Belgique: responsable ou bouc émissaire de l'échec des négotiations Fouchet?" *Res Publica* 31, no. 4 (1989), p. 521.

19. Silj, "Europe's Political Puzzle," p. 13.

20. Lacouture, *De Gaulle,* p. 325.

21. To this list, Strauß would also add the solidarity of Northern Protestants versus Southern Catholics. Strauß, *Die Erinnerungen,* pp. 421–22.

22. Willy Brandt, *Erinnerungen* (Zurich: Ferenczy, 1989), pp. 246–7.

23. The battle between "Gaullists" and "Atlanticists" was largely fought between Franz Josef Strauß and Gerhard Schröder. See Strauß, *Die Erinnerungen,* pp. 446–50.

24. Strauß, *Die Erinnerungen,* p. 416.

25. De Gaulle's conversations with Soames were directed toward reviving the spirit of the Fouchet Plan, but including the British. This marked a "sea–change" in de Gaulle's perceptions of Great Britain, but ultimately ended in failure. See Helen Wallace, "The Conduct of Bilateral Relationships by Governments," in Morgan and Bray (eds.), *Partners and Rivals,* pp. 150–1.

26. The characterization of German 'Atlanticism' as being 'North German' is borrowed from Strauß. And, perhaps it is best understood from the Bavarian viewpoint. Gerhard Schröder, in Strauß's opinion the leader of the Atlanticist movement, was born in Saarbrücken and made his political career in North–Rhine Westphalia.

27. Brandt, *Erinnerungen,* p. 257; Strauß, *Die Erinnerungen,* p. 416. The term "protocols of renunciation" is a loose paraphrase of Lacouture, but captures, I believe, the sentiments of de Gaulle. Lacouture, p. 308.

28. Spaak, *Combats inachevés,* pp. 403–12. Francophone Belgium has long been recognized as an obstacle to Benelux unity, not because of its inherent affinity with France, but because of its distrust of the Dutch–speaking majority within the three–state grouping. See Alfred Pijpers, "Keeping the Spirit of Fouchet in the Bottle," in Christopher Hill (ed.), *National Foreign Policies and European Political Cooperation* (London: George Allen and Unwin for the Royal Institute of International Affairs, 1983), p. 172.

29. Spaak, *Combats inachevés,* pp. 363–64.

30. See the text of the discourse by Emile Schaus before the West European Union on 27 April 1962, reprinted in: Heinrich Siegler (ed.), *Europäische politische Einigung, 1949–68: Dokumentation von Vorschlägen und Stellungnahmen* (Bonn: Siegler, 1968), pp. 158–9.

31. Ronald Tiersky made this point somewhat differently in his recent analysis of France. "Broadly speaking, the two countries together [France and Germany]

embody most of the contrasting characteristics of the other EC countries: North/-South, industrial/agricultural, Protestant/Catholic and so forth. So where France and Germany can agree, others can usually accept." See Ronald Tiersky, "France in the New Europe," *Foreign Affairs* 71, no. 2 (Spring 1992), p. 144.

32. It has been argued that support of supranationalism in the Fouchet negotiations can be seen as an ironic—or even cynical—change in Dutch foreign policy. Whether or not it represents a real volte–face, it is true, as Richard Griffiths points out, that Dutch support for "strengthening the position of supranational institutions . . . brought it into line with a significant stream of political feeling within the national parliament [of the Netherlands] which was to have important consequences later on." See Richard Griffiths, "The Netherlands and the EEC," in Richard Griffiths (ed.), *The Economy and Politics of the Netherlands Since 1945* (The Hague: Martinus Nijhoff, 1980), p. 281.

33. Christian Franck, "Belgium: Committed Multilateralism," in Hill, *National Foreign Policies,* p. 85.

34. The Italians also mediated in the interests of France. See Spaak, *Combats inachevés,* p. 412.

35. This was the position taken by Spaak and cited above. Jean Rey, a well–respected Belgian member of the Commission of the European Economic Community, made a similar point about the treatment of the French during the Fouchet negotiations, and the resulting French veto of the British application to join the EEC. See "Discourse de Jean Rey à l'Université de Gand, 21 février 1963," in Jean Poorterman (ed.), *Jean Rey nous parle* (Brussels: E. Guijot, 1984), p. 242.

36. Strauß argues that by the summer of 1962, Adenauer had already lost much of his political influence in Germany. Strauß, *Die Erinnerungen,* p. 416.

37. The Fouchet Plan allowed any state the absolute right of veto. Presumably the small countries would be reluctant to exercise that right. Germany, and particularly a Germany unhappy with Gaullist leadership of the Community, would not be so reticent.

38. It is useful to recall that the "new Europe" was, at that time, still a very delicate thing. As Ludwig Erhard confessed to Jean Monnet: "If I criticize the German constitution, no–one would say that I am a bad German. But if I criticize the Community of Six in the name of a larger Europe, I am immediately accused of being a bad European. . . . By contrast [with Germany], the Constitution of the Six is still fragile and unrealized. By attacking it, you break down its foundations and push it off balance." Jean Monnet, *Mémoires* (Paris: Fayard, 1976), p. 528.

39. This divergence is argued most forcefully in Peter Ludlow, "Beyond 1992: Europe and Its Western Partners," *CEPS Paper, No. 38* (Brussels: Centre for European Policy

Studies, 1989), p. 10. There is obviously a wide literature on corporatism. Perhaps the best survey of small countries is Peter Katzenstein, *Small States in World Markets: Industrial Policy in Europe* (Ithaca: Cornell University Press, 1985).

40. See Ludlow, "Beyond 1992," p. 22. See also Peter Ludlow, *The Making of the European Monetary System* (London: Butterworths, 1982).

41. See Paul de Grauwe and Wim Vanhaverbeke, "Exchange Rate Experience in Small EMS Countries: Belgium, Denmark and the Netherlands," in Victor Argy and Paul de Grauwe (eds.), *Choosing an Exchange Rate Regime: The Challenge for Smaller Industrial Countries* (Washington: International Monetary Fund, 1990), pp. 135–55.

42. For a close analysis of this small country strategy, see my "Regional Power and the Corporatist State: Belgium and the Netherlands in the 1990s," paper presented at the Fifteenth World Congress of the International Political Science Association (Buenos Aires, 21–25 July 1991).

43. This argument is made most strongly by Andrew Moravcsik, "Negotiating the Single European Act," in Robert Keohane and Stanley Hoffmann (eds.), *The New European Community: Decisionmaking and Institutional Change* (Boulder: Westview, 1991), pp. 41–84.

44. Patrick McCarthy, "France and the EC: Can a Gaullist Power Find Happiness in a Regional Bloc?" *Bologna Center Occasional Paper, No. 71* (Bologna: Johns Hopkins, February 1992), p. 3.

45. See Patrick McCarthy, "France Faces Reality: Rigueur and the Germans," in David Calleo and Claudia Morgenstern (eds.), *Recasting Europe's Economies: National Strategies in the 1980s* (Lanham, Md.: University Press of America, 1990), pp. 25–78.

46. See Thierry Peeters, "La politique de sécurité dans le contexte Est–Ouest," in Christian Franck and Claude Roosens (eds.), *La politique extérieure de la Belgique: 1987–1988* (Louvain–la–Neuve: Academia, 1988), pp. 57–67; Jean–Luc Bodson, "Les partis politiques belges et la politique étrangère," in ibid, pp. 281–95; Erik Jones, "The Benelux and the Financing of Western Defense," *CERI/CSIR Topical Papers, No. 3* (Brussels: Center for the Study of International Relations of the Free University of Brussels, October 1989); Hugo de Ridder, *Geen Winnaars in de Wetstraat* (Leuven: Davidsfonds, 1986), chapter 7.

47. For the gamut of interpretations, see Andrew Moravcski, "Negotiating the Single European Act: National Interests and Conventional Statecraft in the European Community," in *International Organization,* 45, no. 1 (Winter 1991). See also David Cameron, "The 1992 Initiative: Causes and Consequences," in Alberta Sbragia (ed.), *Europolitics: Institutions and Policymaking in the New European Community* (Washington: Brookings, 1992), pp. 23–74; Geoffrey Garret, "International Cooperation and Institutional Choice: The European Community's Internal Market," *International Organization* 46, no. 2 (Spring 1992), pp. 533–60.

48. Robert Cohen, "The Netherlands and European Integration," *International Spectator* 43, no. 11 (November 1989), p. 710.

49. Cameron, "The 1992 Initiative," p. 63.

50. Ibid., p. 61.

51. See Banque Nationale de Belgique, *Rapports 1984* (Brussels: BNB, 1985), pp. xlii–xliv.

52. Moravcsik, "Single European Act," p. 62.

53. In the words of one observer: "When the chips were down and the voters' choice was real rather than hypothetical, a majority would stick to the EC." See Kenneth E. Miller, Denmark: A Troubled Welfare State (Boulder: Westview, 1991), pp. 175–81. See also Rudolf Hrbek and Thomas Läufer, "Die Einheitliche Europäische Akte—Das Luxemburger Reformpaket: Eine neue Etappe im Integrationsprozeß," *Europa Archiv* 41, no. 6, 25 March 1986, pp. 182–83.

54. The citation is from President Mitterrand. See *Agence Europe* 4796, 4 June 1988, p. 3. See also Elke Thiel, "The European Economic and Monetary Union: Economics and Politics," manuscript, 4–5 May 1991.

55. The citation is taken from the Belgian Minister of Finance. See Philippe Maystadt, "The Intergovernmental Conference: The State of the Negotiations and Emerging Options," *De Pecunia: Special Issue, European Union in a Turbulent World Economy* (June 1991), pp. 35–50. See also, J-rgen Mortensen, "Federalism vs. Coordination: Macroeconomic Policy in the European Community," *CEPS Paper, No. 47* (Brussels: CEPS, 1990).

56. See Christian Thune, "Dänemark," in Werner Weidenfeld and Wolfgang Wessels (eds.), *Jahrbuch der Europäischen Integration: 1988/89* (Bonn: Europa Union Verlag, 1989), p. 309.

57. "Rede des belgischen Ministerpräsidenten, Wilfried Martens, abgegeben am 28. September 1988 in Brüssel," *Europa Archiv* 43, no. 24, 25 December 1988, D 687.

58. *Agence Europe* 5148, 8 December 1989, p. 4. See also the press conference held at the end of the Strassbourg summit: *Agence Europe* 5150, 10 December 1989, pp. 15–17.

59. An important passage of the letter reads: "The European Council should initiate preparations for an intergovernmental conference on political union. In particular, the objective is to: strengthen the democratic legitimation of the union, render its institutions more efficient, ensure unity and coherence of the union's economic, monetary and political action, define and implement a common foreign and security policy." *Agence Europe* 5238, 20 April 1990, p. 3.

60. The citation is in reference to the 3 June 1988, Franco–German summit mentioned earlier. For a complete text of the press conference, see *La politique étrangère de la France: Textes et documents* (Paris: Ministry of Foreign Affairs, May/June 1988), pp. 25–26.

61. The Belgian memorandum (19 March 1990) predates the Franco–German letter to the Irish presidency, and so arguably understates the conviction of the Belgians toward supranationalism. See Sophie Vanhoonacker, "Belgium and European Political Union," in Finn Laursen and Sophie Vanhoonacker (eds.), *The Intergovernmental Conference on Political Union: Institutional Reforms, New Policies and International Identity of the European Community* (Maastricht: European Institute of Public Administration, 1992), pp. 37–48.

62. Finn Laursen, "Denmark and European Political Union," in Laursen and Vanhoonacker, *Intergovernmental Conference,* p. 67.

63. René van Beveren, "Belgium and the Gulf Crisis, August 1990–March 1991," in Nicole Gnesotto and John Roper (eds.), *Western Europe and the Gulf* (Paris: West European Union, 1992), pp. 7–16.

64. Armand Clesse, "Europe and the Gulf War as Seen By the Luxembourg Presidency of the EC," in Gnesotto and Roper, *Western Europe and the Gulf,* pp. 89–96.

65. Robert Wester, "The Netherlands," in Laursen and Vanhoonacker, *Intergovernmental Conference,* pp. 177–88.

66. See *Agence Europe* 5571, 20 September 1991, p. 3; *Agence Europe* 5577, 28 September 1991, p. 4.

67. The text of Mr. Major's 20 November speech is reproduced in Laursen and Vanhoonacker, *Intergovernmental Conference,* pp. 419–28. The citation is from p. 420.

68. M.P.C.M. van Schendelen, "Dutch Private and Public Lobbying in the European Community: The Vice or Virtue of Multiple Lobbies," paper presented for the International Political Science Association Study Group (22) on "Politics and Business," (Buenos Aires, 20–25 July 1991), pp. 11–13.

69. This analysis of the Danish veto is taken from Peter Ludlow, "The Treaty of Maastricht and the Future of Europe," *CEPS Working Document No. 68* (Brussels: Centre for European Policy Studies, 9 June 1992), pp. 41–50. See also "Danes Appear to Reject Pact," *International Herald Tribune,* 3 June 1992, pp. 1, 6.

70. Cited in William Drozdiak, "Danish Vote Shakes EC but 11 Vow to Press On," *International Herald Tribune* 4 June 1992, p. 1.

71. *Agence Europe* 5744, 5 June 1992, p. 6.

72. Drozdiak, "Danish Vote," p. 1.

73. Ian Davidson, "Mitterrand Gambles on Referendum," *The Financial Times,* 4 June 1992, p. 4.

74. For business criticism of Mitterrand, see Ben van der Velden, "Ondernemers: Mitterrand zet Europese belangen op het spel," *NRC Handelsblad,* 19 September 1992, pp. 1, 18.

75. As of 21 October 1992, the White Paper is available only in Danish. This analysis is therefore drawn from a press release (Nr. 101/92) issued by the Danish Ministry of Foreign Affairs. Citation, p. 4.

76. Danish Foreign Ministry press release, p. 7.

77. "Europese top bevestigt geloof in Maastricht," *De Standaard,* 18 October 1992, p. 1.

78. See, for example, Karel Lannoo, "Risico neen–stem was pokerspel niet waard," *De Standaard,* 22 September 1992, p. 8.

79. See, for example, Willem Beusekamp, "Bundesbank onverbiddelijk bewaker van D–mark en economie," *de Volkskrant,* 3 October 1992, p. 31; Jos Grobben, "Helmut Schlesinger: Zoon van een keizer," *Knack* 22, no. 39, 7 October 1992, pp. 50–1.

Chapter 7

The Franco–German Security Partnership

Philip Gordon

INTRODUCTION

The paradox of postwar security cooperation between France and Germany has been the ability of the two countries to build and maintain a military partnership despite their very different perspectives on international security. How have two countries with such contrasting historical legacies, attitudes toward the use of military force, and foreign policy ambitions managed to develop the closest bilateral security relationship in all of Europe? Was Franco–German military cooperation from 1949 to 1989 a result primarily of the Cold War, in which enduring national differences were overshadowed by a common and overwhelming threat? Or was it the product of a genuine rapprochement over time of French and German perspectives and the realization that the two countries have most security interests in common?

This paradox—divergent perspectives yet common policies—is also the fundamental challenge for the future of the Franco–German partnership. For if French and German perspectives on security have indeed remained very different, and the Franco–German couple was no more than a marriage of convenience in the circumstances of the Cold War, one would expect that marriage to run into great difficulty now that the circumstances have so profoundly changed. Without the common Soviet threat, will France and Germany be able to maintain their postwar patterns of increasing military cooperation? Were French and German policies during the Persian Gulf War and the Yugoslavia conflict evidence of divergence between Paris and Bonn and precursors of more divergence in the future? Has German unification disturbed the fundamental balance between France and Germany that many saw as a prerequisite for cooperation?

This chapter explores some of these questions by examining the ebbs and tides of Franco–German security cooperation over the past several decades. It begins with an overview of the distinct French and German security paradigms that have been maintained since World War II, examines the *relance* of Franco–German security cooperation in the 1980s (as well as some of the reasons for that *relance*), and concludes with an assessment of the prospects for the Franco–German security partnership in the post–Cold War world.

CONTRASTING STRATEGIC CULTURES SINCE WORLD WAR II

All countries have what might be called a national strategic culture, a set of attitudes and policies toward defense and security that arise from history, geography, and political culture.[1] Although France and Germany have obviously shared a preoccupation with the overriding Western security concern of the postwar era—the Soviet threat—the two countries have had very distinct perspectives and priorities within that overarching consensus. France and Germany agreed that Western Europe had to be defended and that cooperation between the two countries—within the context of an Atlantic Alliance—was a critical element in that defense. Yet at both the public and elite levels, French and German attitudes toward security and defense have been highly divergent.

For France, the overriding foreign policy goal after World War II was the restoration of French status as a great—or at least significant—power, including in the military domain. This was not, as is sometimes suggested, a uniquely Gaullist ambition that emerged in the 1960s, but one that was present from the very start of the postwar era. Humiliated by their sudden and shocking defeat in June 1940, French leaders set out quickly to recover their lost status and prestige by insisting on a French occupation zone in Germany, demanding a seat on the United Nations Security Council, and seeking to reestablish French colonial possessions around the globe. When General de Gaulle came back to power in 1958, he made the pursuit of grandeur the cornerstone of his foreign policy and built an independent nuclear force to support France's claim to great–power status. None of his successors abandoned this aim, and throughout the 1970s, 1980s—and so far in the 1990s as well—maintaining and augmenting France's status and rank has been a primary element of French strategic culture.[2]

Germany's postwar foreign policy goals have been both more modest and more parochial. Not only did defeat and occupation prevent the Germans from seeking a prominent postwar military role, but the experience of the war, and the guilt it engendered, also seemed to sap from the Germans any will to do so. Rather than seek prestige through the reestablishment of its military might and international responsibilities, Germany's postwar leaders have sought to avoid a prominent world role and to concentrate on domestic and economic objectives. Although its economy and population have long been greater than those of France, Germany is neither a member of the United Nations Security Council nor a nuclear power, and it does not play a global military role. Germany has not sought to display its power proudly and prominently like France but has, rather, gone out of its way to play it down or cover it up.

A second fundamental element of postwar France's strategic culture that differs from Germany has been the pursuit of national military independence. Again, not only for Charles de Gaulle but for his predecessors and successors, maximizing French autonomy has been an overriding political and military goal. French leaders who had lived through World War II had seen the consequences of French reliance on the "Anglo–Saxons" for security, and many had resolved never to be so dependent on others again. De Gaulle, who was obsessed with independence, insisted on the total autonomy of the French nuclear force and in 1966 withdrew France from NATO's integrated military commands. While the theme of independence has always been implemented pragmatically and France never had any intention of trying to "go it alone," even its most cooperative leaders—Valéry Giscard d'Estaing and François Mitterrand—have been careful to uphold this aspect of the Gaullist legacy. Even as the 1980s came to an end France still chose to remain outside NATO integration, refused to discuss publicly any coordination of its nuclear force, and produced more than 95 percent of its military forces at home.

The German attitude toward military independence has been quite different. After World War II, Germany was not only militarily "dependent," but in fact did not exist as a country until 1949 and had no army until 1955. Once the Cold War began, Germany—divided, nonnuclear, and on the border of a Soviet Empire occupied by the huge Red Army—had no choice but to rely heavily on the support of its western allies, and in particular on the United States. Whereas France, with no direct dispute with the Soviets and inevitably protected by the Allied forces in Germany, had the "luxury" of trumpeting its independence from Washington, Germany was condemned to accept its interdependence or even outright dependence. The tragic legacy of German unilateralism from the 1890s to 1945, moreover, prohibited the

Germans from acting alone, especially where military affairs were concerned. Germany's strategic culture thus has emphasized cooperation, multilateralism, and integration—not independence like France's.

Finally, France and Germany have since World War II had very different attitudes about military force. Each country drew very different lessons from the war itself. France's precipitous defeat taught it never again to be caught unprepared militarily, and its ultimate achievement of victor status produced the obvious message that it was better to be on the winning side in a war. Germany, on the other hand, learned of the dangers of possessing an excess of military might and felt most directly the tragedy of what military conflict on one's own territory can bring. Whereas France has associated military force with victory, independence, power, and glory, Germany has associated it with defeat, dependence, ignominy, and disaster. What has been true of military forces in general has been all the more true of nuclear forces: for France, these ultimate weapons were symbols of the country's security, independence, and technical prowess, whereas in Germany—the potential battleground for a European nuclear war—they were ever–present reminders of the horrific fate that awaited them if war ever broke out.[3]

To put it baldly then (and describing national strategic cultures briefly always requires some simplification), French–German military cooperation in the postwar period seems to have taken place despite important differences in perspective between the two countries, not because of a fundamental rapprochement of views. What France sought in the security domain, Germany often shunned. What France pursued with vigor, Germany largely avoided. What France was allowed or got away with, Germany was prohibited or did not want.

THE RELANCE OF FRANCO–GERMAN
COOPERATION IN THE 1980s

As Patrick McCarthy's introduction demonstrates, Franco–German security cooperation has developed unevenly since the early 1950s. If its successes included the relatively rapid overcoming of the animosity between these former enemies, the signing of the 1963 Elysée treaty, and some progress in joint armament production, those successes were not without their limits. France's insistence on an independent national defense policy was incompatible with Germany's desire for integration and its reliance on the United States, and the two countries' different strategic cultures made a "fusion" of their security policies impossible. Even under such like–minded supporters of the Franco–German partnership as Valéry Giscard d'Estaing and Helmut Schmidt, military cooperation lagged well behind financial and economic cooperation; as the 1970s ended the Franco–German security rapprochement was far from complete. Schmidt recounts in his memoirs that he and Giscard had made far–reaching plans to relaunch the partnership at the start of the 1980s, but fate—in the form of domestic politics—intervened: by the end of 1982 both leaders were out of office.[4]

The changes of government in Paris and Bonn did not derail Franco–German partnership, however, and those changes may in fact have been prerequisites for future cooperation. The French and German socialist parties were moving in opposite directions on security questions at the end of the 1970s; the French PS was rallying to nuclear deterrence and the Atlantic Alliance while the SPD was joining the anti–nuclear camp and abandoning the pro–defense Schmidt. Thus it was only the arrival of the socialist Mitterrand (now a strong supporter of the Atlantic Alliance, the *force de frappe,* and a hard–line policy toward the Soviet Union) and the conservative Kohl (similarly firm on NATO, nuclear deterrence, and the USSR) that brought about a convergence of French and German views, and made a convergence of their policies possible.

Mitterrand and Kohl wasted little time and already in October 1982 devoted their first bilateral meeting to military questions.[5] Although the French president reasserted France's independence and refused German participation in French nuclear planning (eternal French prerequisites), and the German chancellor reaffirmed the Federal Republic's primary tie to NATO and the United States (eternal German prerequisites), the meeting produced some significant results, including the commitment to implement the long–dormant and far–reaching defense clauses of the 1963 Elysée treaty.[6] To expedite the treaty's implementation, the two leaders also decided to create a Franco–German Commission on Security and Defense that would seek to institutionalize the exchange of views between the Germans and the French on security policy. Defense and foreign ministers of the two countries would meet at least twice per year, and the Commission's three specialized working groups—on arms collaboration, military cooperation, and politico–strategic issues—would meet even more often, in small groups just below the ministerial level.[7] The success of the treaty's revival should not be exaggerated, but the fact that French and German officials were now meeting regularly at the highest level to discuss security—and that they finally managed to reverse the dismal record of military–industrial cooperation during the 1970s by agreeing on the coproduction of a combat helicopter—did lend a certain amount of momentum to the relationship.[8]

At the start of the following year an even more powerful expression of Franco–German solidarity took place: to celebrate the twentieth anniversary of the Elysée treaty, Mitterrand travelled to Bonn to make a historic speech before the Bundestag. Breaking with the ambiguity of his predecessor on the Euromissile issue (Giscard had failed to support publicly the Pershing II and cruise missile deployment on the grounds that France was not concerned by NATO's nuclear decisions), Mitterrand called on the Germans to support deployment of the Pershing missiles and denounced those who wanted to "decouple" Europe from the United States. The speech was not only an effort to ensure the reelection of Mitterrand's partner Kohl but an eloquent personal plea for Franco–German cooperation and peace after generations of war.[9]

Like many other examples of France's commitment to the Franco–German relationship, however, the Bundestag speech was ambiguous. As German observers did not fail to point out, it was rather easy for Mitterrand to call on the Germans to accept the missiles while France, of course, refused to do so itself. Bonn may have been pleased to see France supporting NATO policy and backing a highly controversial deployment, but did not fail to notice that Mitterrand was calling on German leaders to take all the political heat. Still, the Bundestag speech turned out to be a boon to future bilateral cooperation; even ambiguous French support for German policy was better than no support at all, and Helmut Kohl—the eventual winner in the March 1983 Bundestag elections—was grateful for the political boost.

By 1984, the momentum of the Franco–German couple was strong enough to act as the motor for the relaunching of another long–dormant institution of European defense cooperation, the Western European Union (WEU). Such a move had, of course, been tried ten years before under French Foreign Minister Michel Jobert—during the fateful American "Year of Europe"—but German suspicions of French motives at that time made progress impossible. This time, however, with the French showing increased interest in European cooperation (and having ceased to portray such cooperation as a means to undermine NATO), and with the Germans themselves coming to believe more sincerely in the need for a "European pillar," the proponents of the WEU were able to give it new life. After France pushed to have the remaining restrictions on German conventional armament removed from the original WEU Treaty, Germany agreed to reactivate the organization.[10]

Even more important to Franco–German defense cooperation than these diplomatic acts were the changes made in French conventional force structures, including, most importantly, the creation of a 47,000–strong Force d'Action Rapide (FAR) designed to intervene quickly in Central

Europe. In many ways a microcosm of the French attitude toward German security in the postwar era, the FAR was a classic example of France's desire to show concrete interest in European solidarity while holding on to the pretense as well as the reality of national autonomy. On one hand, the FAR was a major sign of growing French support for Germany that would, in the words of French defense minister Charles Hernu, "permit [us], infinitely better than today, to commit ourselves at the side of our allies."[11] At the same time, however, the French commitment to defend Germany remained ambiguous. French leaders continued to assert that the French government's autonomy was "complete" and that the FAR's independence from NATO structures was "total;" it was unclear whether the FAR would really be capable of playing an important military role.[12] Because the force was designed to intervene in conflicts not only in Europe but abroad (where fighting conditions would be very different), many military experts wondered whether this lightly armed, untested, and extremely heterogeneous force could have much of an impact even if French leaders were prepared to send it to the front.

During the mid–1980s, as leaders in both Paris and Bonn began to doubt American reliability and fear U.S.–Soviet "collusion," Franco–German military cooperation increased commensurately. The Strategic Defense Initiative (which undermined deterrence and drew scarce funds away from European defense), swollen U.S. budget deficits (which put pressure on Washington to reduce defense spending), the October 1986 Reykjavik summit (where Reagan appeared willing to bargain away Europe's nuclear guarantee), and the 1987 intermediate–range nuclear forces (INF) treaty (which raised fears of decoupling) all contributed to a sense in Europe that the longstanding American guarantee for European security would have to be supplemented, or perhaps one day even replaced. As French Defense Minister André Giraud warned at the time, "American consciousness about the problem of European security might not always be so acute."[13] Even in traditionally Atlanticist Germany, security experts had begun to wonder about the long–term American commitment and to call on Europe to take on a greater and more autonomous military role.[14]

Mitterrand and Kohl responded to this situation by moving ever further down the road toward European—and more specifically, Franco–German— defense. In February 1986 the two leaders met (for no less than the twelfth time since the beginning of the previous year) and announced studies on the use of the FAR in Germany, future joint military maneuvers, a telephone crisis "hotline" between Paris and Bonn, and a French commitment—albeit a qualified one—to consult with the Germans before using tactical nuclear weapons in Germany.[15] The military maneuvers planned at this time took place in September of the following year and would prove to be the largest and most significant ever between the two countries. In Operation Kecker Spatz/Moineau Hardi (Bold Sparrow), 20,000 French troops, operating for the first time under German command, joined 55,000 German soldiers deep in the territory of the Federal Republic (in Bavaria and Baden–Wurtenburg, well outside the normal French zone of operation). The operation was not without technical and logistical hitches—French helicopters, for example, arrived late to their designated point of intervention—but it did show that France was serious about contributing to forward defense and that the FAR could indeed have a role in Central Europe. The maneuvers were also significant for Germany, which agreed (albeit reluctantly) to French demands that Kecker Spatz take place outside of the NATO structure. This was a Franco–German exercise; NATO's Supreme Allied Commander Europe (SACEUR) was not invited.

What explains the renewed enthusiasm in both Paris and Bonn for this Franco–German "alliance within the alliance"? How were Mitterrand and Kohl able to make progress in the very areas in which progress had eluded their predecessors? Why did it seem more imperative for France and Germany to cooperate after 1982 than after 1962, and why was this cooperation easier to achieve? Three different sets of factors can be identified that in the mid–1980s pushed the French and the Germans closer together.

The first was the combination of an unfavorably evolving military balance in Europe and new uncertainties about the United States. With tensions rising across the continent, the Soviets deploying multiple–warhead nuclear missiles targeted at Western Europe, and a growing conventional force imbalance between East and West, the French and the Germans reached the obvious conclusion that Western defense had to be bolstered. But they also realized that the United States and NATO, in its present form, would not be around forever and that France and Germany thus had a growing interest in contributing more themselves. The French and German perceptions of American policy, of course, were not identical. For France, military cooperation with Germany meant most of all preparing Europe for the day when long–standing French predictions of an American withdrawal from Europe would come true. For Germany, cooperation with France was primarily a way to augment the European contribution to European security so that the day of the American departure would never arrive. This was not the first, or only, example of divergent motivations producing similar policy results.

A second set of factors that contributed to increased Franco–German cooperation were the political developments within the Federal Republic discussed in chapter 2. With the German SPD having abandoned Schmidt to join the pacifist and anti–nuclear camps and now outflanked on its left by a Green party opposed to the military and to the Atlantic Alliance, the governments in both Bonn and Paris saw more reason than ever to work together. For Chancellor Kohl, a neutralist coalition on the left was a powerful reason to emphasize Western cooperation and show voters that Germany was well anchored in its European and Atlantic alliances (and that it would be safest if it remained so). The particular cooperation with France also sent the message that Germany was no "vassal" of the United States but could look after its own security interests in Europe. For Mitterrand and the French, the prospect of a neutralist Germany seeking accommodation with the East and leaving France on the hypothetical "front line" was a frightening prospect, one that led the French government to do all it could to reassure the Germans. More than anything, changes in French military policy during these years were designed to anchor what was perceived to be an unsteady Germany to Europe and thereby protect France's postwar "buffer zone."

Finally, there was an economic impetus to Franco–German military cooperation during the 1980s. The debates about European security, after all, were going on at the same time as debates over European economic policy, and the two issues were closely linked. With France in dire need of support from Germany after its disastrous economic experiment of 1981, a French failure to support the German government on security questions—such as the Euromissile issue, for example—would have been extremely risky. After France's decision in March 1983 to remain in the ERM and to join Germany in a strong economic partnership, it would have been implausible for France to reject the German desire for a strong security partnership in favor of a more nationalist option.[16]

By 1986, Franco–German security relations were as good as they had ever been, and the Germans were not unhappy to see changes taking place in Paris. A German *droit de regard* was not given over French nuclear weapons, but the issue was at least confronted and discussed; the French nuclear force was not extended to German territory as some Germans might have hoped, but that force was expanded and made more credible; France's interest in a more autonomous European defense distinct from the Atlantic Alliance that the Germans preferred was not abandoned, but it was no longer presented as an alternative to NATO; French conventional forces were not built up to the levels the Germans might have liked, but they were better organized for participation in Europe; and the French commitment to intervene on the central front with those forces was not made automatic, but it was given more substance.

Yet for all this, it could still not be said that the Franco–German military couple of the 1980s was free from problems. First, it must be remembered that one of the main catalysts on the French side of the relationship was the French suspicion of German intentions—not the best grounds on which to build a close and enduring relationship. Second, the two countries continued to have different views about nuclear weapons and about armed forces in general, with Germany still much less comfortable with military power than France. Third, as long as Germany was divided, different French and German attitudes towards the Soviet Union were inevitable: whereas France had no territorial or minority rights disputes with the Soviet bloc and no major role to play in the East–West military confrontation, Germany had vital national interests—such as *Ostpolitik*—at stake. France had become a status quo power while Germany retained an underlying and growing desire for change. Fourth, despite the increased Paris–Bonn dialogue and frequent high–level meetings, a number of conflicting perspectives remained: to the French, Bonn was still seen as more interested in East Germany, *Ostpolitik,* and the United States than in France (which it probably was), and to the Germans, the French remained more concerned with their national independence and international prestige than with Franco–German relations (which they probably were). Finally, one of the greatest lingering problems of all was that whereas the French believed they had made great strides toward a full commitment to German and European defense—and congratulated themselves for their efforts—the Germans saw how much further the French had yet to go. Many in the Federal Republic found France's European defense policies under Mitterrand long on symbolism but woefully short on substance; even the most successful of marriages have their differences and misunderstandings.

Toward the end of the 1980s—at least after 1987—the Franco–German security relationship took on a new character. As the reforms of Soviet leader Mikhail Gorbachev began to appear more and more credible, the most visible impetus to Franco–German defense cooperation of the past thirty years—the Soviet threat—began to fade. Germany, because its stake in detente was by far the greatest, was probably the first country to "take Gorbachev at his word" (as Foreign Minister Hans–Dietrich Genscher requested), and the Germans were the first to welcome the Soviet leader's "new thinking" in foreign policy.[17] By 1988, nearly 60 percent of Germans surveyed had a favorable opinion of the Soviet Union (compared to less than 10 percent in 1981), and by 1989 more Germans trusted Gorbachev than they did any Western leader with the exception of German head of state Richard von Weizsäcker.[18] Just as the Germans had cheered de Gaulle and Kennedy when those leaders visited the Federal Republic in the early 1960s, they now enthusiastically welcomed the Soviet leader, who made a triumphant visit to West Germany in June 1989.

In this sort of climate, progress in the Franco–German security partnership no longer consisted primarily of French efforts to augment their commitment to forward defense or to nuclear deterrence, as it had in the past. Instead, as Germany sought to take advantage of change in Moscow to pursue disarmament and detente, Franco–German cooperation meant most of all French solidarity with Bonn's new security policy stance. Nobody perceived this shift better than François Mitterrand (who in the late 1970s had similarly perceived and taken advantage of the move away from detente), and a different kind of Franco–German security cooperation began to thrive. Already in early 1987, overcoming widespread reservations in France about the INF treaty that would eliminate the Euromissiles, Mitterrand went along with the wishes of the German government and public opinion and backed the agreement. Similarly, in contrast to Gaullist Prime Minister Jacques Chirac, who in 1988 opposed a further treaty banning short–range nuclear forces (dubbed by some Germans as "German–range nuclear weapons" because they could not reach beyond German borders), Mitterrand supported such a ban and backed Kohl and Genscher at NATO's Brussels summit in March.[19] Finally, Mitterrand also went out of his way before and after his 1988 reelection to stress that French nuclear policy was a policy of deterrence and "non–war," and that France's "final nuclear warning" would not be delivered on Germany territory.[20] Better than his conservative partners in the cohabitation government, and better than the British and American leaders as well, the French president understood—for the time being, at least—the critical importance of showing his trust in Bonn.[21]

With French support for Germany's priorities of disarmament and detente made clear, and a major potential obstacle to Franco–German cooperation thereby removed, the bilateral relationship could be pursued. On 22 January 1988, Mitterrand and Kohl celebrated the twenty–fifth anniversary of the Elysée treaty with the creation of a Franco–German Defense and Security Council that would build on the success of the 1982 Commission on Security and Defense. The Council, to meet twice per year, would consist of the two heads of state and government as well as the foreign ministers, defense ministers, and (ex–officio) the general inspector of the Bundeswehr and the chief of staff of the French armed forces. The Council would have at its disposal a Council committee, a permanent secretariat (to be located in Paris and initially headed by a German general), and the already existing Commission on Security and Defense.[22] Franco–German cooperation at the end of the decade was also manifested in a historic military exercise in Champagne during September 1989 when 5,000 German soldiers maneuvered with 25,000 French soldiers on the World War I battlefield of the Marne. Added to this was the October 1990 constitution of a 4,200–strong Franco–German brigade. First proposed by Chancellor Kohl in 1987, the joint brigade was insignificant militarily but was a powerful symbol of cooperation and reconciliation between the two former enemy armies as well as a testing ground for future forms of bilateral military integration.[23]

Thus, on the eve of the revolutions that were about to fundamentally change the basic European security situation that had existed for more than forty years, Franco–German military cooperation was perhaps at its peak. Patrick McCarthy is doubtless right when he points out in chapter 3 that French apprehensions about growing German power and different French and German interpretations of Soviet policy began well before German unification. But perhaps the more important point is that the French government overcame the temptation to break with Bonn and instead responded to the new situation by augmenting its efforts to reach joint French and German positions. In short, it can be said that despite continued differences in strategic culture and only limited progress in certain key areas such as nuclear policy and industrial military cooperation, France and Germany had by the end of the 1980s managed not only to decisively overcome their past enmity, but to actually develop a number of common institutions, policies, practices, and views. All things considered, de Gaulle and Adenauer would not have been disappointed.

THE FRANCO–GERMAN COUPLE
AND THE POST–COLD WAR WORLD

How have the dramatic developments of the late 1980s and early 1990s— including German unification, the disintegration of the Soviet Union, and the Persian Gulf War—affected the Franco–German security partnership? What have been the French and German responses to the shocks of the past few years? Have developments in Europe and around the world since 1989 pushed France and Germany closer together or moved them further apart?

The period that immediately followed the revolutions of 1989–90 did not augur well for Franco–German relations, and a series of events during 1990 revealed important differences between Paris and Bonn. Despite Mitterrand's assertion on 3 November 1989 that he was "not afraid of German unification," his actions over the following months betrayed a certain hesitation to accept a united Germany and stood in marked contrast to the confidence and support that Mitterrand had shown for Bonn during the 1980s.[24] When Chancellor Kohl proposed a ten–point plan for a German confederation on 28 November without consulting Paris, Mitterrand was visibly troubled, and in December 1989 the French president visited Kiev (in an apparent attempt to persuade Gorbachev to oppose German unification) and East Berlin (in an effort to bolster the rickety East German regime). Seven months later, in what seemed at the time a serious blow to Franco–German security cooperation, Mitterrand announced suddenly and unexpectedly that at least half, and perhaps all, French troops would be withdrawn from Germany despite a reiterated German invitation that they remain. For Mitterrand, French soldiers had been stationed in Germany in "conditions that could leave a certain bitterness," and it was "logical that they come back to their [own] country."[25] As the legal and historical basis for French troops in Germany was not the postwar occupation but a bilateral agreement following the Brussels Treaty of 1954, this was a curious formulation, especially from a man who had so strongly supported Franco–German security cooperation.

During 1990, the French and the Germans became disillusioned with each other's behavior, and the Franco–German summit in Munich in September of that year was one of the least amicable ever. France was upset because Germany had initiated the unification process without consulting its neighbors, waffled on the key question of the new Germany's eastern borders, and unilaterally negotiated the size of the German army with the Soviet Union. Germany was distressed that France had attempted to delay or prevent unification, decided unilaterally to pull its troops out, and refused to accept NATO's new plans for multinational military corps. The summit ended not with the traditional assertions of bilateral unity but with an observation by Mitterrand that "there will be no lack of conflicts, rivalries and misunderstandings [in the future]," followed by the biting comment, "Indeed, I don't know why I speak in the future tense."[26]

By the beginning of 1991, the Franco–German relationship was back on track and it was clear that despite their differences, both Paris and Bonn saw cooperation and enhanced European integration as the best, or even the only, option for the future. Indeed, it seemed that the differences themselves were a catalyst for expanded cooperation. Already in April 1990, the foundation of this more positive approach had been outlined in a joint Kohl–Mitterrand proposal to create a European "political union" by 1992.[27] At the time, the proposal seemed an exaggerated and overtly cosmetic attempt by France and Germany to show the world (and each other) that the new Germany would remain fully integrated and fully committed to Western Europe. In retrospect, however, the vague Kohl–Mitterrand political union initiative may prove to have been the beginning of a new and even more successful phase of Franco–German cooperation.

Since the April 1990 proposal, France and Germany have joined together in a series of subsequent joint initiatives to relaunch Franco–German and European cooperation. Where European security is concerned, the Franco–German proposals describe a process by which Europe would develop a "true security policy that would ultimately lead to a common defense."[28] This common defense would initially be built around a re-vamped WEU that would eventually "fuse" with the Community itself, perhaps in 1998 when the WEU's original fifty–year statute conveniently runs out. At the EC's December 1991 Maastricht summit—the culmination of the process Kohl and Mitterrand had launched the previous spring—France and Germany overcame British, Dutch, and Portuguese objections that an EC–based defense might undermine NATO, and EC leaders agreed to "the eventual framing of a common defense policy . . . which might in time lead to a common defense."[29] The Twelve also agreed with the French and German view that the European Union should be able to call on the WEU "to elaborate and implement decisions and actions of the Union which have defense implications."[30]

For the Franco–German security partnership, the most significant of all the pre–Maastricht Paris–Bonn initiatives was a 14 October 1991 statement that concluded with a proposal to expand the existing Franco–German brigade into a much larger joint corps.[31] Apparently conceived of by the Elysée and the German chancellery without substantial input from their respective defense and foreign ministries, the design of the joint corps only gradually took shape over the following months before being announced formally at the May 1992 Franco–German summit in La Rochelle, France.[32] According to the summit communiqué and French and German officials, the corps would consist of 35,000 troops (two German mechanized brigades, the first French armored division, and the Franco–German brigade) under alter-nating French and German commands, with headquarters in Strasbourg, France. It would have three types of missions: (1) the defense of Western Europe in the context of the NATO and WEU treaties; (2) peacekeeping and peacemaking (either in Eastern Europe or outside of Europe); and (3) humanitarian tasks. From the beginning, France and Germany emphasized that other EC member–states were welcome to join their plan and that it was a "European"—not simply a "Franco–German"—corps. Nonetheless, the joint corps proposal was a clear sign that Paris and Bonn were frustrated with the inability of the Twelve (in the EC) and of the Nine (in the WEU) to reach a consensus on the divisive subjects of security and defense. As has happened so often in the past, France and Germany decided to move forward bilaterally, hoping to draw their European partners in their wake.

While the French and Germans have presented the corps proposal as a shining example of post–Cold War Franco–German military cooperation, it must be noted that like so many other examples of this cooperation, this one is not without ambiguities or problems. First, of course, is the different status of the troops involved: German troops are integrated in NATO's military command structure, but French troops are not. Bonn went out of its way to reassure Washington that no German forces would be withdrawn from NATO commands, but at the same time promised Paris that their "priority" would be the European corps.[33] Second, there are serious questions about Germany's political ability to perform all the missions assigned to the corps: the German Basic Law (at least as interpreted at the time of the corps's inception) prohibits the deployment of German soldiers in any operations outside the NATO area and in any operations other than defense. As the most likely security risks to which the corps might have to respond are, in fact, outside the NATO area, and given the substantial SPD resistance to a major constitutional revision, the chances that the corps will have a significant role to play anytime soon are very limited.[34] Finally, there are important differences in French and German goals for the corps: whereas French leaders seem to see it as the basis for a European army that would eventually be able to ensure European security without the United States, Germany has portrayed it as a means to strengthen the European contribution to NATO and link France more closely to NATO's integrated commands.[35] Even if the corps is fully functioning by 1995, as planned, it will be far from the unified and capable fighting unit desired by some of its more ambitious designers.

Despite these questions and ambiguities, the decision to create a joint corps is strong evidence of the continued desire in both Paris and Bonn to pursue the Franco–German security partnership. On the French side, the creation of the corps reverses the July 1990 decision to pull French forces out of Germany and establishes a new basis for that deployment; it accepts for the first time since the late 1950s the logic of peacetime military integration; and it provides for—through the joint headquarters in Strasbourg—the first permanent stationing of German soldiers in France. Along with some recent indications that France might be willing to discuss the Europeanization of its nuclear deterrent, the Franco–German corps proposal is a sign that some of the French obstacles to a more far–reaching Franco–German partnership may finally be disappearing.[36] On the German side, the corps proposal is also significant. It makes the German interest in developing European defense autonomy clearer than ever before: the Germans formally agreed that the corps would "provide the European Union with the possibility of conducting its own military affairs." And it is one more step—limited, to be sure—toward the surmounting of post–World War II restrictions on the German role in international security.[37] Rather than having spelled the breakup of the Franco–German couple, the end of the Cold War seems to have given the relationship a new vitality.

How likely, though, is this vitality to last in the future? Have the efforts since 1989 been worthy but futile attempts by political leaders to prevent the inevitable stalling of Franco–German security cooperation? Are France and Germany likely to remain intimate military partners or are they more likely, despite the attempts by Kohl and Mitterrand to hold the relationship together, to drift apart? The argument can certainly be made that despite all the recent efforts, France and Germany will not prove capable of sustaining the momentum of the past decade and that, while renewed war between the two countries is probably forever excluded, a true common security and defense policy may be just as unlikely.

The first cause for pessimism about the future relationship is that German unification has thrown off the balance that has been a necessary factor in Franco–German reconciliation. The new Germany is now 78 million inhabitants to France's 55 million, a 31 percent difference. The united Germany's economy is nearly 40 percent greater than France's, that is, almost as large as the French and British economies combined.[38] Even more importantly, Germany is no longer constrained by the division, political de–legitimization, and military dependence inherited from World War II and imposed by the Cold War. While France thus needs Germany as much as ever, Germany needs France much less: even former president Giscard d'Estaing admitted in 1990 that the Franco–German dialogue is "no longer at the center of the debate."[39]

Second, the geopolitics that made military partners of France and Germany have changed. Whereas the bipolar division of Europe facilitated Franco–German cooperation by foreclosing Germany's historic Eastern options, the end of the Cold War has reopened all sorts of new German markets, temptations, and responsibilities in the East. (As some French critics have observed with some resentment, the new Germany has become "polygamous" while France remains faithful to its old partner.) And whereas until 1989 the hostility of the Soviet Union and the existence of the Warsaw Pact harmonized French and German security threats and interests, the end of the Cold War renders those threats and interests quite different. Surely

Paris and Bonn would have different perceptions of—and perhaps reactions to—crises such as a civil war in Eastern Europe or a fundamentalist coup in North Africa.

A third cause for skepticism is that French and German strategic cultures, despite the political rapprochement over the years, remain very different. The French still believe in their global military role, independence from Washington, the pursuit of grandeur, and the necessity of military force; the Germans remain militarily parochial, reliant on the United States, geopolitically humble, and strongly averse to the use of military force. As the specific case of the Franco–German corps shows, a true harmonization of French and German perspectives on security remains a long way off.

Finally, skeptics about the future of the Franco–German security link can easily find evidence for their views in the actual security policies France and Germany have pursued since 1989. In the Persian Gulf War, for example, the French and German responses could hardly have been more different. Whereas France initially sought to pursue an independent diplomatic line and then took part in allied military action, the German response was to avoid any military role, even to the point of resisting the symbolic deployment of German Alpha–jet trainers to Turkey in the context of NATO's Article Five. The German contribution to the coalition, in fact, was more substantive than it initially seemed, but it is worth noting that Bonn sought to play down the German contribution while Paris sought to emphasize France's role. Similar arguments can be made about French and German policy toward the Yugoslav civil war, with Germany supporting recognition of Croatia and Slovenia while France opposed it, and with France willing to send military forces to the region but Germany unable to do so. Also worth noting are the differences in French and German policy toward NATO, with Germany—but not France—having fully supported the Alliance's efforts to adapt to the post–Cold War era by their support of the June 1990 declaration that nuclear weapons would henceforth be weapons of "last resort," the decision to create multinational corps, the formation of a NATO Rapid Reaction Corps, and the creation of a North Atlantic Cooperation Council with the former members of the Warsaw Pact.[40]

As these arguments and examples demonstrate, French and German views in a number of areas remain quite different, and it would be naive to believe that the future will be free from serious bilateral differences or that a common foreign and security policy—let alone a true political union—will be easy to achieve. France and Germany are two historic entities, each with its own perceptions and interests, and all the goodwill and European enthusiasm in the world cannot change that. The compelling forces of a common Soviet threat and a mutual desire to lead a European Community (fortuitously limited in size by the Cold War) will no longer serve to overshadow differences between Paris and Bonn.

Must we therefore conclude that France and Germany begin to drift apart and eventually split as the "realities" of the post–Cold War world set in? Such a conclusion, despite the continued and perhaps growing differences between the two countries discussed above, would be based on an incomplete, and therefore inaccurate, reading of the past forty years. Analyses that assume the inevitable breakup of the Franco–German couple in the absence of a clear threat fail to understand that the Soviet threat was by no means the only glue holding France and Germany together in a security partnership and that the desire for—indeed, the necessity of—bilateral reconciliation and European construction played just as prominent, or even more prominent, roles.

As argued above, divergent security interests, threats, and perspectives were an enduring characteristic of the Franco–German relationship from the 1950s to the 1980s, but they never prevented the two countries from consistently augmenting their military cooperation. In this sense, it can be said that the Franco–German military couple has been a product of political will prevailing over geopolitical realities.

NOTES

1. For a good discussion of the concept of strategic culture and application of the concept to Germany, see Stephen F. Szabo, *The Changing Politics of Germany Security* (London: Pinter, 1990), pp. 1–22.

2. As recently as March 1991, 72 percent of French people surveyed believed that France was a great power. See "La France est–elle encore une grande puissance," *L'Express,* 1 March 1991, pp. 28–33. On the pursuit of grandeur by de Gaulle's successors, see Philip H. Gordon, *A Certain Idea of France: French Security Policy and the Gaullist Legacy* (Princeton: Princeton University Press, 1993).

3. Public opinion polls support the case that France and Germany have very different views of the use of military force. When asked in May 1991 whether they agreed with the statement that their country "must have a strong defense in order to defend its territory," 46 percent of French people surveyed "agreed strongly" in contrast to only 17 percent of the Germans. When asked whether war was sometimes necessary to protect a country's vital interests, 68 percent of the French agreed strongly or somewhat, compared to 42 percent of the Germans. It is not surprising, then, that in the heat of the Persian Gulf crisis just before the war began, 60 percent

of the French supported the use of military force to drive the Iraqi army out of Kuwait while only 22 percent of the Germans supported the use of force. For the first two polls, see the May 1991 Commissioned Personal Interview Surveys provided by the United States Information Agency. For the Gulf War poll results, see Dominique Dhombres, "Britanniques et Français restent les plus favorables au recours à la force," *Le Monde*, 23–24 December 1990, p. 3.

4. According to Schmidt, Giscard had told him in July 1980, "I want to take great steps together with you after my reelection; until then let us please not disturb French public opinion." The chancellor answered that he would "be as ready to do that next year as this. But please do not forget that my term in office has its limits." Schmidt's sense of the future seems to have been more prescient than Giscard's. See Helmut Schmidt, *Die Deutschen und ihre Nachbarn* (Berlin: Goldman, 1990), p. 320. On the domestic developments in France and Germany at this time, see chapters 2 (Allin) and 3 (McCarthy).

5. See the "Déclaration du Président de la République à l'issue des consultations franco–allemandes des 21 et 22 octobre 1982 à Bonn," in Ministère des Relations Extérieures, *La politique étrangère de la France: Textes et documents. Octobre–novembre–décembre 1982* (Paris: Documentation Française, 1983).

6. The Elysée treaty had called for regular meetings between the French and German defense ministers (every three months) and sought to promote a "rapprochement of military doctrines" and "common conceptions" about European defense. For the text, see the annex of Karl Kaiser and Pierre Lellouche, (eds.), *Le couple franco–allemand et la défense de l'Europe* (Paris: Institut Français des Relations Internationales, 1986), pp. 329–33; or the German version, *Deutsch–Französische Sicherheitspolitik* (Bonn: Europa Verlag, Forschungsinstitut der Deutschen Gesellschaft für Auswärtige Politik, 1986), pp. 308–313.

7. For details on the Franco–German Commission, see André Adrets (pseudonym of a former defense ministry official), "Les relations franco–allemandes et le fait nucléaire dans une Europe divisée," *Politique étrangère*, no. 3 (Fall 1984), pp. 649–664.

8. See Jacques Isnard, "Relance spectaculaire de la coopération militaire franco–allemande," *Le Monde*, 30 May 1984, p. 1.

9. See the 20 January 1983 Bundestag speech printed as "Il faut que la guerre demeure impossible," in Mitterrand, *Réflexions sur la politique extérieure de la France* (Paris: Fayard, 1986), pp. 183–208.

10. The terms of Germany's entry into the WEU in 1954 (after the failure of the European Defense Community) included limits on German conventional armaments production and military logistics. The removal of these limits took away the stigma of discrimination that had always marked the WEU in German eyes. On the 1954 Paris Accords providing for German accession to the WEU, see Alfred Grosser, *La IVe République et sa politique extérieure*, (Paris: Librairie

Armand Colin, 1961), pp. 320–326. On the agreement to "relaunch" the WEU, see *Le Monde*, 25 February 1984.

11. These are Hernu's words cited in Yost, "Franco–German Defense Cooperation," p. 2.

12. See Hernu cited in *Le Monde*, 5 November 1983, p. 9.

13. See "L'offensive Giraud," *L'Express*, 10–16 July 1987, p. 40. Also see President Mitterrand's warning that American disengagement was "a real danger." Interview with Mitterrand by Jean Daniel entitled "La Stratégie, par François Mitterrand," *Le Nouvel Observateur*, 18–24 December 1987, p. 25. (Subsequently cited as Mitterrand, "La Stratégie.")

14. See, for example, Christoph Bertram, "Europe's Security Dilemmas," *Foreign Affairs* 65, no. 5 (Summer 1987), pp. 942–57; Alfred Dregger, "Entwurf einer Sicherheitspolitik zur Selbstbehauptung Europas," *Europäische Wehrkünde*, no. 12 (December 1987); Helmut Schmidt, "Deutsch–französische Zusammenarbeit in der Sicherheitspolitik," *Europa–Archiv*, no. 11 (1987): pp. 303–12. For a general discussion of German views, see Wolfram F. Hanrieder, *Germany, America, Europe: Forty Years of German Foreign Policy* (New Haven: Yale University Press, 1989), pp. 113–30.

15. The statement issued by Mitterrand following the meetings announced that: "Within the limits imposed by the extreme rapidity of such decisions, the President of the Republic declares himself disposed to consult the Chancellor of the FRG on the possible employment of prestrategic French weapons on German territory. He notes that the decision cannot be shared in this matter. The President of the Republic indicates that he has decided, with the Chancellor of the FRG, to equip himself with technical means for immediate and reliable consultation in time of crisis." See the 28 February 1986 declaration in *Le Monde*, 2–3 March 1986, p. 4; or excerpts from the declaration as "Press conference of François Mitterrand, President of the Republic of France," 7 March 1986, *Survival* 28, no. 4 (1986), p. 367.

16. For the link between French and German security and economic issues in the early 1980s, see the analysis of Patrick McCarthy, "France Faces Reality: *Rigueur* and the Germans," in David P. Calleo and Claudia Morgenstern (eds.), *Recasting Europe's Economies: National Strategies in the 1980s* (Lanham, New York, London: University Press of America, 1990), p. 67. On the French economic policy during this period, see chapter 4 (Boche).

17. For Genscher, see his 2 January 1987 speech to the World Economic Forum in Davos, Switzerland, printed as "Nehmen wir Gorbatshow ernst, nehmen wir ihn beim Wort," in Hans–Dietrich Genscher, *Wir wollen ein Europäisches Deutschland* (Berlin: Goldman, 1991), pp. 135–48.

18. For the polling data as well as a good discussion of changing German attitudes toward the Soviet Union, see Szabo, *Changing Politics*, pp. 47–51.

19. For Chirac, see "M. Chirac prône la vigilance à l'égard de l'Union soviétique," *Le Monde,* 2 March 1988, p. 2. For Mitterrand, see Claire Tréan, "M. Mitterrand se déclare hostile à la modernisation des armes nucléaires de l'OTAN," *Le Monde,* 27 February 1988.

20. See Mitterrand's remarks in "La stratégie nucléaire de la France s'adresse à l'agresseur et à lui seul," *Le Monde,* 21 October 1987; and "Le chef de l'Etat confirme son intention de réviser la doctrine sur l'emploi des armes préstratégiques françaises," *Le Monde,* 22 October 1987.

21. See Gordon, *Certain Idea,* chapter 6.

22. See Peter Schmidt, "The Franco–German Defense and Security Council," *Aussenpolitik* (English edition) 40, no. 4, pp. 367–68.

23. See Christian Millotat and Jean–Claude Philippot, "Le jumelage franco–allemand pour la sécurité de l'Europe," *Défense nationale* (October 1990), p. 67.

24. See Pierre Haski, "Mitterrand n'a pas peur de la réunification allemande," *Libération,* 4 November 1989; and Julius W. Friend, *The Linchpin: French–German Relations, 1950–1990* (Washington: Center for Strategic and International Studies, 1991), p. 81.

25. See Mitterrand's 6 July 1990 press conference cited in "La logique voudra que l'armée française stationnée en Allemagne regagne son pays," *Le Monde,* 8–9 July 1990, p. 5.

26. See "A relationship in the balance," *The Economist,* 6 October 1990, p. 53.

27. For the text of the proposal, see "Text of Statement by Mitterrand and Kohl on EC Union," Reuter Press Agency, transcript, 19 April 1990.

28. See the 6 December 1990 Kohl–Mitterrand letter to the Italian presidency of the EC printed as "La lettre commune de MM. Kohl et Mitterrand," *Le Monde,* 9–10 December 1990.

29. See the "Treaty on Political Union, Final draft by the Dutch Presidency as modified by the Maastricht summit," *Europe Documents,* no. 1750–1751, 13 December 1991, p. 19.

30. Ibid.

31. In fact, the original joint corps proposal was no more than a footnote appended to a Kohl–Mitterrand proposal on political union. See the text of the proposal as "MM. Mitterrand et Kohl proposent de renforcer les responsabilités européennes en matière de défense," in *Le Monde,* 17 October 1991, pp. 1, 4–5.

32. On the initial proposal, see David Buchan, "Europeans called to join ranks," *Financial Times,* 17 October 1991. For the press release following the La Rochelle summit, see "Summit of the Franco–German Defense and Security Council on 22 May 1992 in La Rochelle," text provided by Embassy of the Federal Republic of Germany, Washington, D.C.

33. See Henri de Bresson and Claire Tréan, "Paris et Bonn protestent de leur fidélité à l'OTAN," *Le Monde,* 22 May 1992, pp. 1, 6.

34. On the obstacles in Germany to a full German participation in the corps' stated missions, see the insightful editorial by the head of the foreign desk of the *Frankfurter Allgemeine Zeitung*, Günter Nonnenmacher, "Ambiguïtés franco–allemandes," *Le Monde*, 23 June 1992, p. 10. For background on the constitutional issue, see Karl–Heinz Kamp, "Die Debatte um den Einsatz deutscher Streitkräfte außerhalb des Bündnisgebietes," Interne Studie no. 22/1991, Forschungsinstitut der Konrad–Adenauer–Stiftung (March 1991).

35. For the German argument, see German Defense Minster Volker Rühe cited in Pierre Servent, "Pour M. Joxe et M. Rühe, les Européens doivent assumer leurs responsabilités en matière de sécurité," *Le Monde*, 5 June 1992, p. 4.

36. The French willingness to consider whether it was "possible to conceive of a European nuclear doctrine," was first broached by President Mitterrand on 10 January 1992 and was followed up by a series of other official statements to that effect over the following months. Discussions of a European nuclear doctrine based on the *force de frappe* have remained limited, however, and even as 1992 ended little progress has been made. For a discussion of recent French ideas on the subject, see Philip H. Gordon, *French Security Policy after the Cold War: Continuity, Change and Implications for the United States*, R–4229 (Santa Monica: RAND, forthcoming), pp. 26–27.

37. The statement on European autonomy is from the press release of the La Rochelle summit, "Summit of the Franco–German Defense and Security Council," pp. 1–2.

38. For economic and population figures, see OECD, *Main Economic Indicators* (Paris: OECD, April 1992), p. 174; and *European Economy*, no. 50 (December 1991), p. 40.

39. See Giscard quoted in *Le Figaro*, 30 July 1990.

40. On the French reluctance to support some of NATO's recent policies, see Gordon, *French Security Policy*, pp. 9–20.

Chapter 8

U.S. Policy toward
Franco–German Cooperation

Julius W. Friend

It is not entirely clear whether the United States has ever had a clearly articulated policy toward Franco–German cooperation, despite some general statements. This cooperation is in any case not a unitary concept susceptible to a single policy attitude. Once the cooperation of the Franco–German couple was largely economic, usually operating in the framework of the European Community. Since 1984, however, it has increasingly concerned security questions. Ratification of the European Single Act in 1986 also gave a new dimension to the Community's older economic aspect, arousing American fears of a Fortress Europe excluding the U.S.

This discussion must therefore, at the risk of some duplication, discuss U.S. policy attitudes toward the French–German couple in the older EC (since perceptions of the post–1992 EC were not immediately apprehended by U.S. officialdom), then toward the couple as major actors in the EC understood as "the Europe of 1992," and finally as proponents of the West European Union as a purely European defense organization.

Queried for a rapid description of U.S. policy toward the forms of Franco–German cooperation which began to take shape in 1983–1984, one former high official concerned with European affairs replied "benign neglect;" another and later occupant of the same post said the U.S. had welcomed Franco–German cooperation, but the details, especially concerning NATO, frequently made Washington nervous. These responses are of course not contradictory; both reveal a good deal about U.S. policy on this question.

Insofar as Franco–German cooperation did not affect what U.S. official-dom saw as U.S. policies or interests (as in the early or mid–1980s) it could be thought good and be regarded benignly. As soon as conflicts or potential conflicts were perceived, the U.S. reacted sharply. But most of these conflicts took place in multilateral frameworks, those of NATO affairs and the EC, where Germany is the key NATO ally and the Franco–German relation the linchpin of the EC. An examination of U.S. policy toward the Franco–German relation is thus necessarily a discussion of problems in European security questions and in multilateral economic–political relations.

American multilateral diplomacy has been principally directed toward NATO, and to a lesser extent to the EC, and even in these venues the U.S. has traditionally preferred bilateral diplomacy. When directed toward the Federal Republic, this diplomacy had much to do with Germany as the central theater for NATO forces, where France has been self–excluded since 1966. Arms–control questions affected France differently than they did the Federal Republic.

Patrick McCarthy remarks in chapter 1 of this book that the French–German alliance "is not primarily . . . against outside powers, but a way for one partner to control the other and for the other to control itself." To this I would add that the Germans recognize that they need a partner to play a major role in Europe without being overly suspected of trying to dominate. Fur-thermore, while the French do not see their alliance with Germany as precisely "against" the United States in any old–fashioned sense, since 1963 France has often used the link with Germany to try to create European resistance to American influence in the affairs of Europe. The U.S. has thus repeatedly had difficulty in maintaining its official policy of benevolent regard (or benign neglect) toward the Franco–German relationship. Given American suspicion of France's intentions in influencing Germany, the target of American displeasure or criticism has usually been France.

Where France has attempted to "control" Germany using European institutions, American officials have instead believed that the way to "con-trol" Germany is through the American–German bilateral relation, together with NATO. The U.S. thus could not but worry about too close and exclusive a relation between the two major West European nations. Whether these worries are well founded or justified is quite another question.

The period 1984–1992 is obviously broken by the caesura of 1989, when the revolutions in East Europe ended the Cold War and began a period which invalidates all previously existing formulations of international relations, almost immediately rendered still more confusing by the collapse of the Soviet Union in 1991. The "control" of now–united and sovereign Germany has an entirely different meaning in the new era, and the relevance of NATO is far less clear. Germany's need for France in their EC relations, however, gives France a certain leverage not shared by the U.S. one that is not easily subject to U.S. pressure tactics.

FRANCO–GERMAN MILITARY LINKS, NATO, AND THE UNITED STATES

The Franco–German military cooperation that began in 1982–1984 renewed an idea that had disappeared from an earlier Franco–German agenda almost as soon as it was announced, because of American objections. The 1963 Franco–German friendship treaty as first drafted stipulated that the two governments would consult together on all important questions of foreign policy prior to any decision—including those concerning the European Community, East–West relations, NATO, and other international organizations. Soon after Konrad Adenauer returned from Paris, where he had signed the treaty, he was visited by U.S. Ambassador Walter Dowling, bearing a warning message from President Kennedy. U.S. popular and congressional sentiment, wrote the president, might think that U.S. presence in Europe was no longer desired either by France or Germany. Nor was Washington sure what was meant by German–French cooperation in defense. When Adenauer assured the ambassador that Bonn held fast to NATO, Dowling suggested that the Bundestag might add a resolution to the treaty on NATO. Presumably American diplomatic efforts did not stop with this visit to the chancellor. In ratifying the treaty, the Bundestag attached a preamble stating that it was intended "to further common defense within NATO and integration of the member countries' armed forces." For de Gaulle, this "unilateral preamble . . . changed the whole meaning [of the treaty]."[1]

After de Gaulle took France out of the NATO integrated command, Franco–German military cooperation was almost a dead issue. François Mitterrand and Helmut Schmidt, however, agreed in February 1982 to pursue deeper consultations on security matters (following up on earlier and abortive plans roughed out by Schmidt and Giscard). In October 1982, soon after becoming chancellor, Helmut Kohl went to Paris to inform himself on the arrangements made by Mitterrand and Schmidt, and a Franco–German Commission for Security and Defense was organized to promote cooperation.[2]

Bilateral cooperation still had to yield to the priorities of NATO integration. An Independent European Program Group was created to obviate the fact that France was not in the Eurogroup and to work more closely within NATO.[3] Ministers of defense and foreign affairs now met in conference before the convening of the statutory governmental summits, and military officials from these ministries met in working groups on weapons cooperation, military cooperation, and political–strategic affairs.

In the period immediately before and after the difficult German decision to station Pershing rockets and cruise missiles in the Federal Republic, French influence on German security policy and closer French cooperation with NATO was entirely welcome in Washington. The high point of this policy came with Mitterrand's famous visit to Bonn in January 1983, where he comforted the new conservative majority and enraged the SPD by urging the Germans to accept American missiles. When Mitterrand visited Washington in late March 1984 he was given the warmest of receptions and was thanked by President Reagan for his "courage and decisiveness." On 28 February 1984, however, just prior to a Kohl visit to Washington, the *Washington Post* reported that Kohl intended to convince Reagan that plans for joint military projects with France did not decrease Germany's need for cooperation with the U.S.

Franco–German relations continued to show progress. Although Kohl angled in vain for an invitation to the ceremonies marking the fortieth anniversary of the Normandy landings (he argued that Germany too had been liberated), Mitterrand applied balm by organizing a commemorative joint pilgrimage to the World War I slaughterhouse of Verdun, where a famous photo shows a diminutive Mitterrand and a giant Kohl standing in meditation, hand in hand. Joint exercises of French and West German forces were scheduled: in June 1985 *Alliance,* a small–scale bilateral exercise, involved 3,100 German and 1,500 French troops from armored divisions, and in September 1986 *Fränkischer Schild* was a corps–level exercise with the French First Armored Division. It was presented as a bilateral exercise, outside NATO, but actually saw the presence of a large U.S. contingent alongside German and Belgian troops.

Kecker Spatz in 1987 was a German exercise involving territorial troops not assigned to NATO, with major French participation. At France's request, NATO commander General Galvin and the German general who headed the NATO military committee were not invited. In June 1987 Kohl suggested establishment of a joint French–German brigade, using German territorial troops and French troops. The idea was rapidly welcomed by Mitterrand as a possible "embryo of a European defense structure." The brigade of 4,000 soldiers was finally constituted in October 1990.

As long as the imperatives of NATO defense against a seemingly solid Warsaw Pact prevailed, Washington could see French attempts to work more closely with the Germans as ancillary to the NATO effort. The collapse of the Soviet system in East Europe and of the Warsaw Pact changed all that. Questions on the future of NATO were immediately raised, not least by the French. The candidate for an all–European defense organization was clearly the West European Union (WEU).

Subject to lengthy fits of sleeping sickness since its founding in 1948, the WEU was revived in 1984 on French initiative despite reservations on the part of Britain and the Netherlands, which feared a weakening of NATO. Foreign and defense ministers of seven countries laid plans for the enhancement of a "European identity" in arms control, disarmament efforts, and weapons procurement policy.

In October 1987 the WEU adopted a platform pledging closer cooperation on security matters, while carefully emphasizing the importance of cooperation with the U.S. under NATO. One important passage of the declaration read, "We are convinced that the construction of an integrated Europe will remain incomplete as long as it does not include security and defense. We see the revitalization of the WEU as an important contribution [to that end]."[4]

STRATEGIC DEFENSE INITIATIVE (SDI)

Ronald Reagan's March 1983 proposal of a satellite–borne laser defense against incoming rockets, a sort of celestial umbrella promptly dubbed "Star Wars" by its opponents, became the occasion of new French and German problems with Washington, which each handled differently. SDI disturbed the French, whose strategic doctrine rested on the premise of a small but invulnerable nuclear submarine force that could if necessary hurl missiles at Soviet cities. They reasoned that if the Americans developed such defenses, so would the Soviets.

The Germans, who took no official stand on Reagan's idea for nearly a year after its first announcement, shared this fear of encouraging Soviet missile defenses, which would then make European conventional or even limited nuclear war conceivable. When Defense Secretary Weinberger first presented the scheme officially to the April 1984 Nuclear Planning Group, the German attitude was rather skeptical. Defense Minister Manfred Woerner did hedge his opinion, however, noting that the Federal Republic had no objection to laser research. France, on the other hand, opposed the idea, and instead promoted an EC initiative on high–tech research called EUREKA— which was however not presented as the European alternative to SDI. In December 1985 the German government finally decided to let German firms participate in SDI program research. Once again the German need not to get too distant from the United States had proved a decisive factor.

The October 1987 Reagan–Gorbachev summit in Reykjavik, where the president came close to bargaining away U.S. strategic missiles—but stopped because of disagreements on SDI—could not but unite the Europeans, who were "vastly disturbed to discover that such revolutionary changes in the Western security system affecting Europe could be proposed and negotiated without prior consultation. But they were perhaps even more disturbed by the sudden realization that the American negotiators apparently proceeded at Reykjavik without the slightest understanding of the basis of the system of Western security."[5]

The Kohl–Mitterrand summit on 27 October 1987, supposedly concerning cultural affairs, turned into a discussion on Reykjavik. Kohl told a news conference, "European security must not be decoupled from the security of the United States and . . . it must not be possible in the future to conduct wars in Europe." Mitterrand agreed with Kohl's remarks.[6] Richard Smyser writes:

> For the Germans, Reykjavik meant that an American president had come perilously close to giving up the nuclear deterrent that defended West Germany and Berlin, leaving the Soviet Union militarily superior with its conventional forces on the European central front. . . . After Reykjavik, Bonn and Paris turned to each other (and, to a lesser degree, toward London as well). Paradoxically, Bonn turned to Paris because it wanted to have a connection that would be less susceptible than Washington to Gorbachev's diplomatic charm, a suspicion that Paris felt toward Bonn. Both watched each other, even as they watched the superpowers. Consultations intensified, as did high–level visits. Franco–German discussions ranged into much broader areas of security cooperation than ever before, and those discussions were conducted at a higher level with both Mitterrand and Kohl personally and intensely involved.[7]

Discriminate Defense, a January 1988 report by a commission co–chaired by U.S. Under Secretary of Defense for policy Fred Iklé, was interpreted as suggesting that Western Europe was no longer uniquely relevant to U.S. security. "Some Germans saw in it, as they had in SDI, Washington's determination to avoid risk–sharing." German State Secretary for Defense Lothar Ruehl warned that the report "left Europe no choice but 'to take more responsibility for its defense with its own forces.'" As Smyser sees it:

> As the 1980s drew to a close, German officials and defense analysts came gradually to the conclusion that the role of extended deterrence in U.S. strategic

policy had become increasingly fuzzy, not because the United States seemed to be walking away from its commitments but because those commitments were not at the forefront of American senior–level thinking.[8]

As noted above, Reykjavik had evoked the same reactions in Paris as in Bonn. France by mid–decade had already recovered from the fear of "German drift," and was beginning to see in SDI the threat of American decoupling from Europe. Dominique Moisi wrote in 1988: "Reykjavik and its after–shocks revived in France an old and rather negative image of the United States. The Iran–Contra scandal only confirmed French apprehensions. Not only were the Americans unpredictable and adventuristic, their diplomacy was unreliable and probably incompetent."[9] The United States, which at the beginning of the decade had incurred German suspicions that it was dangerously and mindlessly anti–Soviet, was now alternately suspected by both the French and Germans of cooperating with the Soviets to their detriment and of having no clear policies.

American disposition to rethinking, plus the new policies of Mikhail Gorbachev, encouraged the Germans to hesitate at the U.S. proposal to "modernize" short–range nuclear weapons, now that intermediate–range ones had been forbidden. Mitterrand's disposition to back the Germans on this, while pursuing the French short–range Hadès program, might have led to more tension between Paris and Washington. However, the new Bush administration was reconsidering the value of a weapon its German ally so much disliked. At the Brussels NATO meeting of 29–30 May 1989, the modernization question was downplayed by being put off until 1992 (and dropped at the July NATO meeting in 1990).

When Bush met the chancellor in Mainz in May after the 1989 NATO meeting, he extended an invitation to West Germany to "join a partnership in leadership," which was widely interpreted as meaning a recognition of the Federal Republic as the U.S.'s most significant ally. The notion, whether seriously meant or not, caused more disquiet in Britain than in France, already excluded and self–excluded from this role. In any event, its portent was substantially affected by events later in the year. The process of German unification that began with the opening of the Berlin Wall in November 1989 ended with unification and Soviet agreement that the new Germany might remain in NATO. This was certainly a victory for American policy, which had worked hard for this result—even while France and Britain showed an initial lack of enthusiasm for unification.

The new dispensation removed the constraints on Germany on which France had based much of its German policy. France had feared a "new

Rapallo"—a German diplomatic temptation to work closely with the Soviet Union, and distrusted the tendency of German public opinion to Gorby-mania. But France had thought it had political advantages a divided Germany did not possess; now it feared the possible ambitions of a united Germany. The U.S., despite State Department suspicions of Hans–Dietrich Genscher and worries about continued German adherence to NATO, had been less fearful, largely confident that German need for security would, as always, keep the Federal Republic in the American camp.

Elizabeth Pond, one of the best observers of the contemporary German scene, argues that the United States was not disturbed by the prospect of German unification because Europe had already agreed on a single market by 1992 and, implicitly, on political unification thereafter, while Gorbachev had decided to cut radically his half–million troops in Eastern Europe. Also, President Bush had already fixed on a strongly pro–European and pro–German stance at the NATO summit in May 1989.[10]

Pond concluded that the United States might otherwise have feared that Moscow might play the "German card" and offer unity in return for neutrality. Instead, the U.S. stuck with the decision made six months earlier to give Bonn the status of the U.S.'s senior partner "and welcome Western European integration fully, without the reservations of previous American administrations."

The American stance during the unification process was far more confident than the French one, but unification also removed German constraints upon which the U.S. had depended. As the East bloc and the Warsaw Pact melted away, Germany's need for security against a weakened Soviet Union with no military frontier facing its territory became less imperative, and the NATO scenario of instant response to counteract (hence to forestall) a Soviet attack became more questionable. Less than two years later, when the Soviet Union itself had ceased to be, the value and the future of NATO were much in question. But the instability in the countries of the former Soviet Union, and the presence of several hundred thousand FSU troops in the Eastern German Länder, diminishing until a final departure set for 1994, reinforced caution. An alliance was still desirable.

Still, what sort of alliance, against what enemy, under what circumstances? The United States's presence in Europe had been indispensable to the old Federal Republic because only the U.S. disposed of sufficient atomic force to make Soviet attack or Soviet armed blackmail too risky. (Not that American nuclear might did not make Germans nervous as well.) If the nuclear threat to Germany and Western Europe had diminished (and indeed existed only in the scenario of a Fascist and aggressive involution in Russian policy) then German policy need not see the American tie as vital—though perhaps desirable.

The French, who had long accepted the value of the American guarantee of West Germany as an implicit part of their own solo performance, rapidly recognized the strategic implications of the new situation. Franco–German military cooperation could now be more than a means to keep Germany bound to France and proof against temptations—it could become the foundation stone of Western security. In this new world, as Paris saw it, the United States would, because of its own interior dynamics, play a reduced role in European affairs. French policy has of course expected such a turn in American policy at least since de Gaulle's time; in its old form this idea was the "Will the U.S. sacrifice Chicago to protect Hamburg?" thesis.

Suddenly it became apparent to Washington that although it counted on German goodwill (goodwill among nations being, however, a notoriously perishable commodity), NATO was its principal institutional link to Europe and one almost certain to be weakened. Voices were soon heard in Washington proclaiming that NATO had to be given a broader meaning—it must become more political, and have more economic meaning. Secretary of State Baker's speech in Berlin on 12 December 1989, linking NATO, the EC, and CSCE as elements of a three–track role for the U.S. in European affairs, expressed such thinking. On closer inspection, these ideas turned out to be less than convincing, even to Americans. Western Europe was moving closer to economic union. If it needed to spell out its relation with the U.S., what did this have to do with NATO?

Washington also began to take an increased interest in CSCE, an institution long discounted, but where the U.S. presence as a kind of "honorary European power" was recognized. Yet CSCE has no strong institutions, something like a *liberum veto,* and by 1991 had swelled to more than 50 members.

Before the July 1990 breakthrough Kohl achieved with Mikhail Gorbachev, winning Soviet agreement to united Germany's remaining in NATO, American foreign policy was not entirely confident that Germany would not accept its departure from NATO as a price for unification if the Soviets insisted. At the Bush–Mitterrand summit in Key Largo, Florida, on 20 April 1990, Bush therefore made a pitch for French return to the NATO integrated command and acceptance of U.S. missiles on French territory. There had earlier been discussion of a French general becoming SACEUR, and French officials had been hinting that American flexibility might bring about new departures, including in NATO.

Whether because Bush did not make the SACEUR offer or because Mitterrand, now at least as Gaullist as de Gaulle, could not accept an idea which may have seemed to him a refurbishing of old concepts, the meeting failed, and the relationship between the two men cooled considerably.[11]

Soviet acceptance of united Germany's membership in NATO made European security questions less urgent. In August 1990, with Iraq's invasion of Kuwait, security problems shifted to the Middle East. In the ensuing hostilities, logistic and planning capabilities produced by NATO were immensely valuable, while the WEU provided plausible cover for European countries that wished to participate in the naval effort against Iraq under a European umbrella.

After initial hesitation and a show of unilateral diplomacy in the Persian Gulf crisis, France put troops under American command. For a brief time, there were better relations between Paris and Washington than Washington and Bonn; the Americans looked askance at German unwillingness to get too deeply involved in a non–European adventure. But some French officials emerged from the conflict both resentful of what they saw as insufficient communication and consultation on the part of the dominant Americans, as well as a newly heightened appreciation of real–time satellite intelligence uses in a combat situation.

Defense Minister Pierre Joxe told the National Assembly: "Without intelligence from the Allies, that is to say the Americans, we were almost blind. To leave our systems in their present state of insufficiency and dependence would be to weaken considerably our present and future defense efforts." This theme was repeated in the press and by the RPR leader Edouard Balladur (a likely future prime minister): not France but Europe needs its own observation satellites "in order to avoid [a situation in which] European countries are blind if they do not benefit from information supplied by the Americans."[12] The French push for a European intelligence satellite capability has been met to some extent by Italian and Spanish agreements to fund the Hélios intelligence satellite, but the very expensive system required to place and maintain a number of satellites in orbit, coordinate their use, and interpret and distribute the take has so far not encountered much enthusiasm from the Germans, whose financial cooperation would ultimately be necessary.

The Gulf War once over, the question of the future of NATO emerged again. NATO had shown its usefulness as a logistical base, but politically it had not and could not have been used against Iraq. The "out–of–area" problem continued to limit NATO usefulness in any likely scenario for the near future. In the meantime, the EC nations, with France and Germany leading, had proceeded with plans to create a more articulated Europe. The Kohl–Mitterrand joint letter of 6 December 1990 on common French–German positions for European Political Union, developed in considerably greater detail the principles they had espoused in their April 1990 summit meeting.

The two leaders declared that "foreign policy will have a vocation to extend to all areas," to include a real common security policy and eventually a common defense. They further suggested that the European Political Union establish a "clear organic relation with the WEU." In time the WEU could become part of the political union and work out its common security policy. This language seemed to challenge U.S. views on the future of NATO, although another phrase added "the Atlantic alliance will be reinforced by the increase in the role and responsibilities of the Europeans."[13]

On 4 February 1991, Foreign Ministers Dumas and Genscher announced a plan for the development of this organic relation of WEU to the EC, which might come to fruition by 1996. The foreign and defense ministers of the nine–nation WEU, meeting on 22 February, endorsed the idea of making the WEU the central vehicle for a future defense policy plan, with reservations by the Dutch and, to a somewhat lesser extent, the British. The report, which became a contribution to the EPU negotiations, stressed the urgency of reappraising NATO structures. The French and Germans proposed a close tie to the EC, while the Dutch, in particular, were unhappy at the idea that EC summits should have the power to issue guidelines to the WEU.

The U.S. government was sufficiently displeased to send two senior diplomats to Europe with a message (the so–called Dobbins–Bartholemew letter) strongly against the concept of changing NATO structures or allowing the WEU to take instructions from the European Council. This official reaction stemmed from an instinctive fear in Washington that European desires to set up a European defense organization, whether or not they professed to believe so, constitute a zero–sum game which could only end by weakening NATO. It followed that vigorous diplomatic action was necessary to make this American unhappiness entirely clear. The message was not well received, but its importance was noted.[14]

On 20 May, during a visit to the U.S., Kohl issued a placatory statement, saying that despite moves to strengthen West European defense NATO remained the cornerstone of the Western alliance. The NATO meeting of late May 1991 saw the organization of a NATO rapid reaction force, which Mitterrand countered on 30 May with a waspish statement rejecting any idea of France joining it, and expressed reservations on NATO restructuring. "NATO is not the whole of the Atlantic Alliance, and not all questions can be settled at that level."

In early October 1991 the French were expressing their irritation at the American and German proposal that most of the states of Eastern Europe be brought into a NATO Coordinating Council (NACC), which was intended to give former East bloc states some sort of tenuous relation with NATO. *Le Monde* wrote bitterly: "Mr. Genscher, who will make pledges Friday to Mr. Dumas in Paris, did the same last week in Washington with Mr. Baker to play a dirty trick on France. He and the secretary of state launched a project intended to reinforce NATO relations with the East. France, hostile to this project in which it sees the means for the United States to maintain its influence in European affairs, is once again alone in a bad posture."[15]

In their meeting of 16–17 October 1991, Kohl and Mitterrand announced plans for establishing a 30,000–strong Franco–German corps, designed to be expanded later to a Euro–corps—but not with U.S. participation. They reiterated the idea that the WEU should become the basis of a common European security and defense policy. *Le Monde* reported that Paris and Bonn had taken the precaution of informing the White House in advance, explaining that it was not an attempt to rob NATO of its content. The newspaper added that Paris was not optimistic about the U.S. reaction, since the State Department and Secretary Baker in particular were suspected of trying "systematically to torpedo any European defense project." Quoting an unnamed French official, it wrote: "As long as the question of European defense was theoretical, the Americans were in favor of it. Now, when it is becoming a real possibility, they are against it."[16]

British Foreign Secretary Douglas Hurd immediately reacted, saying that it would be "useless and dangerous" to duplicate what NATO is already doing. But a French spokesman insisted that the new organization would not rival but complement NATO, while a German spokesman in Bonn explained that the creation of a European army was a "long–term proposal," recalling that the U.S. had frequently urged its European partners to assume greater responsibility for their own defense. Unnamed but presumably American military experts cited by the *New York Times* noted that Germany was moving closer to French ideas.[17]

Speaking at a Socialist party meeting in early September 1991, Foreign Minister Dumas evoked French fears of U.S. dominance, saying that the deterioration of the Soviet Union meant that "American might reigns without a balancing weight." Dumas and Delors told the meeting that the EC and the UN should seek to balance American power.[18]

At the Rome NATO summit in November 1991 President Bush, departing from his advance text, chose frontal confrontation to express U.S. fears of being edged out of Europe. "Our premise is that the American role in the defense and the affairs of Europe will not be made superfluous by European union. If our premise is wrong, if, my friends, your ultimate aim is to provide individually for your own defense, the time to tell us is today."[19] All ministers present hastily announced that no one intended to push the United States out of Europe, and Secretary of State Baker told reporters that the dispute was "a red herring." But the *New York Times* quoted an anonymous American official (elsewhere identified as National Security Council chief Brent Scrowcroft) who said "There's a concern on our part that they are considering going their own way without the U.S.," and referring to Chancellor Kohl, "We really don't know what he's up to, not yet."[20] The meeting issued a compromise statement: "The challenges . . . cannot be . . . addressed by one institution alone."

Certainly the French and Germans do not think in 1992 that the American role in the defense and affairs of Europe is now superfluous, nor that the troubled projects for greater European union will rapidly make it so. NATO still exists, and if the security problems it was designed to meet still exist, why replace it? If the problem has disappeared, why would an EC/WEU or the CSCE be better able to face it? As German editorialist Josef Joffe puts it:

> Why should 12 profoundly diverse nations, joined, above all, by the quest for economic gain, succeed where NATO is said to falter? How is [the WEU] to organize a common defense in the absence of a clear threat? Certainly, the in–house challenge of war in Yugoslavia has not proven strong enough to spawn EDC II. And, if the task is to balance the successor(s) of the Soviet Union, then NATO, by dint of previous performance and U.S. power, has a better claim to the future.[21]

The only raison d'être for what Joffe calls EDC II would be as a shadow organization existing for the contingency of the U.S. indeed pulling its forces out of Europe. American official objections to it are certainly nourished by apprehension that if the Europeans were perceived in Congress as asking the Americans to leave, that perception would combine all too easily with the feeling that the U.S. does not need to spend money it does not have to defend a Europe which is not now threatened and is quite rich enough to defend itself.

FRANCE, GERMANY, AND AMERICA: THE ECONOMIC REALM

The institutional security link to Europe, now in question, is paralleled by the non-institutional, but very important, economic link. Once the European Single Act of 1986 acquired momentum, an America that had looked with some indifference at the Eurostagnation of the early 1980s began to fret about the possibility of a Fortress Europe that would exclude American business and services. But as with "security Europe," the European Community as an economic entity centers on the Franco–German couple, as not only its political but also its economic motor. For example, 43.8 percent of the foreign trade of the twelve EC nations in 1990 came from exports by France and Germany. American attention has always been directed, therefore, at the French and German role in negotiations with the EC—and in EC dealings in the GATT, with these two nations as well.

While the State Department had closely followed the possible implications for U.S. business of the Single Act, official public statements were slow in coming. In a speech of 4 August 1988, then–Deputy Treasury Secretary M. Peter McPherson accused the EC bureaucracy of having already drafted directives for 1992 that would deny U.S. banks equal treatment. McPherson said, "The creation of a single market that reserves 'Europe for the Europeans,' would be bad for Europe, bad for the U.S., and bad for the multilateral economic system." The Reagan administration had called press attention to the speech in advance as an important policy statement.[22]

There had, of course, also been particular quarrels between the U.S. and the EC on matters affecting American interests, such as the threat to ban American meat products injected with hormones or the "pasta war." The first of these reflected German and Italian fears; the second concerned the Italians; others affected the French. But these were essentially sectoral quarrels. Fear of Fortress Europe, on the other hand, often came down to fear of schemes urged by one or another of the leading EC countries, i.e., France or Germany. From 1987 on, the cockpit for larger struggles was the Uruguay round of General Agreement on Tariffs and Trade (GATT) negotiations.

These negotiations have continually run into difficulty on the issue of EC agricultural subsidies, where both Germany and France have interests in a solution not too distant from the status quo, but where the U.S. has always seen France as the main stumbling block, and Germany as the somewhat erring ally that can presumably be "brought around" to see reason and then influence the French—a technique the French refer to as "trying to drive a wedge between us."

President Bush extracted promises from Chancellor Kohl that he would intervene with the French to solve the GATT problem, most notably at the Houston G–7 meeting in 1990. The problem persisted, and in May 1992 the Germans did press successfully for changes in the subsidy method. The U.S. did not, however, think that the export subsidy cutback was sufficient, and the problem continued. A recent study on German–American relations puts the situation thus: "The Germans say that they genuinely want to solve the trade problem but their hands are tied. They complain that the Americans appear to believe that Germany must be the American stalking horse in the Community, a task the Germans say they can not and will not undertake."[23]

In late 1992 a much–weakened Mitterrand administration that feared a farmers' revolt was still having great difficulties in making the kind of concessions on agricultural supports demanded by the U.S., thereby threatening the future of the GATT negotiations themselves. And France continued to fear U.S. wedge tactics coming from pressure on Kohl, as spokespeople blamed the Americans for the GATT problems.

GATT has seen some of the most severe U.S.–French–German tensions. On EC matters, Reagan–era policies toward the EC, which one author refers to as on a "war footing," gave way under the Bush administration to a more conciliatory policy. In May 1989 Assistant Secretary of State for Economic and Business Affairs Eugene McAllister said, "The U.S. unequivocally supports [EC] economic integration . . . and we see the [EC 1992] plan as good for the United States and the world." Commerce Secretary Robert Mosbacher, however, declared in 1989 that the U.S. should "have a seat at the table when the EC sets standards on products and other areas."[24] The State Department has consistently worried about such language, without disagreeing with its content. Officials there remember very well the European reaction to Henry Kissinger's patronizing notions in 1973 of the Year of Europe.

In his Berlin speech on 12 December 1989, Baker nevertheless suggested a three–track role for the U.S. in NATO, the EC, and the CSCE. "We propose that the U.S. and the EC work together to achieve, whether in treaty or some other form, a significantly strengthened set of institutional and consultative links." The reaction was mixed. EC Commissioner Karel van Miert, a Belgian, said, "I don't believe in such formal arrangements with rigid procedures. This could imply co-decision and . . . lead to obsessive patronizing. The seat–at–the–table formula is not a good idea."[25]

Jacques Delors told the European Parliament: "There is something ambiguous about linking the transatlantic partnership with European integration as Mr. Baker did. Some member–states might interpret it as a deliberate attempt to interfere in our affairs, something which would be unacceptable between two equal partners. . . ."[26] Delors went on, however, to rejoice at the emergence of new attitudes which would sweep away the quarrels of the past such as the one on hormones.

An unnamed U.S. official cited by the *Economist* remarked: "European leaders, especially the French, should cease to have an inferiority complex and stop fearing that if America takes part [in EC affairs] it will dominate proceedings and try to slow European integration."[27] European leaders, not least the French, feared exactly that. They might have cited as evidence of U.S. thinking remarks such as those made in August 1989 by Deputy Secretary of State Lawrence Eagleberger:

> Regardless of how big the EC gets, or what issues European governments devolve to common decision–making, the need for a strong American voice in Western affairs will not be diminished. The EC is and will remain a group of separate and sovereign states deeply attached to the transatlantic community, each of which values and counts on the United States to help craft the Western agenda.[28]

Eagleberger's statement is hard to refute—but the tone of his remarks was still reminiscent of his mentor Henry Kissinger and his "Year of Europe."

The development of American official thinking on institutional relations with Europe in the following months is reflected in a speech in September 1990 by Baker aide Robert Zoellick, architect of a rethinking of U.S. policy on the EC, who expressed the hopes of the Bush administration for the emergence of an international Europe "cognizant of its capabilities and responsibilities," progressing toward political integration in foreign and security policy. Commenting on these remarks, the *Financial Times* wrote: "Previous American uncertainties about whether a stronger Community was really in the American interest have been set aside and Washington is hoping that a framework agreement will be signed in November affirming common values. . . ."[29]

The Europeans, all of them, continued to reject the idea of an American seat at the EC table, but as a senior U.S. diplomat, wise in the ways of both Washington and Brussels puts it, Mosbacher made a mistake in demanding a 13th seat, because "we are an unacknowledged member, which means we couldn't be acknowledged, since others, especially the Japanese, would want in too."

Even before the revolutions in Eastern Europe, the consultative links between the U.S. and the EC that evolved in the 1980s were too infrequent and unstructured to be useful in relations with the Europe of 1992. U.S. recognition of this fact urged a rethinking of the relation.[30] If there was to be no 13th seat and no formal treaty, there could at least be a declaration of purpose. On 6 April 1990, German Foreign Minister Genscher, speaking to American newspaper editors in Washington, stated that a new and long–term political perspective was needed for U.S. and Canadian relations with the EC. He called on the North American democracies and the EC members to "issue a joint declaration encompassing all the political, economic, techno-logical, and cultural aspects of our relationship. . . ."[31]

Subsequent discussions on a draft declaration during 1990 concerned the number and level of joint meetings, whether there was to be binding language on ecological questions, and monetary cooperation (dropped at American urging, since the Treasury prefers to deal on such matters in the G–7). A final draft of the declaration was not quite ready when Jacques Delors and Italian Prime Minister Giulio Andreotti, heading the Italian presidency of the Commission, came to Washington in mid–November for a presidential consultation, henceforth biannual.

It was decided that the declaration should be signed at a special ceremony coinciding with the November CSCE summit in Paris. But President Mitterrand then refused to sign the document, objecting to a clause specifying the number of meetings and consultations between the U.S. and the EC through the European Political Cooperation working groups, which would, the French feared, give the U.S. too much influence. When agreement was finally reached, there was no time for a formal signing, and the document was anticlimactically announced, on 23 November 1990, to little accompanying publicity.[32]

The declaration reaffirms and celebrates bilateral cooperation between the U.S. and the EC. Its novelty lies in listing biannual consultations to be held between the president of the United States and the presidents of the EC Council and the EC Commission; between EC foreign ministers and the American secretary of state; ad hoc consultations between the EC presidency's foreign minister or the troika (the past, present, and succeeding presidencies) and the secretary of state; and biannual meetings between the European Commission and U.S. cabinet–level government.

French objections struck out specifications for regular meetings between the State Department and EPC working groups, which in fact take place regularly. In the past, however, biannual meetings of this last type, between political directors of the troika countries and their State Department counterparts were "very casually prepared and . . . usually little more than a superficial diplomatic chat about current issues."[33] In 30 years of regularly scheduled bilateral consultations at top, high, and middle levels between the French and German governments, the French have learned the usefulness of coordinating in this way. Their objection to specified EPC consultations, therefore, was not just pro forma, but rather reflected their abiding distrust of what they see as nearly irresistible hegemonic inclinations on the part of the Americans. Tensions in Franco–American relations grew worse in 1992. Disagreements persisted on GATT negotiations and on plans for a French–German corps. A bilateral summit between Bush and Mitterrand, like those on Key Largo in 1990 and Martinique in 1991, was dropped because it seemed only likely to exacerbate relations, while the relation between Foreign Minister Dumas and Secretary of State Baker degenerated badly, to the point that Baker reportedly asked his French counterpart: "Are you for us or against us?"[34]

At the same time, the U.S. began to have increasing doubts about its "partnership" with united Germany. German reticence in the Persian Gulf War could be explained by the sudden strains of impending unification, with its accompanying problems, though Washington was hardly pleased. German unwillingness to pressure the French on GATT was a further problem. Increased cooperation with France on defense matters, in the shape of the planned 35,000–strong Franco–German corps, suggested that the Germans were tilting too far toward French ideas. The *Washington Post* quoted a senior French official as saying: "The Germans share every one of our concerns toward the Americans, only we have the courage to tell them."[35] (The French have, to be sure, been saying this about other Europeans since de Gaulle's time, which does not mean that they are necessarily wrong.)

German–American relations continue to be a great deal smoother than Franco–American ones. But there is little reason for the confidence which obtained in Washington in 1989 that the German partner would necessarily support U.S. European and global interests. Much depends on the military situation in Europe in 1994 and the years after, when Soviet troops are no longer in eastern Germany—but Russian behavior may not necessarily be confidence–building.

CONCLUSION

In 1992 it is easier than ever before to see that Europe, as a political–economic and security expression, exists only insofar as France and Germany are closely associated. In security affairs, this Europe could not have existed before 1989–1990 because the American guarantee was absolutely necessary to West European security, France stood aside from NATO, and Germany could have no nuclear force. In the South Slav crisis of 1991–1992, with the U.S. standing aside, the cry that "Europe" could not cope with the crisis in ex–Yugoslavia was reducible to the statement "France and Germany could not combine to cope." The Germans furthered the emergence of new South Slav states, but were constitutionally unable to take or even envisage military measures to cope with the ensuing problems. Whether or not the French were willing to act—the indications are mixed—they could not act alone.

Security Europe was conceived as a development of the Western European Union, and as a possible and eventual replacement for NATO. Political–economic Europe was designed by the Maastricht Treaty. In all these cases, Franco–German accord was the necessary precondition, and its absence the premise for failure.

American policy has not, however, historically viewed the French–German relation in this strong light, in part because, as noted above, the relation has only emerged as a central one since the mid–1980s, with the U.S. slow to see that in its emerging new form Franco–German cooperation has become crucial to the existence of a Europe that is more than a geographical expression.

An American objection to acquiescence in Franco–German plans, never admitted by official America, is continuously voiced by the French: that American leaders have comfortably adjusted to a hegemonic role in the affairs of Europe based on the Cold War, and are extraordinarily reluctant to give it up now that the Cold War is over.

In late 1992, after presidential elections, future American policy toward a Europe making slow and contradictory progress toward union was still uncertain, nor was it clear how the Clinton administration would handle the interaction of U.S., French, and German interests. The president–elect's declarations on a probable limit of 100,000 U.S. troops in Europe did not jibe with French assertions that U.S. troops would soon pull out of Europe, but at least suggested that the U.S. might in future not be able (or even want) to keep its former position in NATO or a post–NATO organization, with an American officer as its supreme commander. Some scenarios, perhaps drawing on hints thrown out by senior members of the conservative French opposition, prefigure France's return to a North Atlantic military force with a French general in command. Other scenarios, however, suppose that the U.S. Congress would not long support major expenses for an organization of this description.

The United States, for military, economic, cultural, and political reasons, would like to play a major role in the affairs of Europe. The Europeans, even the French, have no desire to see the U.S. withdraw now, but the French appear more convinced than ever that the historically inevitable American withdrawal predicted by de Gaulle has now met the circumstances that will bring it about. The corollary of this belief, however, in the 1960s as today, is that France can best assert future leadership by anticipating future history—even at the risk of repelling the U.S. by prophesies that could be self–fulfilling. Whether Germany—demographically and economically more than one–half of the Franco–German couple—will continue to play the role of cooperative French and European partner, is another matter.

Ultimately, the justification for a future U.S. role in Europe is not NATO alone, but the fact that leadership in Europe has been accorded more easily to a non–European power than it could to any single European country, or even any two countries. The question is whether this leadership is seen as cooperative or hegemonic. France clearly sees it as the latter, while Germany, which has in the past sometimes bowed to American desires and sometimes resisted them (especially on monetary questions) is still getting accustomed to its new role in Europe.

The waning of U.S. hegemony, which David Calleo concluded in 1987 was increasingly inviable, has been greatly accelerated by German unification, Soviet collapse, and American fiscal weakness. The U.S. could not now prevail in a head–to–head struggle with the Franco–German couple, if they stuck together. The question is whether the U.S. will consider the Franco–German alliance a threat to its European position and continue to "drive wedges" between the partners, or whether they will see the Franco–German couple as the chief building block of a European Union which, if it comes to fruition, would be a powerful force for economic (and military) security. "As its fundamental tenet, the hegemonic approach assumes that stable peace and prosperity in the world require a benevolent hegemonic power—a predominant state managing the world system in the general cosmopolitan interest."[36] U.S. policy attitudes have still not taken leave of this tenet, if constant remarks about the U.S. as the only superpower are to be taken seriously.

If the confused security situation in Eastern Europe and the Middle East does not take a severe turn for the worse in the remainder of the decade, the call for the U.S. as a federator of military forces may never come, while the importance of the European Community will grow despite current setbacks, and perhaps move toward European Union. In reassuring conditions such as these, any attempt by the U.S. to maintain what the French, at least, would describe as hegemony would be self–defeating. But the U.S. would be more likely to fulfill the old French prophecy and pull more and more out of European military affairs.

If the horizon should grow darker, particularly in the next few years, then U.S. military capabilities would be welcome—both to Germany and to France. The United States cannot insist to its allies that it is needed unless they agree. America, however, remains at least nominally free to conclude that it is not needed. No decision has been made, and tensions remain.

NOTES

1. On this incident, and de Gaulle's reaction to the Bundestag preamble, see Horst Osterheld *Ich gehe nicht leichten Herzens. Adenauer's letzte Kanzlerjahre, ein dokumentarischer Bericht* (Mainz: Matthias Grünewald Verlag, 1986), p. 201, and François Seydoux, *Dans l'intimité franco–allemande* (Paris: Editions Albatros, 1977), p. 18.

2. On the 1980 plans, see Hans–Peter Schwarz, *Eine Entente Elémentaire* (Bonn: Forschungsinstitut der Deutschen Gesellschaft für Auswärtige Politik, new edition, 1990), p. 97.

3. See W. R. Smyser, *Restive Partners: Washington and Bonn Diverge* (Boulder: Westview Press, 1990), p. 53.

4. *Facts on File World News Digest,* (New York/Oxford: Facts on File, 1987), p. 848.

5. James Schlesinger, "Reykjavik and Revelations: A Turn of the Tide?" *Foreign Affairs* 65, no. 3 (1987), p. 435.

6. *Facts on File* 1987, p. 803.

7. Smyser, *Restive Partners,* p. 59.

8. Ibid., pp. 62–64.

9. Dominique Moïsi, "French Foreign Policy: The Challenge of Adaptation," *Foreign Affairs* 67, no. 1 (1988), p. 155.

10. Elizabeth Pond, *After the Wall* (New York: Priority Press Publications, 1990), p. 26.

11. See Frank Costigliola, *France and the United States: the Cold Alliance since World War II* (New York: Twayne Publishers, 1992), pp. 228–229.

12. Quoted in Philip H. Gordon, "French Security Policy After the Cold War. Continuity, Change, and Implications for the United States," Rand Arroyo Center Report R–4229–A, 1992, pp. 40–41.

13. *European Affairs,* no. 4 (1990), p. 25.

14. Interview with former Assistant Secretary of State for European Affairs Rozanne Ridgway, December 1992. (Amb. Ridgway was no longer at the State Department in 1991. Her comments, however, reflect long experience of U.S. attitudes on this question.) Also see *The Economist,* 16 March 1991.

15. *Le Monde,* editorial, 10 October 1991.

16. *Le Monde,* 17 October 1991.

17. *The New York Times,* 17 October 1991.

18. *Facts on File,* 1991, p. 746.

19. *The New York Times,* 8 November 1991.

20. Ibid.

21. Josef Joffe, "Collective Security and the Future of Europe: Failed Dreams and Dead Ends," *Survival* 34, no. 1 (Spring 1992), p. 47.

22. *Facts on File,* 1988, p. 585.

23. W. R. Smyser, *"America and the New Germany,"* chapter 3, American Institute for Contemporary German Studies publication forthcoming in 1992. I would like to thank Mr. Smyser for allowing me to read and quote from the working draft.

24. Roy H. Ginsberg, "EC–U.S. Political/Institutional Relations," in Leon Hurwitz and Christian Lequesne (eds.) *The State of the European Community: Policies, Institutions, and Debates in the Transition Years* (Boulder: Lynne Riemer, 1991), pp. 392, 394.

25. Ginsberg, "Institutional Relations," p. 397.

26. Ibid.

27. Ibid., p. 398.

28. Cited in Gordon, "French Security Policy," p. 301.

29. John Wyles, "U.S. Reaches Out to Hesitant Europe," *Financial Times,* 26 September 1990.

30. This point is made in a useful study by Roy H. Ginsberg, "The United States and the Transatlantic Declaration," conducted for the Institut für Europäische Politik, Bonn, final draft, October, 1992. I am grateful to Prof. Ginsberg for sending me a copy of the final draft and allowing me to quote from it.

31. Speech to the American Society of Newspaper Editors, cited from Ginsberg, "Transatlantic Declaration," p. 10.

32. See Ginsberg, "Transatlantic Declaration," p. 11.

33. Jean de Ruyt, "European Political Cooperation: Toward a Unified European Foreign Policy," *Atlantic Council of the United States Occasional Paper,* October 1989, p. 34.

34. *The Washington Post,* 27 May 1992.

35. Ibid.

36. See David Calleo, *Beyond Hegemony: The Future of the Western Alliance* (New York: Basic Books, 1987), p. 130.

Conclusion:
France and Germany
in the New Europe

David Calleo

How durable is the Franco–German partnership? After three decades, it seems beyond a merely episodic converging of distinct national interests. Conventional wisdom now finds it almost unthinkable that France and Germany would ever again go to war with each other. Perhaps our historical experience is too short for such blind confidence, but a network of institutional structures does frame the bilateral relationship in a cooperative mode. Ministers and heads of government do meet regularly, along with numerous joint commissions of civil servants and private experts. And there are voluminous organized cultural and academic exchanges. Today, there is even a joint army corps in the making.

Beyond these bilateral ties is a common Franco–German project—the European Community—which puts the Franco–German relationship into a dense network of cooperative arrangements that enmeshes all Western Europe. Franco–German partnership has always been that Community's foundation and generally its driving force as well. So long as that joint project endures, some reasonable degree of Franco–German partnership is likely to endure with it.

In its more than three decades, the EC has certainly been a great success. No one denies that it profoundly conditions relationships among its member–states. Nevertheless, it has not superseded those states, as many hoped it might. The EC is less a replacement for the traditional nation–state than an imaginative extension of it. The role of the Community's "supranational" Commission has essentially been as *amicus curiae* to the Council of Ministers, where the member–states are the decisive actors. The states remain, moreover, the chief interpreters and administrators of Community decisions within their own borders.

In many respects, the Community has given traditional states a new lease on life. Cooperating and bargaining within the EC, Europe's states have generally been able to exert more influence over their external environments than otherwise would have been possible. Moreover, national governments have often used the EC to bolster their domestic authority. Participating in the European Monetary System, for example, allowed the French government to impose a policy of *rigueur* on its own economy. Through the EMS, the French socialist government was able, in effect, to borrow the German Bundesbank. The European Community has thus developed into a very complicated and quite novel confederal structure for governing the European continental system. But it has remained a confederacy of national states rather than a federation in the making. As a confederacy, it has been highly efficacious, precisely because it has permitted Europe's nation–states to retain their self-determination and, with it, their high degree of administrative efficiency and democratic participation. At the same time, it has made it possible for states to surpass their traditional limitations—their lack of economic scale and their tendency to self–defeating quarrels with each other. The advantages of such a confederacy are also its vulnerability. It depends on maintaining a consensus among the partners, among whom are several relatively major powers.

Historically, a working consensus within the EC has been highly dependent on Franco–German cooperation. The two governments usually have held the initiative in developing and imposing new directions for the Community as a whole. When they have agreed on basic policies, the Community has moved forward. When they have not, it has stagnated. This is not to say that other states have had no weight in shaping the Community's policies. Leadership in the EC is naturally a complex process. The Commission often takes initiatives. Smaller countries protect their interests and sometimes decisively affect policies, often by borrowing support from important interests within France or Germany. Nevertheless, the Franco–German axis has been the vital relationship at the Community's center. Thus, while the Community greatly encourages and facilitates close Franco–German cooperation, it also depends on it. Furthermore, within the Community France has not ceased being France, nor Germany ceased being Germany. Each has its own distinctive national interests, as well as its independent capacity to pursue those interests, within and outside the Community.

In the end, therefore, Franco–German partnership and the European Community it has fostered depend not only on institutions and public opinion, but also upon a basic geopolitical and economic climate—one that encourages Europe's states to participate collectively in the definition and pursuit of their national interests. Neither the postwar Franco–German axis nor the EC developed in a geopolitical vacuum. Both are logical European adaptations to the very special environment created by the postwar bipolar order. That order set unusually favorable conditions for West European cooperation in general and Franco–German cooperation in particular. The other essays in this book discuss most of these conditions in detail. Here they are reviewed only to note how much the overall geopolitical character of the postwar European order has changed since 1989.

The Soviet occupation of Eastern Europe, including the eastern half of Germany, greatly simplified relationships among West European states. A looming and seemingly permanent Soviet military threat was a great incentive to Western unity. It also removed Eastern Europe's perennially unstable states as a zone of contention among West European powers. And a divided and occupied Germany was small and vulnerable enough to be a manageable and eager partner for France and the rest of Western Europe.

The Soviet threat also made the United States, through NATO, the manager of West European security. Thanks to the static character of a military balance based on nuclear weapons, the American protectorate was effective and involved little risk of war. It also eliminated any serious military competition among West European states themselves. West Germany was soon rearmed, but its forces were integrated into NATO, and its territory was still occupied by the American, British, and French forces there to defend it. Britain and France ultimately developed significant nuclear forces, but a nonproliferation treaty constrained Germany from doing the same. In effect, the bipolar order deprived West Germany of a good deal of its legal and practical sovereignty in military and diplomatic matters. All these conditions together gave West European states a degree of security against military threats unprecedented in modern times.

While the bipolar order imposed a high domestic political and economic price on Eastern Europe, West European states enjoyed stable democratic regimes together with unprecedented economic growth and prosperity. The Federal Republic not only resumed Germany's customary high economic performance, but built stable democratic political institutions, well–rooted in what developed into a genuinely democratic society. France performed its own economic miracle and greatly strengthened its own political institutions. Both countries developed distinctive and highly successful models for welfare capitalism. Among other big European states, Italy's economic performance was still more impressive.

Part of the explanation for Europe's rapid economic development lay in the liberal global regime that went with American hegemony. Being open to American investment and competition, and to world trade in general, spurred Europeans to modernize rapidly and gave them a powerful incentive for economic cooperation with each other. A sort of transatlantic compromise emerged whereby the U.S. occupied a hegemonic position in Western Europe's military defense while West European states developed an economic bloc of their own. In effect, Europeans allied with the Americans against the Soviets in the military sphere, and with each other to balance the Americans in the economic sphere.

This bifurcated arrangement, despite its serious tensions over the years, was workable nonetheless. The Soviet military threat was all too clear and required an essentially military response, for which the Americans were the obvious source. The Americans dared not risk a Russian–dominated Europe. For the West Europeans the political and budgetary costs of American protection were low, while a prosperous and liberal global economy kept transatlantic economic competition within mutually tolerable limits.

Aside from general conditions favoring European cooperation, there were special incentives for a close Franco–German partnership. France was never America's favorite ally and was therefore eager to develop a European bloc—both to keep the "Anglo–Saxons" in their place during the Cold War, and to prepare for an autonomous "Europe from the Atlantic to the Urals" once the Soviet empire had collapsed. The European Community, from which the Americans—and for a long time the British—were excluded, provided France with the necessary machinery. A reduced and vulnerable Germany was the natural partner.

Germany had parallel incentives. The Community became a way to regain sovereignty and legitimacy among West European states. While Germany was more drawn than France to a special relationship with the U.S., Germany's economic interests were deeply engaged in the EC. Moreover, Germany's strategy for reunification lay in encouraging pan–European cooperation to end the bipolar division of Europe. With de Gaulle's "Europe from the Atlantic to the Urals," the French had already pointed the way.

So long as the Soviet Union was an active threat, West Germans, as the front line of defense, could not be expected to push European projects to the point where they seriously threatened ties with their American protectors. But the French had no wish to see the Americans depart from Europe. France was itself no longer subject to direct American military hegemony in NATO. And once America's Vietnam War was over, the French grew increasingly interested in cooperating in global peacekeeping. As the Cold War began to fade in the 1970s, the French joined the Germans in promoting pan–European ties. Even then, the French had no desire to see Germany break with America militarily and turn genuinely "neutralist," as Mitterrand made eminently clear during the missile crisis of the early 1980s.

In the 1970s, and even more in the 1980s, Germany and France grew more and more concerned with using the EC to protect themselves against the vagaries of American economic policy. Both countries thus joined to build a European Monetary System. Both endorsed and reshaped British proposals for a single European market and began also to widen the scope of political cooperation even to the military sphere. This intensification of European integration culminated in the Maastricht agreements reached at the end of 1991. Here again the French and Germans took the lead in shaping and negotiating the agreements.

From a long historical perspective, the geopolitical incentives to Franco–German cooperation and postwar European unity seem obvious. At the beginning of the twentieth century, the European states were still at their collective apogee of relative prosperity and power in the world. By 1945, after two internecine wars of appalling savagery and destructiveness, the European powers had come close to destroying themselves. Their region was dominated by two external powers. Eastern and much of Central Europe were occupied by a backward and totalitarian Eurasian "superpower": Western Europe preserved its political independence by becoming the military protectorate of the Americans. It was only logical that West European states should band together to regain as much of their autonomy as possible and prepare for the day when the overextended Soviets would collapse and the overextended Americans could depart. Both developments were long anticipated, particularly by the French. If Europe meanwhile built a Community, it could take its rightful place in building the "multipolar" world that might be expected to unfold. The alternative was that Europe should resume its internecine quarreling as soon as the superpowers had left.

The Cold War's geopolitical framework began to disintegrate with Gorbachev's new European policy in the late 1980s, followed by the abrupt collapse of the Soviet empire and of the Soviet state itself. These dramatic events soon raised the issue of America's place in Europe, since no military threat now seemed to justify the commitments and privileges of the old NATO role. Yet any sudden American departure was ruled out by bureaucratic and political inertia, particular interests and loyalties bound up in the NATO relationship, plus a large reservoir of caution, goodwill and shared interests. Nevertheless, shortly after the Soviet collapse, American forces in Europe were being cut sharply.

These cuts corresponded to what seemed a major shift in American public opinion. The end of the 1980s saw signs of a new political will for serious domestic reform in America. Throughout the decade, America's federal government had labored under a very heavy fiscal deficit. By the beginning of the 1990s, the deficit was larger than ever and federal debt was accumulating at the rate of a trillion dollars every two or three years. Meanwhile, a stubborn recession hung over the economy, bound up, many people believed, with the heavy load of public and private debt. At the same time, the U.S. continued to run a large external deficit despite a sharp depreciation of the dollar in the second half of the 1980s. A large external deficit under such circumstances naturally fed public fears about a secular national decline in competitiveness and general economic vitality. In 1992, Clinton's successful campaign for the presidency combined this concern over economic decline with outrage at the low state of public investment, health care and education. Thus, despite the great foreign successes of his first term, President Bush was unable to win a second. His supposed lack of interest in domestic problems was widely assumed to be the reason. Under these circumstances, continuing domestic support for America's traditional military role in NATO could hardly be taken for granted. Moreover, as will be discussed below, the kind of hegemonic American leadership that was embodied in NATO no longer seemed appropriate to the security threats emerging in the new Europe.

While Europe was having to consider changes in transatlantic relations, it was also being faced with the often unsettling consequences of Soviet disintegration: Central and Eastern Europe were unfrozen, Germany was quickly united, and the other nation–states freed from Soviet communism— including Russia itself—were trying with great difficulty to democratize and liberalize themselves rapidly. Several countries were disintegrating into their ethnic components, and Yugoslavia's disintegration became a ferocious military conflict that threatened to spill over into neighboring states.

Western Europe's broad reaction was embodied in the Maastricht agreements. The strategy was to deepen the integration of the Community, while at the same time preparing to extend membership eventually to several additional states, including former communist states like Poland and Hungary. In effect, the internal European scene at the beginning of the 1990s could be characterized as the troubled confluence of two powerful currents: the trend toward tighter West European economic and political integration built up in the 1980s, and the disintegrating expansion of Europe to the East since 1989. The Community's basic reaction was to accelerate the first integrating trend as a way of strengthening its core before widening membership to contain the second disintegrating trend. This seemed to repeat the successful pattern of the Community's past expansions. Traditionally, periods of enlargement tended to be preceded by periods of internal strengthening. An increased federal authority would compensate for the increased diversity of the membership.

Under the circumstances of the early 1990s, however, a more centralized federalism could not be the panacea that many people hoped it would be. In hindsight, the problems with such a strategy seem obvious: with so many radically different new states waiting to be brought within the ambit of the confederal system, deepening was incompatible with widening, if widening meant full membership for newly liberated Central European states within a few years. Deepening, moreover, confronted a more immediate difficulty. Germany's reunification meant that the Community had already been widened. And Germany's policy to cope with its own widening has already made the harmonizing of national interests much more difficult within an EC of twelve members. High German interest rates put monetary integration in a bad light, and popular support for further integration has since fallen alarmingly low in several member countries.

These points become clearer with a closer look at the goals embodied in the Maastricht Treaty signed at the end of 1991. One principal goal is a monetary union that aims not merely at fixed exchange rates, but at a common currency, presumably with all the attendant implications for convergence of macroeconomic policies. Another goal is to clear away obstacles to the "single European market." This is seen to require rules of fair competition. On the one hand, it means curbing national subsidies, regulations and industrial policies that distort free trade and competition; on the other, it means setting minimum standards for social benefits, job conditions, compensation, taxation, or environmental regulation.

Deepening of this kind obviously makes full membership more, rather than less, difficult for the countries of Central and Eastern Europe. It is essentially a strategy to protect the Community's present members, with their high labor, social, and environmental costs, from "unfair" competition from the new entrants. The would–be entrants may appreciate and aspire to the more rigorous and opulent standards of the older members, but their own radically different situations make adhering to such standards counter-productive. For a newly democratic and liberalized country trying to phase out obsolescent industries in order to enter a market economy, high inflation is probably unavoidable. It will seem the most realistic way, politically, to accommodate adjustments too radical to be paid for in a more straightforward fashion. Renouncing the capacity to devalue its national currency deprives such a nation of the only policy that can sustain its competitiveness. Entering a single market that harmonizes wages and social benefits gives up its principal comparative advantage of cheap, intelligent labor. Meeting the Community's monetary and industrial standards, in other words, might well condemn a newly liberated and democratic national economy to prolonged backwardness. As voting members in the EC, the new countries would theoretically be in a position to block every step forward, or to make the definition and management of collective policies extremely difficult. Thus, enlarging the Community to include states like Poland, Hungary, bifurcated Czechoslovakia, or the Baltic states would obviously put European consensus–building under much greater strain.

In theory, such difficulties might be compensated for through Community transfers to the new members—funds directed toward building up general infrastructure or financing promising projects and thereby creating new employment. Private investors seeking access to the rest of the EC market would presumably be attracted by the subsidies and improving infrastructure. Integration would thus tend to raise the poorer new entrants toward the level of the earlier members rather than the reverse. Integration of new members would mean, in other words, leveling up rather than leveling down. This has been the successful formula followed with the poorer entrants of the last decade: Spain, Portugal, Ireland, and Greece. It also seems the solution implied in the new European Bank for Reconstruction and Development (EBRD).

The success of this formula in the past, however, seems much more difficult to replicate under present circumstances. To begin with, the countries of Central and Eastern Europe are a far greater challenge than were Spain, Portugal, Greece, or Ireland, and will require much greater and more problematic investment to be brought up to Community levels. And whereas Europe and the world in general were awash with savings in the 1980s, the early 1990s are a period of acute capital shortage. The Americans, the great dissavers of the last decade, have still not reformed their fiscal practices, while Japan—once a seemingly bottomless pit of savings—has developed a major liquidity crisis of its own. Germany, Europe's principal saver and the Community's former "milk cow," is caught in the colossal demand for capital required to bring its eastern acquisitions up to western standards. The Middle East, formerly another major source of surplus capital, needs heavy investment to recover from the Gulf War. The opening of the Soviet Union has given its successor states a voracious appetite for aid and investment. Not surprisingly, real long–term interest rates have remained high throughout the world, even though by 1992 most national economies were in a serious recession.

In short, finding additional funds for massive transfers to new and relatively backward states in the Community will be more difficult than it might have been in the 1980s. Thus, matching an expanded membership of impoverished states with a more centralized form of "federalism" to transfer resources is unlikely to prove an easy route to success. The center's resources are not likely to be sufficient for such an augmented role in today's more straitened times. Richer members are unlikely to endure the increased taxation and decline in their own living standards required for a federalist policy of heavy direct transfers. The populist backlash after the Maastricht agreements should be a sufficient sign of the growing unease among European national publics over the cost of further European unity. Simultaneous deepening and widening of membership runs the risk of fostering widespread national alienation from the Community's institutions.

Similar reactions may already be seen in the expanded German national state, a microcosm for what an expanded Community might be like. The overall cost of East Germany's adherence to the Federal Republic has turned out to be vastly greater than nearly anyone imagined. In many respects, incorporation has robbed the East of the natural economic advantages that its cheaper labor and lower social and environmental costs might have brought in an open market. In return, it has had massive subsidation of its living standards, and a huge injection of capital for infrastructure and new industrial development. But East German elites, shoved aside by imported West German experts, feel deprived of their birthright. Eastern voters resent their dependent status, while Western electors resent the heavy subsidies. German politics seem more unstable than at any time since the early postwar era. Ugly outbursts against non–German residents are matched by growing tension among West, East and "refugee" Germans themselves. Various German Länder have grown surprisingly rebellious toward the Federal German government.

The burdens of this enlarged Germany are by no means limited to Germany itself. The bigger and more troubled new Germany has already become a major challenge for the consensus of partners within the existing Community. The Kohl government, so courageous in many respects, has nevertheless drawn back from trying to persuade its taxpayers to shoulder the real fiscal costs directly. The resulting huge fiscal deficit imperils Germany's macroeconomic stability, and the consequences do great damage to other economies in the Community. In effect, the German situation imposes high interest rates on all the EMS countries at a time when unemployment is almost everywhere at record levels and rising. If these are the costs of "enlargement" within Germany alone, a nation that gladly chose unification and probably enjoys the world's richest economy, the strains of an early extension of the European Community to newly liberated Eastern countries are clearly more than any confederal consensus could be expected to bear.

The conclusions of such analysis seem clear. There should not be an enlargement of the Community to include even the most promising of the newly liberated states, and even within the EC's present membership there may well have to be some retreat from the ambitious goals of Maastricht. Such reasoning is very difficult for partisans of the Community to accept. On the one hand, it seems to throw away the momentum of the integrating movement built up over the 1980s; on the other, it seems to abdicate the Community's responsibility for the newly liberated states and to renounce the opportunity to organize the new Europe. For many of Europe's current leaders, like Mitterrand, Kohl, or Delors, it probably means they will not themselves see fulfilled the goals they have pursued so constantly, and have seemed so near to grasping. This is particularly unwelcome to Italian leaders, who have used the Community's requirements for monetary union to build up tremendous pressure for long–overdue domestic reforms. But for the Community to retreat under present circumstances is not to fail before history, nor is it to adopt a policy of resignation. It is simply to recognize that the changes of 1989 were a major geopolitical earthquake that has created a new landscape. Obviously the Community will have to rethink its goals and timetables. To plod forward with the unaltered designs of the 1980s is to risk certain disappointment and delay the real adaptation that needs to follow. Indeed, it is to deny the confederacy's real strength, which is its resilient flexibility.

What, then, is to be done about the enormous problems of the newly liberated countries? Quite apart from their moral claims, these beleaguered states pose too much of a threat to the rest of Europe to be ignored. They need not only aid and direction, but some form of intimate association with the Community and its Commission. Accepting the confederal and differentiated nature of the European system indicates the most practical way to provide this link. The European Community has always required a core of leading powers that go forward and, in due course, pressure and persuade the others to follow. This Europe of States has always needed a central mass sufficient to provide enough gravitational force to give order to the rest. In effect, this core attempts to formulate and propose to Europe its general will. A lengthy process of refinement and leadership follows, until all of Europe discovers its collective interest. This distinctive and segmented process of leadership, persuasion, and learning has been the Community's real strength.

Accepting this notion in theory leads to some rather important practical principles. Above all, it makes any doctrinaire rejection of a Europe of variable speeds contrary to the whole history of the European movement. The way to accommodate the reality of the expanded Europe that needs unity but is too diverse for a single uniform organizational structure is to develop the Community's arrangements for association. In effect, it also means embodying the confederal Community in a variety of institutions with distinctive memberships, functions, and perhaps even degrees of participation. This, of course, has always been the real practice. The European Monetary System and the West European Union are the obvious illustrations. Under the present circumstances, nothing but trouble seems likely to follow from the effort to universalize the membership or procedures of the European Community itself in all these parallel confederal organizations. Certainly in the military field Europe's need for the capacity to act is not easily compatible with the EC's heterogenous membership and leisurely procedures.

If membership of the confederacy's various functional organizations must vary, there must also be some compensating general coordination. There is, therefore, a compelling case for having the EC Commission be a partner in all the confederal structures. That same case includes reshaping the Commission to make it more cohesive and efficient and continuing to choose a figure of political weight with intellectual and moral authority as its president. By itself, however, the Commission cannot substitute for the core of leading states. Throughout the Community's history, France and Germany have generally formed that core. Although the present leadership in both countries seems to remain deeply committed to the Community, present circumstances put their relationship under considerable strain. German reunification, with its disruptive economic and political consequences, has disturbed strong dissident nationalist forces in both countries. The reopening of Central and Eastern Europe threatens to revive historical rivalries, as well as divide the two countries over the appropriate EC policy to accommodate the new states. Such differences, however, may already be narrowing. Germany's own experience with unification encourages a more realistic view about expanding the Community's membership, and France's own difficulties with the EMS may promote a more nuanced view of integration.

The European confederacy's prospects for consensus are greatly complicated, however, by the sudden need to develop a real security policy of its own. Military troubles in the East threaten the European confederacy in the West. In time, either effective security arrangements will develop or Western consensus may well start to unravel.

In one obvious way, of course, the Soviet collapse greatly improved Western Europe's security. With luck, Russia will never again seem a nuclear threat to Europe, and a new global order will emerge that will prevent such threats from arising elsewhere. Perhaps it is more realistic to hope that by the time such threats do arise, the military dimension of Europe's confederacy will have evolved to a point where an efficient collective deterrent will seem easy and natural.

Meanwhile, however, Europe faces urgent security threats of a different sort: the mounting disorder within Europe itself. As economic failure and cultural dislocation threaten to overwhelm the underdeveloped political and economic structures of the liberated nation–states, disgruntled and ambitious elites find it easy to mobilize ethnic groups and reopen ancient quarrels. The direct threat to Western Europe is considerable. The violence of such close neighbors may spill over into their emigré communities in the West. And the terrible conflict in Yugoslavia gives a foretaste of how thousands and thousands of refugees, literally fleeing for their lives, may demand entrance to the already crowded West.

A similar set of problems also exists on Europe's Mediterranean borders. Politically and economically underdeveloped Moslem states, caught in profound cultural turmoil and perennial economic failure, threaten to fragment into violently warring factions, spewing out terrorists and waves of refugees in their agony. Again, West European states, often with large Arab populations, will find it difficult to insulate themselves from such consequences. And Europe remains, of course, heavily dependent on Arab oil.

For a European confederation, dealing with such threats now is a very different task from acquiring a credible nuclear deterrent from the Americans during the Cold War. The sharp distinction between security policy and political–economic policy, natural enough in the Cold War, has dissolved. In the new situation, the Americans are far less suited to be Europe's external providers of security. In both Eastern Europe and the Mediterranean countries, Europe requires a concerted long–term strategy combining sustained political and economic aid and pressure with the capacity for selective military intervention to deter violence. The European Community, rather than NATO, is the logical place to concert and manage such a comprehensive strategy. The EC has rich experience in using economic blandishments and threats to coax its relatively underdeveloped neighbors toward productive relations. West European states have far more interest, means, and experience for such a long–term and difficult task than the U.S. Certainly the great bulk of the resources needed must come from Europe, if they are to come from anywhere.

The American military hegemony embodied in NATO seems particularly unnatural in this situation: NATO, by its history and institutional culture, is a military organization designed to counter a massive military threat. While Europe's security does require some effective capacity for selective and timely military intervention, the solution to Eastern and Mediterranean disorder does not lie primarily with military means. The West cannot replace the Russians as Eastern Europe's occupier. Any attempt to do so, particularly if led by the U.S., would almost certainly rekindle a revival of Russian imperialism. Under the circumstances, the less the military dimension is isolated and emphasized, the better for Europe's security. Nevertheless, as Yugoslavia makes clear, the military problems exist, and if not addressed soon enough, can escalate to the point where massive armed intervention seems the only way to bring the situation under control. Paradoxically, it is the European confederation's own military incapacity that threatens, more than anything else, to militarize Europe's security problems.

At the heart of Europe's failure to meet its new security need lies Germany's non–participation. In this increasingly critical sphere for European integration, the Franco–German axis does not function. This institutional schizophrenia was bearable during the Cold War. Today it has increasingly dire consequences. France is unwilling and probably unable to act alone for Europe, and Britain is not a reliable ally for European purposes.

In recent years, European states and Community officials have tried to endow themselves with a military expression of their confederacy. There has been a persistent drive to upgrade the West European Union into a separate but linked military dimension to the EC. A parallel military union has the advantage of leaving out neutralist Community members and lets the WEU depict itself as the long–awaited "European pillar" of NATO. The concept of "double–hatting" would allow the same national forces to be assigned to both NATO and the WEU, and thus permit a flexible use of forces and installations, together with an easier transition to a different American role in NATO.

The Franco–German experiment with creating a joint army corps is another European response. If it can be made to work practically, it offers a formula for the Community's two leading powers to act in concert, in a fashion less likely to arouse either their own mutual rivalry or others' fears that German military power will begin serving national policies.

Meanwhile, the Kohl government has been whittling away at the constitutional and political barriers to using German armed forces for combat roles outside the country. The accompanying political debate seems part of a necessary process by which Germany's political elite and public come to terms with a new world order. For Germany, this is understandably a difficult and delicate moment. A strong American blessing for Europe's own military arrangements—and Germany's full participation in them—would doubtless help greatly. Under the Bush administration, American policy has been too ambivalent about giving up its traditional hegemony in NATO to permit anything other than a half–hearted endorsement for either the WEU or for a more European NATO.

In the absence of any effective European military policies or capacity, the United States is almost inevitably drawn in to take the lead. America's reluctance over Yugoslavia, however, suggests that it is no longer prepared to exercise the hegemony to which it still clings. As was discussed earlier, political conditions in the U.S. do not seem propitious for Americans to lead any prolonged military involvement in Yugoslavia or elsewhere in Eastern Europe. If the military task in Yugoslavia proves as demanding as American military experts have believed it will be, the consequences for the Clinton administration may be traumatic. The 1992 election gave the Clinton administration a mandate for domestic reform, not for building Bush's "new world order" based on American hegemony. Given America's fiscal impasse, heavy U.S. involvement in a major land war in Yugoslavia seems likely to abort any serious domestic reform. Such a situation would call to mind an unhappy parallel with the Johnson administration and the Vietnam War. If the fighting is bloody or prolonged, strong opposition within the U.S. could be expected. The absence of serious European participation would greatly compound American resentment. Perhaps it is unrealistic to expect any major change in the Cold War's U.S.–European military relationship without some sort of traumatic experience along the way.

Whatever happens in Yugoslavia, it seems improbable that the U.S. will, over the long term, continue to manage Europe's security—unless, of course, a Russian threat revives. Even then some kind of more European arrangement, involving France, Germany, and Britain, is the obvious long–range solution. Should German neutralist and pacifist tendencies block progress to a serious military force, it will inevitably signal a lack of German commitment to confederal Europe. Further, the resulting vacuum will imply a rebirth of old ideas of a German–dominated *Mitteleuropa,* cut off from Western Europe. This is an old struggle in Germany, one that has profound implications for the rest of Europe, but which only the Germans can resolve. Perhaps the greatest danger is that Germany's growing national turmoil will no longer permit governments strong enough to play their traditional leading role in the Community. If they cannot, the Franco–German partnership will probably erode, and the European Community with it.

Reflecting on Germany merely reveals, once again, the European confederacy's inevitable dependence on whether a general will for it prevails within the leading states themselves, above all in Germany and France. The basic geopolitical logic that has bound the two middle–sized continental states together still seems valid in the plural world of regional blocs that seems to be emerging. But under present circumstances, probably nothing should be taken for granted. Should the partnership fail to hold itself and the West European system together, the results will not necessarily be dramatic. Most probably, a new alignment will gradually take form. Germany, courting Russia, will once more find itself estranged from France and Britain. As before, Europe's states will consume a good part of their energies keeping each other down and searching for external support. A return to this more intensive and less structured nationalist competition, accompanied by continuing chaos in Central and Eastern Europe or the Mediterranean, does, of course, have ingredients that could combine to produce another European tragedy. In any event, it would spell the end of a once–promising confederal experiment to preserve the strengths and overcome the weaknesses of Europe's traditional nation–states, an experiment that might ultimately restore Europe to a leading role in the world. Intuitively, present French and German leaders understand the dangers and historic stakes, as do many others among Europe's political classes. Only time will tell whether that present widespread intuition will remain deeply rooted in the next generation.

The United States, of course, is more than a disinterested spectator in Europe's drama. A more coherent confederation would eventually alter America's position in the world, whereas a Europe divided in the old ways would allow the U.S. to play an active balancing role or become the indispensable ally to the rump of Western Europe left after Germany's estrangement. Whether such a role, gained at the price of confederal Europe's failure, would really be in America's own interest seems doubtful. A "Fortress Europe" that sought to squeeze out America is certainly a legitimate concern. But assuming that the world economy does not collapse, it seems highly improbable. Europe and America are too interdependent economically and too closely linked culturally. Both, moreover, are open political systems easily penetrated by the other. Europe's confederal character will always leave it susceptible to American influence.

In any event, in a world full of vigorous and untamed new forces, the two great and prosperous liberal continents will naturally share an anxious concern for global order—a concern that will logically encourage them to retain their close alliance. But a Europe better able to manage its own security should greatly reduce America's military burdens and give the U.S. an opportunity to rejuvenate its own continental system. Indeed, Europe's confederal experiment can offer many insights of value to a reform–minded America. But if Europe's great experiment fails, one likely result is an America that continues to be overextended abroad and declining at home. That will provide an unpromising prospect for both sides of the Atlantic.

SELECTED BIBLIOGRAPHY

The literature on the Franco–German relationship is immense, and only works that have been particularly useful to the authors of this book are listed here. For the reader's convenience they are grouped by chapter or by sets of chapters. In general no work is listed twice, although clearly many works are useful for more than one chapter.

Chapter 1

Boche, Jörg. *Franco–German Economic Relations: National Structures and Cooperation in the EC.* Ph.D. diss. SAIS, The Johns Hopkins University Paul H. Nitze School of Advanced International Studies, 1993.

Bulmer, S. and W. Patterson. *The FRG and the EC.* London: Allen and Unwin, 1987.

Documents/Dokumente. 1945 onward.

Friend, Julius W. *The Linchpin: French–German Relations 1950–1990.* The Washington Papers, 155. New York: Praeger, 1991.

Grosser, Alfred. *Affaires extérieures.* Paris: Champs Flammarion, 1989.

"France–Allemagne 1936–1986." *Politique étrangère.* 1/1986 pp. 247–255.

Hanreider, Wolfram F. *Germany, America, Europe.* New Haven: Yale University Press, 1989.

Hanreider, Wolfram F. and Graeme P. Anton. *The Foreign Policies of West Germany, France and Britain.* Englewood Cliffs: Prentice Hall, 1980.

Kolodziej, Edward. *French International Policy Under de Gaulle and Pompidou.* Ithaca: Cornell University Press, 1974.

Morgan, Roger and Caroline Bray, eds. *Partners and Rivals in Western Europe: Britain, France and Germany.* London: Gower, 1986.

Picht, Robert, ed. *Deutschland, Frankreich, Europa.* Munich: Piper, 1978.

Picht, Robert and Wolfgang Wessels, eds. *Motor für Europa? Deutsch–franzoesischer Bilateralismus und europaeische Integration.* Bonn: Europa Union Verlag, 1990.

Simonian, Haig. *The Privileged Partnership: Franco–German Relations in the EC 1969–1984.* Oxford: Clarendon Press, 1985.

Willis, F. Roy. *France, Germany and the new Europe 1945–1963.* Stanford: Stanford University Press, 1965.

Chapters 2, 3, 4

Balladur, Edouard. "Mémorandum sur la construction monétaire européene." *Ecu.* 3/1988, pp. 17–19.

Brandt, Willy. *People and Politics.* New York: Brown & Co., 1978.

Calleo, David P. *Beyond American Hegemony: The Future of the Western Alliance.* New York: Basic Books, 1987.

Calleo, David P. and Philip Gordon, eds. *From the Atlantic to the Urals.* New York: University Press of America, 1992.

Calleo, David P. and Claudia Morgenstern, eds. *Recasting Europe's Economies.* New York: University Press of America, 1990.

Delors, Jacques. *La France par l'Europe.* Paris: Grasset, 1988.

Garaud, Marie–France and Philippe Séguin. *De l'Europe en général et de la France en particulier.* Paris: Le pré aux clercs, 1992.

Gross, Johannes. "Monstrum von Maastricht," *Fueilleton, Frankfurter Allgemeine Zeitung.* 25 July 1992.

Guerrieri, Paolo and Pier Carlo Padoan. *The Political Economy of European Integration.* Savage, Md.: Barnes and Noble, 1989.

Hall, Peter. *Governing the Economy.* New York/Oxford: Oxford University Press, 1986.

Hoffmann, Stanley. "The Case for Leadership," *Foreign Policy.* Winter 1990–91, pp. 20–38.

———. "La France dans le nouvel ordre européen," *Politique étrangère.* 3/1990, pp. 503–512.

Krieger, Wolfgang. "Die deutsche Integrationspolitik im postsowjetischen Europa," *Europa–Archiv.* Folge 18, 25 September 1992.

Le Gloannec, Anne–Marie. *La nation orpheline.* Paris: Calmann–Lévy, 1989.

Le Monde diplomatique: Allemagne, Japon, les deux titans. Paris: Le Monde, 1992.

Lipschitz, Leslie and Donough McDonald, eds. *German Reunification: Economic Issues*. Washington: International Monetary Fund, 1990.

Manfrass, Klaus, ed. *Paris, Bonn: Eine dauerhafte Bindung schwieriger Partner*. Sigmaringen: Thorbecke, 1984.

Minc, Alain. *La grande illusion*. Paris: Grasset, 1989.

Nonnenmacher, Guenter. "Auf verlaesslichem Boden: Frankfreich, Deutschland und die 'Ernstfaelle' in Europa," *Frankfurter Allgemeine Zeitung*. 11 November 1992.

Scharpf, Fritz W. *Sozialdemokratische Krisenpolitik in Europa*. Frankfurt/New York: Campus Verlag, 1987.

Schmidt, Helmut. *Die Deutschen und ihre Nachbarn*. Berlin: Siedler Verlag, 1990.

Teltschik, Horst. *329 Tage: Innenansichten der Einigung*. Berlin: Siedler Verlag, 1991.

Uterwedde, Henrik. *Die Wirtschaftspolitik der Linken in Frankreich: Programme und Praxis 1974–86*. Frankfurt/New York: Campus Verlag, 1988.

Weisenfeld, Ernst. *Welches Deutschland soll es sein? Frankfreich und die deutsche Einheit seit 1945*. Munich: Beck Verlag, 1986.

Weisenfeld, Ernst, ed. *Dokumente—Zeitschrift fuer den Deutsch–Franzoesischen Dialog: Wie geht es jetzt weiter?* Jahrgang 48, Heft 5. October, 1992.

Yost, David. "France and the New Europe," *Foreign Affairs*. Winter 1990–91, pp. 107–128.

Chapter 5

Fritsch–Bournazel, Renata. *Europe and German Unification*. New York/Oxford: Berg, 1992.

Heisenberg, Wolfgang, ed. *German Unification in European Perspective*. London: Brassey's for CEPS, 1991.

Kaiser, Karl. *Deutschlands Vereinigung: die internationalen Aspekte*. Bergisch Gladbach, Lubbe, 1991.

Keohane, R. O. and S. Hoffmann, eds. *The New European Community: Decision–making and Institutional Change*. Boulder: Westview, 1991.

Nicolas, Françoise and Hans Stark. *L'Allemagne. Une nouvelle hégémonie?* Paris: IFRI/Dunod, 1992.

Swann, Dennis, ed. *The Single European Market and Beyond. A Study of the Wider Implications of the Single European Act*. London/New York: Routledge, 1992.

Valance, Georges. *France–Allemagne: Le Retour de Bismarck*. Paris: Flammarion, 1990.

Chapter 6

Calleo, David P. *Europe's Future: The Grand Alternatives.* New York: Norton, 1967.

Griffiths, Richard, ed. *The Economy and Politics of the Netherlands Since 1945.* The Hague: Martinus Nijhoff, 1980.

Hill, Christopher, ed. *National Foreign Policies and European Political Coopera-tion.* London: George Allen and Unwin of the Royal Institute of International Affairs, 1983.

Laursen, Finn, and Sophie Vanhoonacker, eds. *The Intergovernmental Conference on Political Union: Institutional Reforms, New Policies and International Iden-tity of the European Community.* Maastricht: European Institute of Public Administration, 1992.

Ludlow, Peter. "The Treaty of Maastricht and the Future of Europe." *CEPS Working Document No. 68.* Brussels: Centre for European Policy Studies, 9 June 1992.

McCarthy, Patrick. "France and the EC: Can a Gaullist Power Find Happiness in a Regional Bloc?" *Bologna Center Occasional Paper, No. 71.* Bologna: Johns Hopkins, February 1992.

Miller, Kenneth E. *Denmark: A Troubled Welfare State.* Boulder: Westview, 1991.

Spaak, Paul-Henri. *Combats inachevés: De l'espoir aux déceptions, tome 2.* Paris: Fayard, 1969.

Vanhoonacker, Sophie. "La Belgique: responsable ou bouc émissaire de l'échec des négotiations Fouchet?" *Res Publica* 31, no. 4 (1989): pp. 513-25.

Chapter 7

Barzel, Rainer, coordinator. *25 Jahre Deutsch–Französische Zusammenarbeit/25 ans de cooperations franco–allemande.* Bonn: Presse–und Informationsamt der Bundesregierung, 1987.

Garntham, David. *The Politics of European Defense Cooperation: Germany, France, Britain and America.* Cambridge, Mass.: Ballinger, 1988.

Gordon, Philip H. *A Certain Idea of France: French Security Policy and the Gaullist Legacy.* Princeton: Princeton University Press, 1993.

———. *French Security Policy after the Cold War: Continuity, Change and Implications for the United States.* Santa Monica: RAND, R–4229, 1992.

Haglund, David G. *Alliance within the Alliance? Franco–German Military Cooperation and the European Pillar of Defense.* Boulder: Westview Press, 1991.

Kaiser, Karl and Pierre Lellouche. *Le couple franco–allemand et la défense de l'Europe.* Paris: Institut Français des Relations Internationales, 1986. (German version: *Deutsch–Französische Sicherheitspolitik.* Bonn: Europa Verlag, Forschungsinstitut der Deutschen Gesellschaft für Auswärtige Politik, 1986.)

Laird, Robbin F., ed. *Strangers and Friends: The Franco–German Security Relationship.* London: Pinter, 1989.

Schmidt, Helmut. "Deutsch–französische Zusammenarbeit in der Sicherheitspolitik," *Europa–Archiv,* no. 11 (1987): pp. 303–12.

Schmidt, Peter. "The Franco–German Defence and Security Council," *Aussenpolitik* (English edition) 40, no. 4: pp. 361–71.

Szabo, Stephen F. *The Changing Politics of German Security.* London: Pinter, 1990.

Yost, David S. "Franco–German Defense Cooperation." *The Washington Quarterly* 11, no. 2 (Fall 1988): pp. 173–95

Young, Thomas–Durell and Samuel Newland. *The Inevitable Partnership: The Franco–German Security Relationship.* The Land Warfare Papers, no. 4. Arlington: Association of the United States Army, September 1990.

Chapters 8 and 9

Costigliola, Frank. *France and the United States: The Cold Allegiance since World War II.* New York: Twayne Publishers, 1992.

De Ruyt, Jean. "European Political Cooperation: Toward a Unified European Foreign Policy," *Atlantic Council of the United States Occasional Paper,* October 1989.

Ginsberg, Roy B. "The United States and the Transatlantic Declaration," conducted for the Institute für Eurupäische Politik, Bonn, final draft, October, 1992.

Hurwitz, Leon, and Christian Lequesne, eds. *The State of the European Community. Policies, Institutions, and Debates in the Transition Years.* Boulder: Lynne Riemer, 1991.

Moïsi, Dominique. "French Foreign Policy: The Challenge of Adaptation." *Foreign Affairs* 67, no. 1, 1988.

Pond Elizabeth. *After the Wall.* New York: Priority Press Publications, 1990.

Smyser, W. R. *Restive Partners: Washington and Bonn Diverge.* Boulder: Westview, 1990.

BIOGRAPHIES OF AUTHORS

DANA H. ALLIN received his B.A. from Yale University and his Ph.D. from the Paul H. Nitze School of Advanced International Studies of the Johns Hopkins University. He has worked as a newspaper reporter covering state government in Maryland and as a financial journalist in London. He was a professorial lecturer in European politics and American foreign policy at the Johns Hopkins University SAIS Bologna Center, and spent a year as Robert Bosch Foundation Fellow in Bonn and Frankfurt. Mr. Allin is currently a visiting scholar at the Stiftung Wissenchaft and Politick (Research Institute for International Affairs) in Ebenhausen, Germany.

JÖRG BOCHE received his undergraduate training at the Universities of Marburg and Munich in Germany. His M.A. is from the Paul H. Nitze School of Advanced International Studies of the Johns Hopkins University, where he is a Ph.D. candidate. Mr. Boche's specialization is in international economics, and he is currently working with WestLB Capital Management GmbH in Düsseldorf, Germany.

DAVID P. CALLEO is Dean Acheson Professor and Director of European Studies at the Paul H. Nitze School of Advanced International Studies of the Johns Hopkins University. His more recent books include *The Imperious Economy, Beyond American Hegemony,* and *The Bankrupting of America.*

JULIUS W. FRIEND has been lecturer on French politics and history at the Paul H. Nitze School of Advanced International Studies of the Johns Hopkins University, and on European history and comparative politics at the George Washington University. He was also chairman for Area Studies on Francophone Europe at the Foreign Service Institute. He retired in January 1979 from the Central Intelligence Agency as a senior analyst in European affairs. His major publications include *The Linchpin: French-German Relations 1950-1990, Seven Years in France: François Mitterrand and the Unintended Revolution,* and a number of translations from German, and numerous articles on the European Left. His current research concerns investigation into perceptions of national identity in Germany, France, and Great Britain.

PHILIP GORDON is spending 1993 as a Bundeskanzler Scholar and a German Marshall Fund Younger Scholar at the Deutsche Gesellschaft für Auswärtige Politik in Bonn. He received his Ph.D. from the Paul H. Nitze School of Advanced International Studies of the Johns Hopkins University (SAIS) in 1991 and has taught international relations at SAIS, George Mason University, and the European Institute of Business Administration (INSEAD). Gordon is a consultant for the Rand Corporation and has written extensively on French and German security issues. He is the author of *A Certain Idea of France: French Security Policy and the Gaullist Legacy* and is presently working on a study of German foreign policy.

ERIK JONES is a visiting researcher at the Brussels-based Center for European Policy Studies and a doctoral candidate in European studies at the Paul H. Nitze School of Advanced International Studies of the Johns Hopkins University. His dissertation is entitled "Changing the Political Formula: Economic Policy-making in Belgium and the Netherlands in the 1980s." Although specializing in the study of small counties, he has also published in areas ranging from "French Security Policy" to "Fiscal Stabilizers in Monetary Unions" and "Energy Pricing in the Commonwealth of Independent States."

PATRICK McCARTHY is a professor of European studies at the Johns Hopkins University SAIS Bologna Center. He is the author of *Céline* and *Camus* and has edited *The French Socialists in Power 1981-86* in addition to writing many articles on French and Italian politics.

ROGER MORGAN is a professor of political science at the European University Institute, Florence, Italy. He has held teaching and research appointments at a number of institutions, including the Royal Institute of International Affairs (Chatham House) in London and the Bologna Center of SAIS, Johns Hopkins University. His numerous publications include *West Germany's Foreign Policy Agenda* and *Partners and Rivals in Western Europe: Britain, France and Germany*.

INDEX